Programming the Auto_Robot
Unit1 Mark5 Rover

© COPYRIGHT ALL RIGHTS RESERVED

By

ZACHARY M REYNOLDS

GRAPHICS AND PHOTOGRAPHY CURTESY OF

Petaluma California

Other titles by
Zachary M Reynolds

Unit1 Natural Language, Cognitive Execution "The Beaver Lesson" © 1988 Pacific Software Design

Unit1 Natural Language, Cognitive Execution Demonstration Kit © 1988 Pacific Software Design

Unit1 Synthesized Intellect (SI) "Museum Guide" © 1989, 1990, 1991 Pacific Software Design

Unit1 "The MSI Experience, A Summary Report" © 1990 Pacific Software Design

Unit1 "Introduction to Unit1, Natural Language Processing and Machine Intelligence Software" © 1990 Pacific Software Design

Hyperbolic Event Structures for Artificial Intelligence, Book I © 2010 Z-Concepts

Auto- Robot Programming for the Observing Unit, Event Matrix Method for Artificial Intelligence, © 2011 Z-Concepts

Table of Contents

III INNOVATION
[Utilizing sensory feed back to operate a self reliant Unit]

IV PROGRAMMING THE ROVER

V PROGRAMMING THE ROVER INTEGRATING HARDWARE AND SOFTWARE

VI Technical Approach

I
ROVER DESIGN

WHAT IS A ROVER

The **UNIT1** Rover utilizes a **robotic** design to operate over a variety of landscapes, make observations and record the excursion. The Rover travels over non-conforming terrain populated by a variety of obstructions and acts as a recorder of a real landscape. Obstructions may be things such as solid or open frame pieces of work. Objects may be unseen, untouched and only indirectly encountered by the Rover. A group of sensors providing output is routinely polled. Sensor readings are sorted into numerical categories. These categories are refined as Matrix arrays which can be manipulated and "solved."

FUNCTIONALITY

Unit1 Rover is an *automaton* that is capable of making decisions on its own as to how to travel through a maze of obstructions and impedances. While the Unit1 is making this journey, it records the properties of the landscape for immediate or future reference and evaluations. This type of function can be very useful in situations where human presence is dangerous or impossible.

Reaching Locations Too Confined for Humans

Size matters especially when the space to be examined is cramped and littered with debris. The Rover can travel through confined and restricted spaces. Rover movements are autonomous and not controlled by humans. Ordinary tethered guidance is largely unnecessary.

Entering Smoke Filled Spaces

The Unit1 Mark5 Rover is equipped with sensors that are not based upon visible light frequency. They are infra red, ultra sound, vibration and touch activated. With the exception of touch, the signals are evaluated as amplitude. Motor decisions are based upon comparisons of direction, intensity and groupings.

Examining Dangerous Items

Areas and space volumes that pose a hazard may best be approached by intelligent agents, often automatons, at least in the first stages of the exploration. The Rover can be equipped with cameras and other light recording devices and sensors to bring information to the remote operator.

Mapping an Area

The Unit1 Mark5 Rover is fully equipped to record and transmit decisions regarding paths, directions and local course decisions. It also tracks motor revolutions per minute (rpm,) slip and stall conditions. This information allows distance traveled calculations, location tracking and landscape characteristics of slope and clutter.

ALL TERRAIN MOBILITY

The first phase of design (and programming) is to decide what you want the Rover to do. Body design is an essential part of any programming strategy. In the case of the Unit1, it must be able to pass over small obstacles, motor up and down inclines, and move efficiently over a variety of surfaces and landscapes. In the process of choosing what the design will be, important features are examined, such as:

1. Overall size, which would be determined by function.
2. Overall weight of the Unit
3. Motor power, gear reductions and drive transmissions
4. Traction method (track, wheel or a combination of both.)
    a. Surface composition
        i. Hard or smooth (linoleum, wood & slate)
        ii. Textured or rocky (rugs, grass & dirt)
        iii. Soft or yielding (sand)
    b. Slope
5. Stability (is it too high and subject to tipping?)
6. Material and general construction.
7. Power requirements and sources (batteries or engines.)

Once you have the basics of the configuration and the general design, the next step is to build the unit and test it as a Radio Controlled unit. Don't start programming the unit until you have a working chassis that can do all the things you want and are satisfied with the results. Your design will have its peculiarities and will require some adjustments. For example one of the most common adjustments involves the removal of all corners and protrusions that cause the Rover to "catch up" on an obstruction. In line with this adjustment are the placement of fenders and the art of providing smooth surfaces so the unit can glide around obstructions.

UNIT1 MARK5

This version of the Rover has taken into account the above features and design elements and is being presented as a finished product (**Fig 1-1.**) You may add or subtract features, or operate the Unit1 as presented. The finished characteristics include notations which offer some explanation of the selection(s). Although chassis is important, only a general description will be provided. Templates for engine beds, frame works and sensor posts are provided, but it is stressed here that this publication is primarily about programming and code sequences.

Height and Size

The Unit1 is given a certain height to "see" above obstructions and manage navigation around and over simple obstructions. This size also accommodates the number of sensors, drive motors and processing Bricks that will be anticipated for sophisticated operations. Room is allowed for expansions and additions to the devices and sensors, plus power requirements.

Weight

When it comes to traction and the frictional force that can both assist and impede movement, weight is important. Gear trains can be designed to provide sufficient power to the drive axle(s). But friction may still be inadequate to keep the motive method from slipping. Tracks may require exposed "blades" and tires may be "knobbed." Friction can also be too high. It is most important for tracks since they rely upon some slippage to make a turn. Too much traction can cause a tracked turn to stall.

Center of Gravity

Weight distribution can affect how the tractor handles different surface textures, crawls over obstacles and manages velocity changes. It also determines the ability of the Rover to stay upright when it encounters variations in height or slope changes in the terrain. The height of the CG should be approximately equal to the outside width of the track/wheel base. For tracked versions the horizontal center of gravity (CG) is best when it is located slightly forward of the midpoint of the trucks. For wheeled chassis, the CG is best located over the drive tires.

Side View

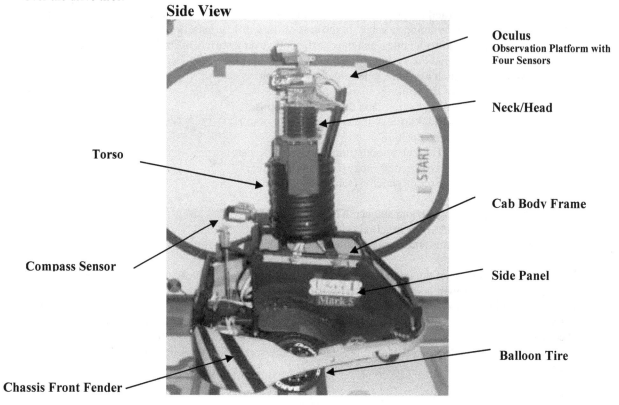

Oculus
Observation Platform with
Four Sensors

Neck/Head

Torso

Cab Body Frame

Compass Sensor

Side Panel

Balloon Tire

Chassis Front Fender

Fig 1-1a

Back View

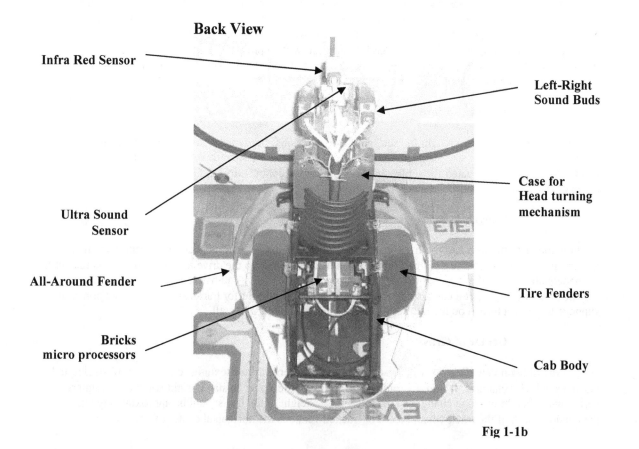

Infra Red Sensor

Left-Right
Sound Buds

Case for
Head turning
mechanism

Ultra Sound
Sensor

All-Around Fender

Tire Fenders

Bricks
micro processors

Cab Body

Fig 1-1b

TRACTOR

The body that provides motive power to the Rover is generally referred to as the tractor. Primarily it houses the mechanisms which propel the body, managing alignment and direction. In this application it also supplies the foundation supporting the robot assembly. The tractor can develop motion by laying down track, turning wheels or using both wheels and tracks. The tractor housing consists of:

- Chassis Base plate & Hardware Mounts
  - Tractor Drivers (servo motors)
- Driven Traction Devices and idler gears
  - Tracks & Trucks
  - Tires (Balloon) "LockUp MT Duratrax C2"
  - Outrigger Idlers or casters

CHASSIS BASE PLATE & HARDWARE MOUNTS

The base plate (**Figs 1-4 & 1-6**) forms the support for the under-slung motors, the track/tire gear, microprocessors, and cab frame struts. The struts support the Cab and Torso. The micros are mounted on rails secured to the base plate.

The plate is polypropylene plastic cut from two left and right hand templates. These plates are fastened together using solvent glue. Inside edges form the center line seam. At the outer edge of each plate segment a vertical rectangular member (**Fig 1-4**) is attached that acts as a reinforcing beam. This beam member is fitted with two reinforced holes that support drive and idler axles. The beam is designed to support either a tracked or tire drive (**Fig 1-6**.)

At one end of the plate assembly (**Figs 1-4 & 1-6**) two palm shaped reinforced surfaces are fitted with support and stabilization casters. These casters are not used for steering. They are preferably ball casters with no edges and no uneven or raised surfaces that would impede motion.

At the other end of the base plate the driven gear boxes are mounted (**Fig 1-2**.) These gears can drive either track sprockets or tire hubs. The boxes house a gear train with a 2:1 power ratio for Track drives and a 2.6:1 power ratio for Wheeled drives.

Tractor Drivers

The two servo motors (**Fig 1-2**) are attached to the underside of the chassis base plate. These motors drive the Rover through a gear train.

Shown here is the wheeled version. The motors are mounted in the same location for the tracked version.

The traction motors are controlled by the micro on the base plate of the body

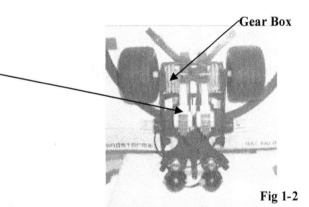

Gear Box

Fig 1-2

Chassis Underside

DRIVEN TRACTION DEVICES AND IDLER GEARS

The base plate is attached to a girder which frames the drive axles. The framing girder (**Figs 1-4 & 1-6**) supports the wheel and driving gear assemblies, and trucks if tracks are used. The trucks act as guides to the tracks, keeping them aligned with the driven and idler gears. The driven gear is run by an axle drive from the motor at the rear of the tracks. An idler gear is positioned at the front of the tracks to maintain track tension and alignment (**Fig 1-4**.)

TRACTOR WITH TRACKS

The track elements (**Fig 1-3**) are plastic and are composed of segmented pads. Each pad is articulated to the adjacent pads so that they are connected but flexible. The individual pads are plastic with raised ribs (blades.) These ribs create gripping power when used on soft terrain, like rug pile, rubber matting or soil. When the bare pads come in contact with smooth surfaces, such as linoleum or wood, they loose gripping power, causing them to slip excessively. In order for the track pads to function on both smooth and textured surfaces, friction tape must be added to the pads.

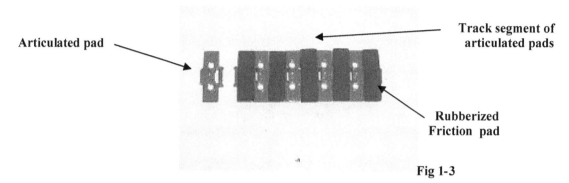

Articulated pad

Track segment of articulated pads

Rubberized Friction pad

Fig 1-3

The friction tape is most effective for multiple surfaces when it is spaced at every other track pad, rather than uniformly on all pads. This is because the friction tape hinders good operation on turns and maneuvers on rugs and soft surfaces. Too much friction prevents the Rover assembly form turning right or left if the tracks cannot slip slightly on the surface.

A second factor affecting proper performance of the tracked assembly is the weight of the completed Rover. Friction is a direct result of applied weight. If the Rover weight is too high, the amount of slip obtained may be inadequate for proper turning.

A third factor is track length. In turning, the slip of the tracks occurs on the inside radius of the turn. If the track length between trucks is long, the leverage against slipping is large. The ratio of track length to width of base is kept low, where the length of track contact (**Fig 1-5**) is app. one half the base width (**Fig 1-4**.)

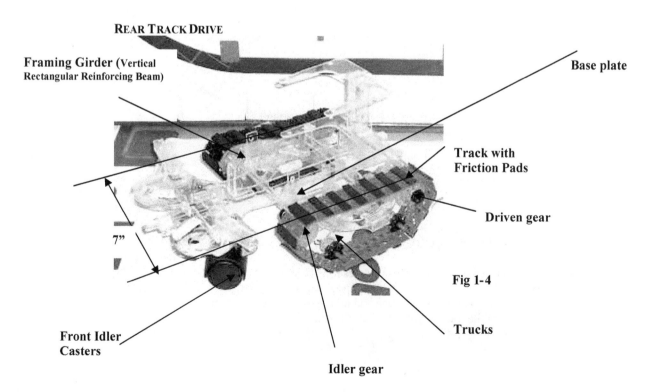

REAR TRACK DRIVE

Framing Girder (Vertical Rectangular Reinforcing Beam)

Base plate

Track with Friction Pads

Driven gear

Fig 1-4

7"

Front Idler Casters

Trucks

Idler gear

Trucks

Trucks (**Fig 1-5**) maintain the spread of the tracks on the traction surface. They also maintain the spread of the tracks between the driven and idler gears. The Trucks are constructed as frames that support sprocket like wheels. They apply pressure to the track pads as well as guide the pads along the line of the track course between gears.

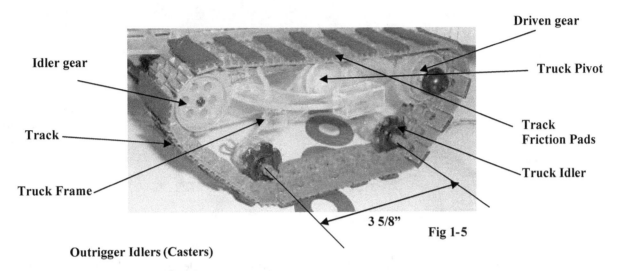

Fig 1-5

Outrigger Idlers (Casters)

With a low ratio of track length to base width, the truck sprockets are usually close to the longitudinal center of gravity of the body & tractor. To keep the Unit from tipping forward or backwards, outriggers are fitted on the longitudinal axis (**Fig 1-4.**) This gives the appearance of the Unit1 operating as a half-track vehicle. This is not completely true, since the idlers are designed to rest slightly above the operational level of the tracks. The outriggers are not designed to touch the ground under normal operating conditions.

This prevents the outriggers from being obstructions to a turn or increasing drag under operating conditions. The fore and aft outriggers come into contact with the ground when the Unit tilts either forward or backwards, and they prevent toppling. The outrigger axles are located from the drive axle a distance 2.3 times the length of the track contact. The width between outrigger axles is the same as the length of track contact.

TRACTOR with Balloon Tires

In this case (**Fig. 1-6,**) the framing girder on the base plate supports the driven axles (left and right) that pass through the drive gear ports. Each axle drives a 4.75 inch diameter balloon tire/wheel. A second set of wheels provide stability. These wheels are idlers, fitted with casters allowing the wheels to automatically track to the direction of motion.

The advantage of a tire drive is the ability to crawl over objects. This is a direct function of three variables: the diameter of the tire, the flexibility of the rim and the size of the object. A small tire diameter requires a greater effort to mount and overcome small objects. The flexibility of the rim depends upon the external tension of the rubberized material. (These tires are not inflated and support the car body weight by the tension of the rubber composition.) they are able to function well upon all types and compositions of surfaces and to effectively crawl over objects.

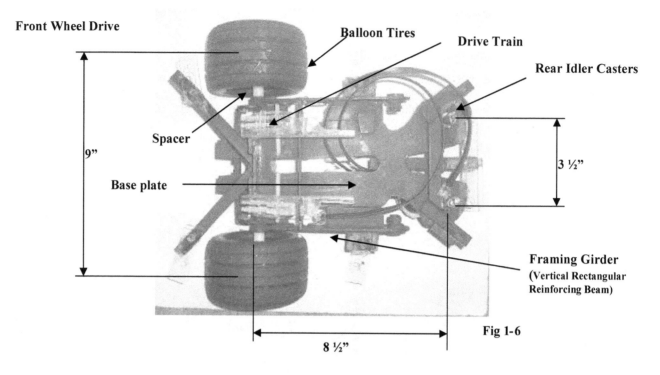

Front Wheel Drive

Balloon Tires

Drive Train

Rear Idler Casters

Spacer

9"

3 ½"

Base plate

Framing Girder
(Vertical Rectangular
Reinforcing Beam)

Fig 1-6

8 ½"

Gear Box

The tires are driven by a gear train similar to the tracked version. The wheeled gear train has a 2.6:1 power ratio. Although the track driver is rear mounted, the best arrangement for the tires is with a front wheel drive (FWD) configuration. The gear box **(Fig 1-6a)** consists of an input, output and idler gear. The purpose of the idler is to keep the tires rotating in the correct direction according to the motor commands for rotation direction.

Because of the added mechanical advantage from the system, the plastic gears (typical LEGO™ parts) are doubled up, increasing wear life to the teeth.

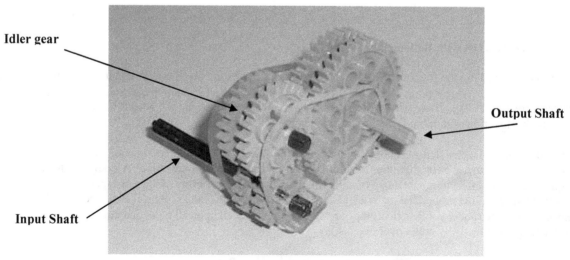

Idler gear

Output Shaft

Input Shaft

Figure 1-6a

Axles

Polypropylene plastic is the preferred structural material of Unit1. In some cases the plastic composition is a specialty molecule that is a LEGO™ manufactured item. For example the gears used in the trains are LEGO™ items. Normally the axles which support the gears and drivers are also plastic materials from LEGO™. However in the case of wheel axles, the cantilevered nature of the wheel requires a greater strength and axle rigidity (resistance to bending) than the plastic elements can provide. In this case a *steel axle* needs to be fabricated. This steel axle (**Fig 1-7**) is cut from a ¼ inch diameter all-thread rod, and is contoured with grooves that match the groove spurs of the LEGO™ gear hubs. The contours are ground by hand with a small high speed grinding tool (like a Dremel.)

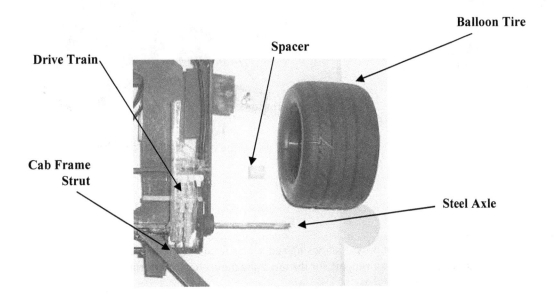

Fig 1-7

CAB BODY

The Rover cab body and the torso it supports (**Figs 1-8 a&b**) are mounted on the chassis base plate. This structure is essentially a box and provides a base for the observation platform, and the compass sensor that registers a specific alignment of the Rover's heading. The cab body provides:

- Housing for microprocessor(s)
- Torso foundation
- Housing for Head motor and gear train
- Touch sensor and Vicinity readings
- Sensor to detect compass alignment of the body

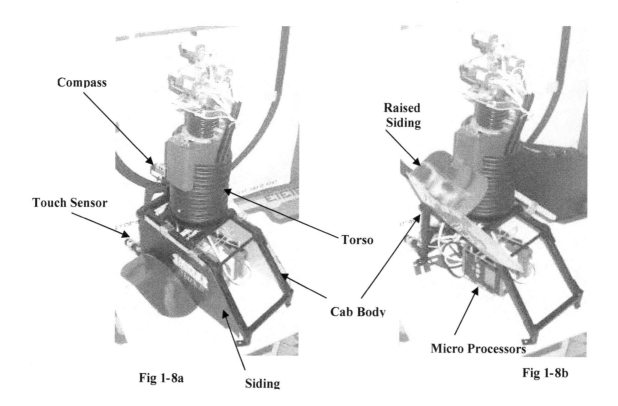

Compass

Touch Sensor

Torso

Cab Body

Fig 1-8a

Siding

Raised
Siding

Micro Processors

Fig 1-8b

FRAME AND SIDING

This structure is an open frame that provides housing and access for the micro processors and battery/power cells. It also provides a support for the torso and observation platform, which is elevated approximately 19 inches above the chassis.

The cab body is fitted with hinged side panels to close off the interior and working parts. Wiring and attachments from the micro processors are kept out of sight and in a compact bundle. The side panels are fitted with fenders for the tires (or tracks) to protect them from debris and/or snags.

MICRO PROCESSORS (LEGO™ BRICKS)

The micro processors are housed in a removable frame (**Fig 1-9 a&b**) that slides on a set of rails installed on the chassis base plate (**Fig1-10.**) There is also room for additional power packs (batteries) that can be wired to the processors, to increase performance range and time.

Current designs of the **Unit1**™ Mark 5 use a LEGO™ style "NXT Brick" **Atmel ARM7 48MHz** processor. Code for **Unit1**™ is **NXC developed by John Hansen** and available through Source Forge network (see **Chapter II.**) Two of these micro processors are used and linked through a BlueTooth connection in a Master/Slave configuration.

Fig 1-9a

Fig 1-9b

Basic programming for the Observer is compiled and run by the Master processor. Drive commands are controlled through the Master Brick. It operates the tractor motors and the head motor. Contact sensors and compass directional readings are processed by the Slave Brick

Support Struts for Cab Body

Mounting Rails for Micro Processors

Framing Girder
(Vertical Reinforcing Beam)

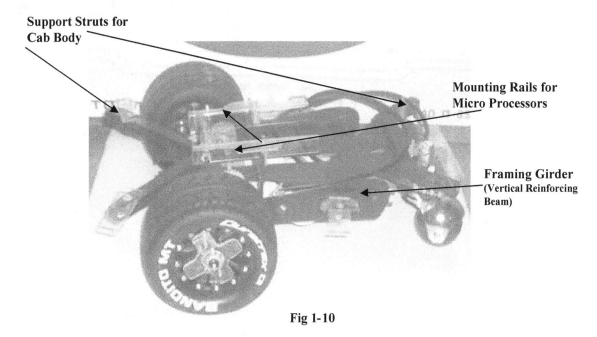

Fig 1-10

TOUCH AND VICINITY SENSOR HOUSINGS

The height of the oculus (observation platform, **Fig 1-19**) allows a greater distance perspective but it misses obstacles and other structures close to the ground. In addition to the effective feed back for stalled movement and improperly executed turns, a series of sensors are provided at the chassis front (**Fig 1-11**) that are close to the ground.

Front Bumper and Side Fenders

The sensors registering touch and vicinity in the front are mounted on a bumper structure. The front bumper (**Fig 1-12**) is spring loaded through the action of the all around fender's elastic properties. The fender and bumper prevent obstructions from being lodged in and under the Unit1 chassis and drive mechanisms

FRONT BUMPER ASSEMBLY

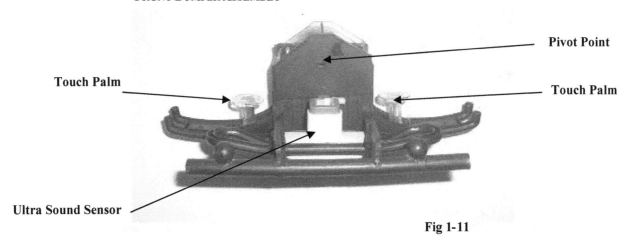

Pivot Point

Touch Palm

Touch Palm

Ultra Sound Sensor

Fig 1-11

Front Vicinity Sensor

An ultra sound distance sensor detects objects very close to the Unit1. It is not used for landscape surveys. Its principal purpose is to measure distance of objects ahead to help determine turning radius or simple avoidance. The ultra sound device is located in the very center of the front bumper at the pivot point

Left and Right Touch Sensors

These sensors are typical contact devices. They are activated by a pivoted front bumper arrangement that is fitted with compression palms on the right and left sides.

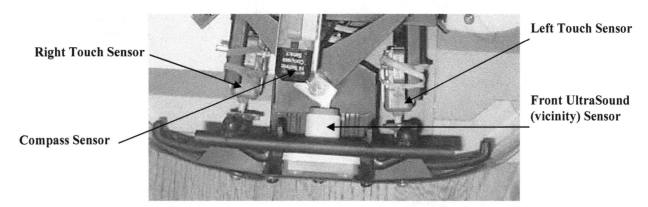

Left Touch Sensor

Right Touch Sensor

Front UltraSound (vicinity) Sensor

Compass Sensor

Fig 1-12

TORSO

The Torso (**Fig 1-13**) has two components. The first is a cylindrical accordion base that houses the wires running to the observation platform, the power/signal wire to the head motor drive servo and the compass sensor. The second is essentially a rectangular box with an open bottom. This box fits into a saddle in the accordion base. It is fitted on the outer front with a cylindrical segment to fit the cylindrical torso base. The back of the box is flat and allows the bundled wires of the observation platform to pass out of the base, up the back of the box and onto the sensor platform.

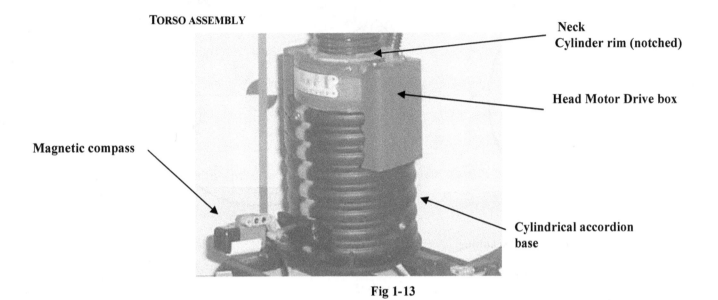

TORSO ASSEMBLY

Neck Cylinder rim (notched)

Head Motor Drive box

Magnetic compass

Cylindrical accordion base

Fig 1-13

HEAD MOTOR DRIVE BOX

The drive box (**Fig 1-14**) is a removable assembly that houses the motor and gear train for head rotation. It also forms the foundation for the neck and observation platform of the oculus. The rim plate for the cylindrical neck hub turns on the top surface of the drive box and is secured to it by notched guides (**Fig 1-23.**)

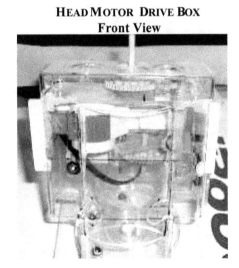

HEAD MOTOR DRIVE BOX
Front View

Fig 1-14

Head Movement Motor and Gear Train

This drive assembly is fitted with a servo motor mounted in the body that turns two vertical axles. A system of gears engages the servo axle to the neck axle, with a ration of approximately 4:1. This ratio keeps the neck axle of the observation platform turning at a relatively low speed, and allows a more precise control of its angular position.

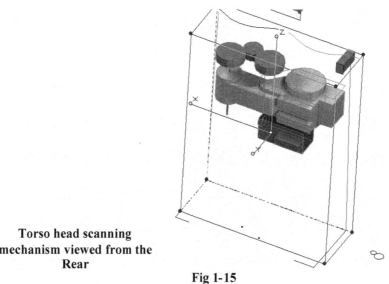

Torso head scanning mechanism viewed from the Rear

Fig 1-15

VIEW OF HEAD TURNING GEAR TRAIN

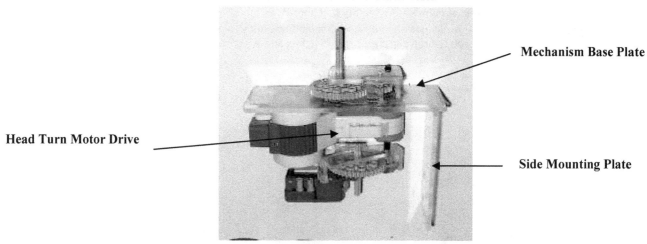

Mechanism Base Plate

Head Turn Motor Drive

Side Mounting Plate

Fig 1-16

Touch Sensor for Head Centering

The drive axle for the neck and head turning assembly extends up to the gear train for head turning and down to a gear train that actuates a touch sensor. This lower train (**Fig 1-17**) is for centering the head to Forward Looking direction (see **Chapter III**.) Rover decisions require a range finder that is forward looking. Ranges that are slightly askew to the actual motor heading lead to decisions that can cause collisions and stalled motor actions.

The lower gear train drives a second axle that is fitted with a cam. The cam turns and compresses the touch button when the axle lines up with a specific point on the right side. This point is a measured number of revolutions from the forward looking exact center. At the activation of the touch sensor, head motion to the right stops. Centering the head is accomplished by the return revolution count.

VIEW OF TOUCH SENSOR FOR HEAD CENTERING

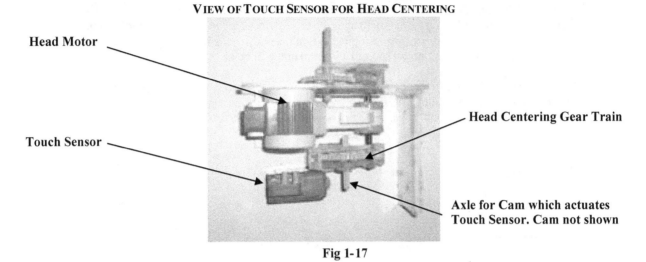

Head Motor

Head Centering Gear Train

Touch Sensor

Axle for Cam which actuates Touch Sensor. Cam not shown

Fig 1-17

MAGNETIC COMPASS

The **Unit1** is fitted with a magnetic compass (**Fig 1-18**.) This compass is sensitive to ferrous materials (such as steel screws, brackets and housings) and electro-magnetic fields (from batteries, motors, etc.) The position of this sensor is far from these sources of error, extended out so as to be clear of the head turn motor in the upper torso and the Brick power cells in the lower Cab Body.

It is also installed upside down. The standard position for a magnetic compass is arranged so the alignment is with magnetic North and the swing is *clockwise* to E, S and W respectively. For the purpose of the Rover, the magnetic alignment favors Cartesian coordinates, where alignment is with 0 (North) and the swing is *counterclockwise* to 90deg, 180, 270. This sequence fits the position coding described in **Chapter III**.

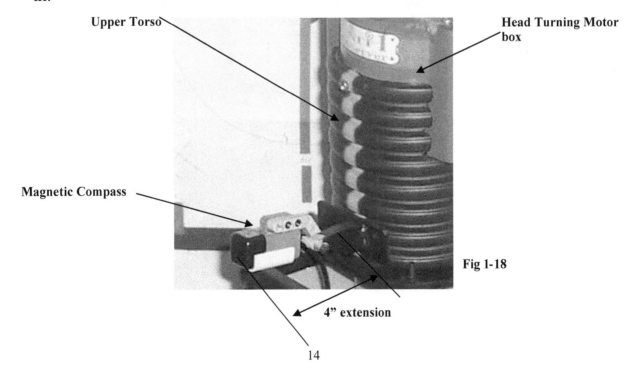

Upper Torso

Head Turning Motor box

Magnetic Compass

Fig 1-18

4" extension

14

OBSERVATION PLATFORM (OCULUS)

The observation platform houses the battery of sensors required for the Rover to observe the landscape. The significance of the platform is its ability to alter the view point of the observation, building a perspective from multiple sources. Other sensors positioned within the body of the Unit1 may verify and/or augment the basic platform. But the principal source of information will come from the platform sensors.

The platform consists of a mounting plate (**Fig 1-19.**) Four sensors are positioned on the plate. The plate or platform is in turn supported by a cylindrical "neck" which positions the entire assembly above the body. A vertical axle turns this assembly by a servo motor mounted in the body.

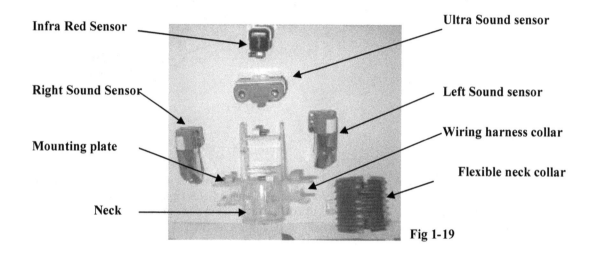

Infra Red Sensor
Ultra Sound sensor
Right Sound Sensor
Left Sound sensor
Wiring harness collar
Mounting plate
Flexible neck collar
Neck

Fig 1-19

A system of gears (**Fig 1-15**) engages the servo axle to the neck axle, with a ratio of approximately 3:1 (that means one gear must turn 3 times for the other gear to turn once.) This keeps the observation platform turning at a relatively low speed, and allows a more precise control of its angular position.

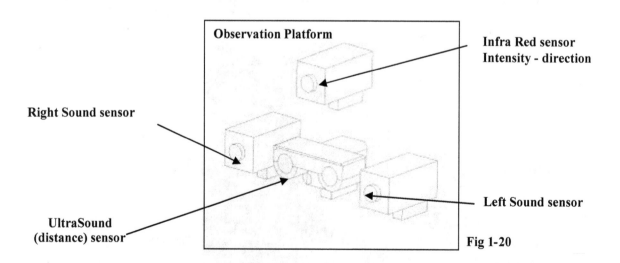

Observation Platform
Infra Red sensor
Intensity - direction
Right Sound sensor
Left Sound sensor
UltraSound
(distance) sensor

Fig 1-20

The Rover uses output from these sensors (**Fig 1-20**) to trigger motor actions. They may be assembled in a *random* format where position is not in any strict sequence. But in our case they are assembled as a group on the observation platform.

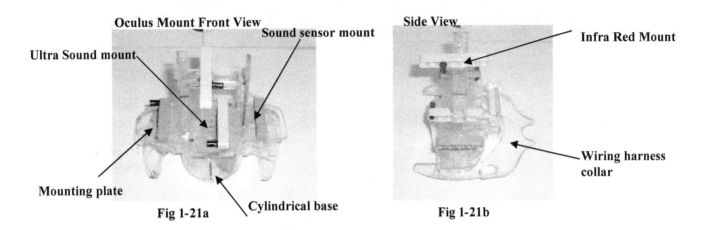

Oculus Mount Front View

Sound sensor mount

Ultra Sound mount

Side View

Infra Red Mount

Mounting plate

Wiring harness collar

Cylindrical base

Fig 1-21a

Fig 1-21b

The oculus mount is fitted with a cylindrical neck at its base (**Figs 1-21 a&b.**) The neck fits into an accordion style collar. The collar allows the oculus head to bend and twist when inadvertently restrained or met with some obstruction. The collar is loosely affixed to the mount's neck by a single vertical stud.

The collar in turn fits over a cylinder with a hub that is turned by an axle driven by the head motor gear train in the upper torso box. This cylinder and hub has a notched rim (**Fig 1-23**) that is kept in place by two notched guides that also serve as stops for neck rotation limits. The axle running through the hub is plastic with a certain amount of twist flexibility. This twist is used to advantage in the design of the stops (see **Chapter II.**)

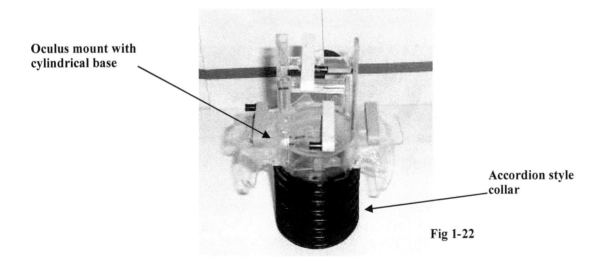

Oculus mount with cylindrical base

Accordion style collar

Fig 1-22

The completed observation platform (**Fig. 1-22**) resembles a head, and is placed appropriately, on the top portion of the Rover.

Using Neck Axle Flex to Position Head

As an alternative to a cam actuated head stop, axle flexibility can be used to position the head. A stud may be placed to stop head rotation. When the neck hits the stop, the excess rotation is taken up by the flexible twist of the axle. When the motor rotation stops, the elastic property of the axle (enabling the twist) releases the pent up twist, reversing the motor drive back to the position of the stops. This is a programming instruction that is described in detail in **Chapter II.**

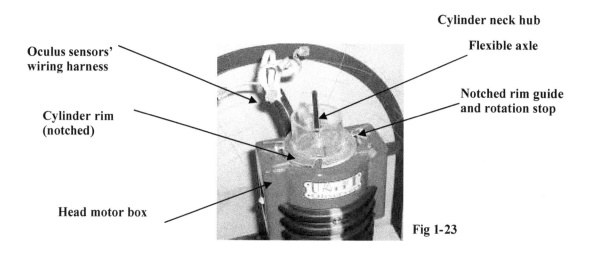

Cylinder neck hub

Flexible axle

Oculus sensors' wiring harness

Notched rim guide and rotation stop

Cylinder rim (notched)

Head motor box

Fig 1-23

ALL AROUND BUMPER AND FENDER

The last item to cover in Rover design is the outer exposed surface of the Unit1. It must be free of snags and other features that could cause the Rover to get caught, impeding its movements. In order to provide a relatively smooth surface a circumferential strip (of varying width) of thin and flexible plastic is held in place by the front bumper and by wheel struts.

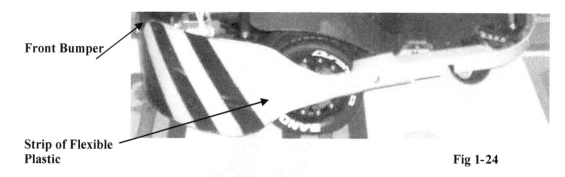

Front Bumper

Strip of Flexible Plastic

Fig 1-24

The plastic fender is also elastic. When it is contacted it tends to give slightly. At the same time it is pushing back at the contacted object. This aspect helps the Unit1 to steer away from obstacles.

It is wider in front to keep debris from collecting under the chassis. This also increases contact surface to initiate a touch signal against an obstruction. The extreme outer side-to-side surface is used to push the Rover away from objects that could snag the tires or tracks.

As the fender extends to the back of the Unit1, it narrows. At the rear of the Rover, low lying obstructions are generally out of the way and tall items can pushed away.

Fig 1-25

DRIVE PROPERTIES AND SWING RADII

The configuration of the wheel base, overall dimensions of the **Unit1** contribute to certain mobility issues. Since there is no flexibility in the chassis and framework, the **Unit1** travels about like a giant insect, susceptible to becoming ensnared in a variety of obstructions. Two of the principal challenges for rover design are 1) the anticipation and consequent strategies for avoiding getting "stuck" and then 2) the specific options for extraction once the **Unit1** is stuck.

Both issues are controlled by the physical dimensions of the Unit1 and its motion restrictions.
Referring to **Figure 1-26,** these dimensions are categorized as Follows:

1. Forward movement equivalent to one body length   - 18"
2. Backup movement to clear front bumper   - 12 5/8"
3. Normal swing radius for front bumper clearance   - 8"
4. Extreme swing radius for front bumper clearance   -12"
5. Swing radius for rear bumper clearance   -10.5"
6. Pass-through width   -16.5"
7. Pass-through height   -24.5"

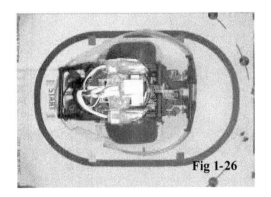

Fig 1-26

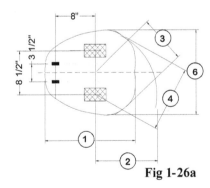

Fig 1-26a

The **Unit1 Rover Mk5** assembly operates at a finished profile of:

Height		24"
Outside Width		16"
Outside Length		18"
Wheel Base		8"
Wheel Width	Front	8 ½"
	Rear	3 ½"
Weight		9lbs
Op Voltage (min)		7.4v
(max)		9.0v

Fig 1-27

Figure 1-27 shows the general position of the sensors, the robot body, servo motors for sensor scanning and tractor functions. This gives a perspective of the functional end result we term the **Observing Unit.**

II
HARDWARE

This chapter is devoted to the qualities and shortcomings of the selected hardware. I have not found significant differences between manufacturers. For that reason I am describing each hardware item and associated programming with the belief that other brands of gear will be similar in character.

Hardware requirements of the **Unit1** Rover have been tailored for the most available off the shelf devices. I have chosen the **LEGO**™ brand of sensors and other hardware because of the variety and adaptability of their line. The Atmel 48mhz processor (**Brick**) is also a fine tool for creating plug in type robotic systems. It is very expandable with additional motor and sensor receivers. The BlueTooth capabilities of the **Brick** are a great plus.

I have designed and detailed the functioning automaton with complex groups or "batteries" of sensors and motor actions, all interconnected in what I defined as a **Real Grid**. Observations in this **Grid** are strictly experience. They do not form a logical progression, they are not abstract. They are formatted on the basis of numerically equal to **1** (in other words **true ;**) but they may be either plus (+1) or minus (-1). I will explain more on this later in **Chapter III**.

OBSERVATIONAL STRUCTURES

The observation platform described in **Chapter I** is populated with the group of sensors shown in **Fig. 1-1a & 1b**. The platform is capable of rotation through 180 degrees, from dead ahead, to left and to right. All the mounted sensors are programmed to register impulses through this arc.
The sensors are:
1. left sound (vibration), **LEGO**™ part 9845
2. right sound (vibration),
3. ultrasonic distance, **LEGO**™ part 4297174
4. infrared seeker, **Hi Technic** infra red seeker 4577327

In addition, a protective smooth outer surface can encase the observation platform. This helps prevent snags on furniture or other natural obstructions.

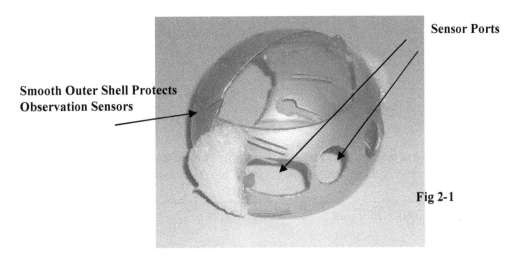

Sensor Ports

Smooth Outer Shell Protects Observation Sensors

Fig 2-1

For this casing (**Fig 2-1**,) a globe is preferred (specifically a hamster ball, with a single large access opening.) Sensor ports are cut in the casing. This draws from the concept of a "skull" in protecting the platform.

ARRANGING THE SENSORS

The primary configuration of the sensors is shown in **Fig 2-2**. These following features need to be part of the design:
1. ability to alter the view point of the observation, building input from multiple perspectives;
2. sensitivity of the sensors is not compromised by other sensors' "noise;"
3. protection for the sensors against snags and impacts.

Other configurations may work just as well, to be determined by the robot designer. Additional sensor may be positioned elsewhere within the body of the robot to verify and/or augment the basic platform. But the principal source of information will come from the platform.

Infra Red sensor
Intensity - direction

Left Sound sensor

UltraSound (distance) sensor

Right Sound sensor

Fig 2-2

Unit1 communicates with these devices through a system of cables. Because the sensor group is always moving in an arc above the body, the attached cables should offer the least obstruction or resistance to the rotating assembly. This is best accomplished by bundling the set, passing from the microprocessor to sensors located near the top of the body, **Fig 2-2a.**

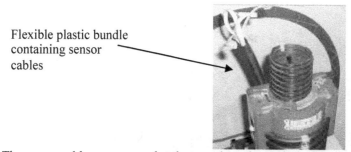

Flexible plastic bundle containing sensor cables

Fig 2-2a

The sensor cables are exposed at the top where they exit the bundle. They enter the opening at the rear of the head to connect to the sockets of the sensors, inside the protective encasement

MICRO PROCESSOR (BRICK)

The micro processor (or Brick) commands the sensors and motors. In the **Unit1** Rover, two Bricks are used to handle eight sensors (**Chapter I.**)

The Brick is programmed using the compiled version of NXC (Not Exactly C.) This version is freeware available on the Source Forge web site. The package can be downloaded and installed on a PC by following the simple download instructions on the site, or shown in **Example 2-7.**

Down Load Instructions from Source Forge Web Site   **Example 2-7**

The Bricx Command Center compiler and code source is a download option offered by the web site

> www.sourceforge.net

Log onto this site and navigate to the **BricxCC** page. This will display options for downloading the sources for code languages that can be used for the LEGO[TM] MINDSTORMS series of programmable microprocessors. The code samples used in this text are written in **Not eXactly C (NXC).**

When you have located the **Bricx Command Center 3.3** page, scroll down to the **Download** paragraph and find the option for **test_releases** folder.
Download these items::

   1.   Latest dated test_release for NXC
   2.   Installation instructions that appear on the BricxCC page
   3.   Installation instruction that appear with the test_release download

Follow the instruction to install the latest version of the NXC source code.

After you have successfully installed the NXC Command Center software:

1.   Bring up the Bricx CC dialogue box.
2.   Bring down the Edit screen and clink on *Compiler* tab
3.   Click on the NBC/NXC tab of compiler options
4.   Set the switches as follows
         4.1.1. Use internal compiler
         4.1.2. Enhanced firmware
         4.1.3. NXT 2.0 compatible firmware
         4.1.4. RICScript
         4.1.5. Optimization level [2]
         4.1.6. Max errors [0]

These setting will match the code levels used in this text. You may view the code samples in text form and/or compile them for use in your NXT[TM] processors.

As a last bit of information, it is highly recommended that you add to your library the edition **Lego Mindstorms NXT Power Programming, Robotics in C** by John C. Hansen, Variant Press second edition.

SOUND AND VIBRATION SENSORS

FUNCTION

The type of sound sensor, as well as all the other sensors, is a typical LEGO™ item.
It is available from the manufacture's retail online store. This device registers sound and vibration in omni
directional signals. Of and by itself the device cannot locate directional attributes. Just placing the bud on
the right side of the platform will not yield satisfactory audio location for the right side.

Locating the Sound Source

The mounted positions of the sound (vibration) sensor (or bud) are indicated as left and right (**Fig 2-2.**)
However some modification of the housing is required in order to register primarily left or right sound
sources, respectively. Drawing from human anatomy, the bony structure of the skull just ahead of the ear is
a great transmitter of sound vibration that can reach the ear drum mechanism.

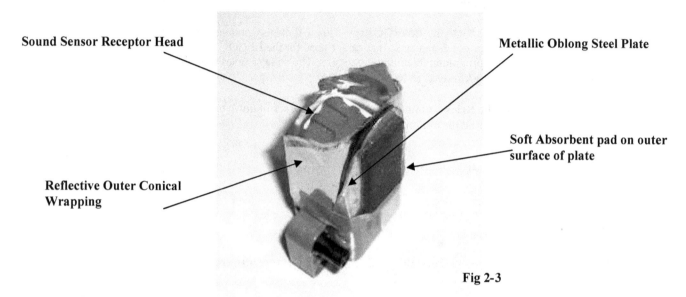

Sound Sensor Receptor Head

Metallic Oblong Steel Plate

Soft Absorbent pad on outer surface of plate

Reflective Outer Conical Wrapping

Fig 2-3

To simulate this bony structure an oblong steel plate (**Fig 2-3**) is affixed to the inside surface of the sensor.
Between the sensor and the steel plate, a conical reflective roll of plastic is placed to focus vibrations. On
the outer surface of the steel plate an absorbent pad is glued to dampen vibrations that travel across the
platform. This provides some isolation of left and right sensors from registering the same acoustical event.

These modifications are summarized:

1. The first modification is attaching a metallic oblong section to the inner edge of the bud. This acts
   to pick up vibrations and accentuate them on the inner side (because it is protected) of the bud.
2. The next modification is to create a polished inner surface to this metallic cone to reflect sound
   waves back to the receiver surface of the bud.
3. The third modification is to house the bud in a protective casing or "skull."
4. The forth modification is providing Styrofoam sound absorbing "ear trumpets" on the outside of
   the protective casing. These act to prevent sound vibrations from being transmitted across the
   casing to the other side's sound bud.

They are further depicted by the break away figure of the assembly shown in **Fig 2-4.** The placement of the
sound bud with the attached modifications is shown in **Fig 2-5**. This figure also locates the position and
mounts for the other sensors that are to be installed.

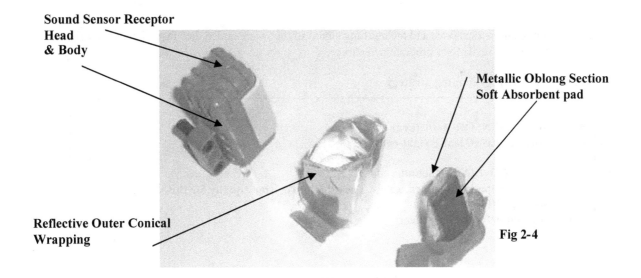

Sound Sensor Receptor Head & Body

Metallic Oblong Section Soft Absorbent pad

Reflective Outer Conical Wrapping

Fig 2-4

Each sound sensor must be calibrated to match as nearly as possible the reading levels of the other. This is done by experimentation and testing of each sensor with a known noise source.

Calibration for the sound sensors must be for very small variation in intensity, between 20 to 50 db. This low range picks up variations in sound when it is reflected off near by obstructions. The reflected sound may be from the robot's own motors, or a programmed sound, giving clues about the robot's surroundings.

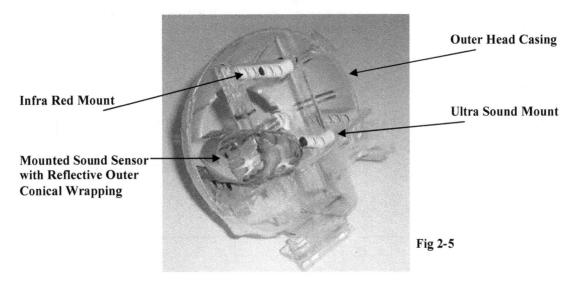

Outer Head Casing

Infra Red Mount

Ultra Sound Mount

Mounted Sound Sensor with Reflective Outer Conical Wrapping

Fig 2-5

Sound and vibration detection are important elements in locating masses and bulk that is near. Bulky landscape features reflect sound and vibrate in sympathy with external sources. They can even be affected by the nearness of the Rover itself. One feature of the sound detection programming is for the Rover to emit a series of sounds while it is taking readings, developing a form of sonar.

Also part of the strategy is to allow the sound signals to accumulate in magnitude (**Exam 2-1**.) As the Rover is taking readings, do not zero out subsequent echoes/readings. If they are allowed to accumulate, stray loud signals will be embedded in the cumulative reading and add value to the polling period. This synthesizes sound magnification.

SOUND COMPOUNDING- ADDING SIGNALS

It's not unusual for the sound signal to be faint. Volume is important, but when volume is low, the direction is of greater interest. In this case, the intensity signal (volume) should be additive, where the sensor is polled more than once and the resulting signal strengths are added. For faint signals, this gives a better order of magnitude for a programmed choice.

Sound Sensors Programming Strategy   **Example 2-1**

```
#define SND1 SENSOR_4  //left ear
#define SND2 SENSOR_1  //right ear

//TextOut(0,LCD_LINE2,"Sound buds");
//task poll_soundbuds(). Calibrate ears. They do not register equally for this set up
SetSensorSound(IN_4); //left ear
SetSensorSound(IN_1); //right ear

xy=0;
xxy=0 ;
                          //TextOut(0,LCD_LINE5,"Listen do loop");
do{
{
//send a sonic ping
//PlayTone(800,500);                //optional sonar ping
//Wait(200);
}
x=SND1+x;                           //receive the ping
                                    //After some experimentation, it is determined that
xx=((SND2)*1.1)+xx;                  //right ear must be notched UP
cntr=cntr+1;

}
//end of Listen do loop
while(cntr<3) ;
//Add the raw data. Use this as the criterion for location. It will be larger than just one
reading
```

ULTRA SONIC SENSOR

FUNCTION

This sensor (**Fig 2-6**) is placed "front-looking" on the observation platform. It receives a lot of attention because of its range finding qualities. But it has its limitations. It doesn't always pick up the correct distance, especially if the surface is soft and absorbent or slanted at an angle to the axis of the receiver/transmitter (transducer.)

If there is a protective "skull" casing (**Fig 2-1**) this sensor is placed inside and "eye-sockets" must be drilled through the casing. These sockets must be large enough to prevent unwanted reflection back to the transducer.

The ultra sound can be very inaccurate in many environments. This can be a mixed blessing. Most of the inaccuracies are a result of the beam spread from the sound source. This spread causes echoes from the sides, as well as ahead, to register on the receiver. Multiple receiver signals can be unwanted signals causing "noise." But they can also indicate a general proximity of peripheral landscape, not just what is directly ahead. For example due to the chassis width, a reading slightly off to the side may indicate an obstruction. Such an obstruction would probably show up as a side lobe reflection on the wide beam of the ultra sound sensor. Although this reflection would be an inaccurate reading of what is dead ahead, it is not an unwanted bit of information.

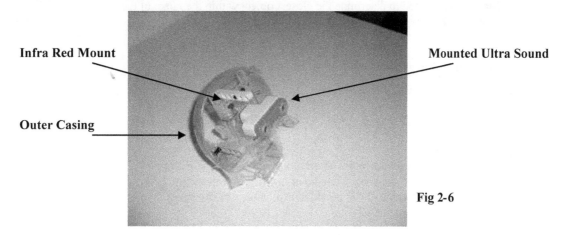

Infra Red Mount

Mounted Ultra Sound

Outer Casing

Fig 2-6

In the case of the Rover, we don't want inaccuracies and doubtful positives to rule when it comes to distance and obstruction avoidance. At the same time we want to allow some peripheral side vision. The ambiguities of what is directly ahead and what is to the side must be significantly reduced before this sensor can be used effectively as a tool. To accomplish this I use high & low range finding programming.

HIGH & LOW RANGE-USND

The first strategy for reducing ambiguity is aimed at distance and range finding. The device is prone to registering a distance that is the default range limit. This default is 250 mm (98.4 inches/8.2 ft.) In some cases the device will not pick up an echo, and it returns a default reading of 250 mm. The approach is to make a bundle of readings, reducing them all to the least range of the sampled readings.

Ultra Sound Sensor Programming Strategy #1 (for Closest mark or least range)   **Example 2-2**

```
//TextOut(0,LCD_LINE4,"Ultra Sound     ");
mutex USndAcc;

SetSensorLowspeed (IN_2);  //USnd
Acquire (USndAcc);
//This segment registers distance based upon a fixed looking position
//It is not a side scanning sequence. The head is either Front or SideL/R
//this finds the smallest value (closest mark)

xs=250;
repeat (10)
{
x= (SensorUS(IN_2));          //these readings are all in mm (not inches)
                              //.3936" per mm

if(x<xs){xs=x;}
}
//xs is the USnd output
```

26

The second strategy is to accumulate the range readings over a measured number of episodes. The average of the range readings (gross sum of ranges / number of readings) determines the reliable proximity of the immediate landscape.

The important point to remember when using these strategies is that they are not compatible.
  Strategy #1 is used to determine the closest object within the range of the sensor.
  Strategy #2 is used to determine the general density (distribution) of mass or bulk in the vicinity.

Ultra Sound Sensor Programming Strategy #2 (for Median mark) **Example 2-3**

```
//TextOut(0,LCD_LINE4,"Ultra Sound     ");
mutex USndAcc;

SetSensorLowspeed (IN_2);  //USnd
Acquire (USndAcc);
//This segment registers distance based upon a fixed looking position
//It is not a side scanning sequence. The head is either Front or SideL/R
//this finds the average value of the marks within range of the beam

        sxxR=0;cntr=0;
    repeat(3)
      {
xChk= (SensorUS(IN_2))
cntr=cntr+1;
sxxR=sxxR+xChk;
        }
zx2=sxxR/cntr;
Release(USndAcc);

//Do not combine this with "Closest mark. "
// You can't have two different ranging calcs competing
```

INFRA-RED SEEKER

FUNCTION

Infra-red seeker is a wonderful sensor when it incorporates direction and intensity. This gives a needed dimensional depth to the sensor matrix, as will be shown in **Chapter V**. This sensor is placed on the center axis of the observation platform, above the ultra-sound, and is front-looking (**Fig 2-8.**) The protective casing must be cut away over the effective arc of IR seeker (**Fig 2-9.**)

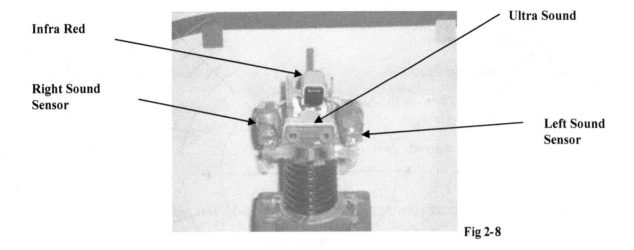

Infra Red

Right Sound
Sensor

Ultra Sound

Left Sound
Sensor

Fig 2-8

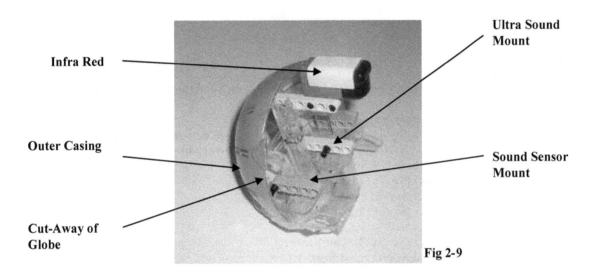

Infra Red

Outer Casing

Cut-Away of
Globe

Ultra Sound
Mount

Sound Sensor
Mount

Fig 2-9

The sensitivity of the sensor must be accounted for by stepping the strength of the infra red emission. This is done in two phases. The first phase involves two steps. The first is amplification of the signal by a multiple of 10 to include fractions as whole numbers. The second is to select the highest value from a series of five readings.

The second phase is to select the number of occurrences over which a high reading is obtained. This series is also set a five (**Exam 2-4.**)

From this selection process two features of the heat source can be detected:
1. Principal direction;
2. Maximum recorded strength.

These values are used to increase the Rover's peripheral sense. At some trigger point the Rover can be directed to "look" to the side.

```
SetSensorLowspeed(SNX4);
{
  float dir, se1, se2, se3, se4, se5, result, cnt,IRcntr;
  //     L  LofC  C  RofC  R
 IRcntr=0;
  SetSensorLowspeed(IRSEEKER);
// ClearScreen();
 //TextOut(0,LCD_LINE1,"from IRSeeker");
 Sdirx=0;Sxx=0;Scnt=0;sxx=0;
 IRrpt:
 se1=0;se2=0;se3=0;se4=0;se5=0;  //zero out variables
 Sx=0;
  do
  {
   ReadSensorHTIRSeeker2AC(IRSEEKER, dir, se1x, se2x, se3x, se4x, se5x);
                                //First, magnify the reading by 10
  if (se1x>se1 ) {se1 =se1x*10;}   //then choose the Highest value
  if (se2x>se2 ) {se2 =se2x*10;}
  if (se3x>se3 ) {se3 =se3x*10;}
  if (se4x>se4 ) {se4 =se4x*10;}
  if (se5x>se5 ) {se5 =se5x*10;}
  cntr=cntr+1;
 }
 while (cntr<5);
 //G4x5b2a2
//NumOut(0,LCD_LINE2,se1);NumOut(15,LCD_LINE2,se2);NumOut(30,LCD_LINE2,se3
);
//NumOut(45,LCD_LINE2,se4);NumOut(60,LCD_LINE2,se5);
              if (se1==sxx) {Sx=Sx+1;Scnt=Scnt+1;}   //record the number of occurrences
                                                  //as the variable Scnt

      if (se1>sxx) {sxx=se1; Sxx=0;Sx=1;Scnt=1;}
              if (se2==sxx) {Sx=Sx+2;Scnt=Scnt+1;}
      if (se2>sxx) {sxx=se2;Sxx=0; Sx=2;Scnt=1;}
              if (se3==sxx) {Sx=Sx+3;Scnt=Scnt+1;}
      if (se3>sxx) {sxx=se3;Sxx=0; Sx=3;Scnt=1;}
              if (se4==sxx) {Sx=Sx+4;Scnt=Scnt+1;}
      if (se4>sxx) {sxx=se4;Sxx=0; Sx=4;Scnt=1;}
              if (se5==sxx) {Sx=Sx+5;Scnt=Scnt+1;}
      if (se5>sxx) {sxx=se5;Sxx=0; Sx=5;Scnt=1;}

 IRcntr=IRcntr+1;
                    //Accumulate & magnify Sxx quantities
 Sxx=Sxx+Sx;
//      TextOut(0,LCD_LINE5,"Sx =          ");NumOut(40,LCD_LINE5,Sx);
// NumOut(60,LCD_LINE6,Sxx);
//      TextOut(0,LCD_LINE7,"   ");NumOut(0,LCD_LINE7,Scnt);
 int xse=0;


if (IRcntr<5) {goto IRrpt; }
                    //This is continued in Example 2-4 cont.
```

```
dirSxx=Sxx/Scnt;
//dirSxx is the principal direction of the heat source
//sxx is the maximum recorded strength
// NumOut(80,LCD_LINE3,sxx);TextOut(0,LCD_LINE3,"strength");
        //ClearScreen();
//        NumOut(50,LCD_LINE3,dirx);TextOut(0,LCD_LINE3,"dirx1 =");
//        NumOut(50,LCD_LINE8,dirSxx);TextOut(0,LCD_LINE8,"dirSxx
=");NumOut(70,LCD_LINE8,sxx);

   // ClearScreen();

}
```

PROTECTIVE CASING FOR OBSERVATION SENSORS

The "skull" casing (**Fig 2-1**) must be cut to allow the ultra sonic signals to pass cleanly beyond the casing surface. This means that the eye holes must be large enough for a clear signal to pass through. From **Fig 2-7**, it can be seen that the eye opening is much greater than the transmitting surface. The 0.34 inch diameter transmitter "eyes" are located 0.625 inches away from the casing opening, and each opening is 0.875 inches in diameter.

The sound sensor ports are large enough for the reflective conical wrapping to pass completely through. The infra red sensor is mounted above and extended forward of the casing to avoid masking sources of heat that are close to the Rover.

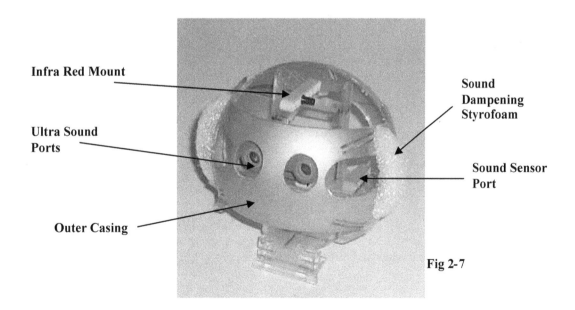

Infra Red Mount

Sound Dampening Styrofoam

Ultra Sound Ports

Sound Sensor Port

Outer Casing

Fig 2-7

HEAD ALIGNMENT & CENTERING

The observation platform is rotated left and right by motor action. The alignment position of the platform is important because the observation platform records all the sensory events in terms of their specific location to the center alignment of the robot body. Misalignments are common after a few cycles of left-right looking. For this reason, a contact sensor is actuated by a cam that stops head rotation when it has reached the left side stopping point. From this stopping point, the servo motor reverses rotation (to the right) at a set time and power to achieve dead ahead alignment of the platform.

Head Centering Programming Strategy – Touch Sensor Stop   **Example 2-5**

```
zxxa=BatteryLevel();
Bx=(7800/zxxa);
Bxx=Bx*100;
pctj=80;
Pwrj=pctj*Bxx/100;

SetSensorTouch(IN_3);              //motor port C turns the head
                                   //sensor port 3 receives touch signals for head location
{
Lk="LR" ;
        //"RR" or "LR" is a self-centering return from a polling turn
    {
        {
        if ((Lk=="L")||(Lk=="LR"))
                                    {
                                    while (IN_3==false)
        OnFwdReg(OUT_C,Pwrj,OUT_REGMODE_IDLE); //Look to the left
                                    }
        Off(OUT_C);
        }
    }

        OnRevReg(OUT_C,Pwrj,OUT_REGMODE_IDLE);
        Wait(850);
        Off(OUT_C);
        //full rotation to the center from left, allowing centering
    }
```

The drawback of this approach is that it requires a sensor port. With the current design of the observation platform, all sensor ports are assigned. Rather than split one of the port, a second alternative is employed to center the "head" or observation platform without a sensor activated stop.

This alternative to the touch sensor for head centering is the use of the head turning axle to automatically position the head motor to a stop position. Since each side location for the head turn is fitted with a stop plate, the head is prevented from rotating beyond a certain point. The motor however is allowed to continue to turn even when the head has reached a stop. This action elastically twists the plastic axle.

31

When the motor stops turning, due to a programming instruction, not a sensor signal, the pent up twist in the axle is released. The released twist causes the motor to turn in reverse to the point where it is aligned with the stop and the axle no longer is twisted.

Head Centering Programming Strategy – Axle Torque   **Example 2-6**

```
zxxa=BatteryLevel();
Bx=(7800/zxxa);
Bxx=Bx*100;
pctj=80;
Pwrj=pctj*Bxx/100;
{
Lk="LR" ;
          //"RR" or "LR" is a self-centering return from a polling turn
          { if (Lk=="LR")  //Look to the left
                   {
              OnFwdReg(OUT_C,Pwrj,OUT_REGMODE_IDLE);
              Wait(950);
              Float(OUT_C);
              //This overshoots the stops
              //at 80pwr and builds extra torque in the neck shaft, twisting it
              //The extra torque is released in counter rotation as the motor "floats"
                   }
          }

  //Execute full rotation to the right timed from the stops, allowing centering
                  if ((Lk=="L")||(Lk=="LR"))
                            {
                            OnRevReg(OUT_C,Pwrj,OUT_REGMODE_IDLE);
                            Wait(850);
                            Off(OUT_C);
                            }
}
```

The motor C then turns the head at a specific power and timing to center head alignment with the center of the Rover torso.

COMPASS SENSOR (ADVANCED OBSERVER)

The Rover follows commands to alter its position relative to local coordinates. In doing this, it performs actions which are specific to its body positions of right, left, etc. Because of variations in motor performance, surface terrain and power fluctuations, servo commands are not always perfectly executed. Eventually, regardless of corrections and performance feed back the Rover will become disoriented. It must rely upon a set of global coordinates which it can detect with minimal error. For this, it uses a magnetic compass.

The compass sensor is mounted at a position on the body, away from disturbing magnetic fields generated by motors or ferrous materials. It is aligned specifically dead ahead, conforming to the coordinates of the Rover. This enables the Rover to sense where it is located relative to magnetic North.

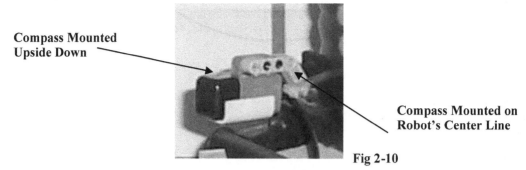

Compass Mounted Upside Down

Compass Mounted on Robot's Center Line

Fig 2-10

However in the Unit1 Mark5 Rover, the compass is modified.

1. The compass sensor is mounted **upside down**. This causes the readings to be expressed in **Cartesian coordinates (0 to 360 deg counter clockwise**) rather than Cardinal compass readings (0 north to 180 south clockwise.)
2. The compass readings are corrected for Deviation, a characteristic of the vicinity of metal to the compass that causes magnetic readings to deviate from magnetic North.

CORRECTING MAGNETIC COMPASS READINGS FOR DEVIATION

As the magnetic compass pivots in a 360 arc, deviation causes the magnetic headings vary from the actual heading change. For example if the heading of 210 deg is changed 45 degrees to 255 degs the new compass heading may read 275 degs. This would be a 20 deg **deviation** error. Such errors are generally caused by internal compass errors and/or local disturbances such as the proximity of metallic parts in the housing.

They can also be caused by a large metallic structure that is nearby and not part of the compass or housing. Errors caused by nearby structures are not easily corrected, but proximity errors can be corrected. This utilizes a process known as swinging the compass.

Swinging the Compass

1. Select a location to swing the compass that does not have any metallic structures within a couple of feet of the compass and housing.
2. Position the housing where it is aligned with the output reading 0 degrees. This should be magnetic North.
3. Rotate the housing 45 deg counter clockwise (CCW.) Note the output.
4. Continue rotating the housing at 45 deg intervals CCW and take readings at each interval.
5. Plot the deviations from actual angle of turn against output reading.
6. For each 45 deg range determine the fraction of error (Mag/Actual = fM.)
7. Create a set of equations that correct the readings to the actual change

Example 2-8

```
//This calibration is for specific positions of the Unit1 and its internal wiring & motor locations
{
if ((DegMag<361)&&(DegMag>300)) {DegMx=(DegMag-300)*0.45;} //fM==0.45
if ((DegMag<151)&&(DegMag>0)) {DegMx= (DegMag)*0.45;}
if ((DegMag<201)&&(DegMag>150)) {DegMx= (DegMag)*0.75;}    //fM==0.75
if ((DegMag<250)&&(DegMag>200)) { DegMx=DegMag;}           //fM==1
if ((DegMag<300)&&(DegMag>250)) { DegMx=DegMag*1.14;}      //fM==1.14

//Some ranges may require complex adjustments. These would take the form shown below

//if ((DegMag<300)&&(DegMag>200)) {DegMx=(210)*0.45+(DegMag-00)*1.2+(50*1.5);}
//if ((DegMag<200)&&(DegMag>149)) {DegMx=(210)*0.45+(100)*1.3+((DegMag-150)*1.65);}
}
```

These equations are then imbedded in the programming at every instance where a compass reading is taken. It won't completely solve the problem of accuracy with heading but it offers a solution to the common problem of deviation errors.

Magnetic Compass Sensor Programming Strategy   **Example 2-9**

```
{
        {
int x, DegMag, DegMx;
float fm;
DegMag=0;
repeat (10){
ClearScreen();
SetSensorLowspeed(IN_2);
x=SensorUS(IN_2);
DegMag=DegMag+(2*x);
        }
DegMag=(DegMag/10) ;
ClearScreen();
TextOut(0,LCD_LINE1,"Read");
TextOut(0,LCD_LINE2,"Mag Heading");NumOut(70,LCD_LINE2,DegMag);
//Wait(SEC_10);
//correct magnetic heading
DegMx=0 ;
//This calibration is for specific positions of the Units and wiring
        {
        //Insert Deviation Calibration Example 2-8
        }

Deg0=DegMx ; if (Deg0==0) {Deg0=1;}
if (Deg0>360) {Deg0=Deg0-360;}

}
```

ADDITIONAL TOUCH SENSORS (ADVANCED OBSERVER)

Touch sensors mounted on the body provide more exploration to a situation already detected. They are not intended as primary alert mechanisms, although they can at times function in that capacity. These sensors are fitted with extensions (antenna and/or bumpers) which sample both the landscape (3 dimension space) and terrain (2 dimensional ground surfaces.)

Since most of the observational data gathered from sampling the landscape/environment is drawn from the sensors housed in the observation platform, the situation(s) involving movement about the terrain requires clarification. The focus on what's going on at track level is left to the motors and their feed back (described in Chapter V.) Motor feed back also alerts the Rover to being stuck, or experiencing a dead end. But there is no three dimensional information with motor feed back alone.

This is where two antennas (left and right,) fill in the gaps of how and by what obstruction motor feed back is causing a jump.

Fig 2-11

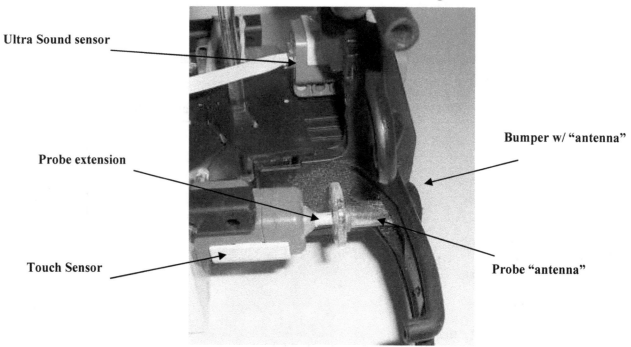

Ultra Sound sensor

Probe extension

Touch Sensor

Bumper w/ "antenna"

Probe "antenna"

HOLDING THE SIGNAL UNTIL IT'S PROCESSED

In many instances during the program, while five tasks are running simultaneously, a sensor may take many readings or reset. In these cases a trigger reading can be lost and a necessary motor action missed. To avoid lost signals, a routine that does not reset the sensor or replace a trigger signal is required. It operates on the basis of "go forward when read." After the reading, or action, the sensor value is reset to a null, or "N." This is shown in the **Example 2-10 (a)** for a touch signal from the Slave to the Master Brick.

Touch Data Gathering Info from SLAVE sensors   **Example 2-10 (a)**

```
TCHx="N";
 SetSensorTouch(IN_4);
 SetSensorTouch(IN_1);

 LISTEN:
Pin="";
ClearScreen();
 TextOut(0,LCD_LINE1,"Listen for Queue") ;
 if ((SENSOR_4==1)&&(TCHx=="N")) { TCHx="L";Wait(100); }
 if ((SENSOR_1==1)&&(TCHx=="N")) {TCHx="R";Wait(100);}

ReceiveRemoeString(INBOX1, true, Pin);
 //INBOX1= 5 Receive Master routing.
//Master sends a signal that it wants info on a touch event.
// If there is no signal in the INBOX1, Pin is a null ("")
if (Pin=="") {goto LISTEN;}
else if (Pin=="Tch")   { goto TOUCH_R; }//Example 2-10 (c)
```

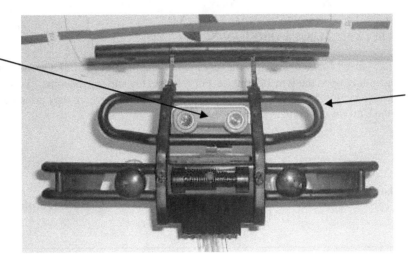

Ultra Sound sensor

Bumper w/ USnd sensor

Example 2-10 (b)

```
TCH3="N";TCHR_L="N";TCHx="N",TCHy="N";
 SetSensorLowspeed (IN_3);

LISTEN:
 Pin="";
ClearScreen();
 TextOut(0,LCD_LINE1,"Listen for Queue") ;

 xs3=250;
repeat (10)
{
x3= (SensorUS(IN_3));            //these readings are all in cm (not inches)
                                //.3936" per cm

if(x3<xs3){xs3=x3;}
}
NumOut(0,LCD_LINE3,xs3); Wait(200);
 if ((x3<10)&&(TCHy=="N"))
        {
        Mevent[4]=1;TCHy=StrCat("F",TCHx);Wait(100);
        TCHx=TCHy;
        }

TextOut(40,LCD_LINE3,TCHy); Wait(200);
ReceiveRemoteString(INBOX1, true, Pin);   //INBOX1= 5 receive Master routing
if (Pin=="") {goto LISTEN;}
TextOut(0,LCD_LINE2,Pin); Wait(200);
 else if (Pin=="Tch")   { goto TOUCH_R; } //Example 2-10 (c)
goto LISTEN;
```

The Ultra Sound distance sensor is used as an assist to the two touch sensors, left and right. The value of this sensor is its ability to detect a 3 dimensional obstruction ahead and to gage if movement by the Rover has effectively cleared the obstruction. Touch sensors cannot do this once the Unit1 has backed away from the contact source.

The approach is to set a limit for closeness, just short of touching and contact. For the Unit1 chassis, this "clear" distance is 10 cm (4 inches.) This signal is registered with the SLAVE as a TCHx variable. The same as for a touch senor signal. It also sets a Motor event value as TRUE [+1] in the Front Touch array.

COMMUNICATION BETWEEN MASTER AND SLAVE

After the SLAVE has sensed contact [Touch] or a very near object in front [USnd] a variable is assigned specific a value, depending upon the type of contact. For a touch, the variable is either **"L"** or **"R."** For an ultra sound, the variable is **"F."** These strings are then sent to the Master, where they are sorted according to how and where the Unit1 is operating.

Routine to Send Touch & Distance Data from SLAVE to MASTER

Example 2-10 (c)

```
TOUCH_R:
      {
      TCHR_L="OK";
      if (TCHx=="N")
        { SendResponseString(OUTBOX,"Nx"); Wait(100);
        goto LISTEN;
        }

TextOut(0,LCD_LINE3,"Found Touch");
TextOut(0,LCD_LINE4,TCHx);
SendResponseString(OUTBOX,TCHx);
TCHx="N";TCHy="N";
Wait(100);
TextOut(0,LCD_LINE5,"Sent touch");
      }


Touchx:
Wait(2000);      //add timeout to avoid double action on touch
goto LISTEN;     //suppress Receive string "OKT"
```

The NXT **LEGO**™ motor (part # 4297008) offers programmable features which enable specialize control of the motorized elements. The basic motor commands FWD or REV direct motor hub rotations. When the Rover uses gear trains, the motor direction of the hub is not always the direction of the driven gear that powers the track or wheel. Care must be taken when developing directional commands that the motor hub rotation is corrected for the driven gear rotation.

These features are very helpful in decisions involving stalled or poorly executed motor commands. They include:

- Head turning
- Forward motion
- Turning differentials in wheel rotations
- Revolution counting
- Power variations
- Speed variations
- Tachometer readings

FORWARD MOTION

Example 2-11

```
//Front Wheel Drive  ::: Head Fwd
 //Located over drive wheels
//aft (at the casters) looking fwd towards
//drive wheels, Motor designations are:
                //A is Left Motor, B is Right Motor, C is Head Motor
//Motor commands (AB) corrected for geared Wheel drives
                //Fwd is now Rev for Front Wheel Drive, Rev is now Fwd
                //Head movement (C) corrected for reverse position on drive
mutex  Fwd_Motr;


     {
  Acquire (Fwd_Motr);
  OnRevReg(OUT_AB,pwr,OUT_REGMODE_SPEED);
//This is a major forward command
  Release (Fwd_Motr);
     }
```

TURNING DIFFERENTIALS IN WHEEL ROTATIONS

Example 2-12

```
//>>>>>>>>>>>>>>>>>>>>>>  this starts a steering turn left w/ no stop time

OnRevSync(OUT_AB,Pwr1,-50);
Wait(1000);
        //turn to LEFT

//>>>>>>>>>>>>>>>>>>>>>>>  this starts a steering turn left w/ no stop time
OnRevSync(OUT_AB,Pwr1,50);
Wait(1000);
        //turn to RIGHT
```

POWER VARIATIONS

Example 2-15

```
 Zxxa = BatteryLevel();
Bx = (7800/zxxa);
Bxx=Bx*100;
Pwr1= 60*Bxx/100;

pctx=90;

Pwrx=pctx*Bxx/100;
//aft (at the drive wheels) looking fwd towards the
//casters, Motor designations are:
     //A is Right Motor
     //B is Left Motor
//keep motor calls one at a time so power goes to one

 repeat(1)
 {
OnRevReg(OUT_B,Pwrx,OUT_REGMODE_IDLE); //Right motor pushes fwd -
turn to left
OnFwdReg(OUT_A,Pwrx,OUT_REGMODE_IDLE); //Left motor pull aft -turn
to left
Wait(1200) ;

Off(OUT_AB);
}
```

REVOLUTION COUNTING

Example 2-13

```
Zxxa = BatteryLevel();
Bx = (7800/zxxa);
Bxx=Bx*100;
Pwr1= 60*Bxx/100;
pctx=90;

Pwrx=pctx*Bxx/100;
 RotateMotorEx(OUT_AB,Pwrx,1080,0,false, true)
          //this drives motors A&B at 90% for 3 complete revolutions and no
          //steering (false). Braking (true) at end of rotation
```

SPEED VARIATIONS

Example 2-14

```
 Zxxa = BatteryLevel();
Bx = (7800/zxxa);
Bxx=Bx*100;
Pwr1= 60*Bxx/100;
pctx=90;                        //alter (pctx) to vary the motor power & speed
Pwrx=pctx*Bxx/100;
OnRevReg(OUT_AB,Pwrx,OUT_REGMODE_SPEED);
```

TACHOMETER READINGS

This routine tests the revolution counter against an observed standard to determine whether or not the motor is stalled (barely turning or slipping) or rotating at a proper rate. The observed standard is simply a value determined by the applied power divided by a constant that has been shown to closely fit the actual rpm at the time of the observation (or experiment.)

Example 2-16

```
Rtaz=0;
Rtac0=0;
Rtaxx=0;

tEXs=CurrentTick();
ResetRotationCount(OUT_AB);

TextOut(0,LCD_LINE5," tac*          ");
NumOut(60,LCD_LINE5,hitBmp); //NumOut(80,LCD_LINE5,pwr);
ArrayInit(Mevent,0,14);
ctickx:
 tEXf=CurrentTick()-tEXs;
if (tEXf<2300) {goto ctickx;}        //this must allow 23000ms to elapse w/ motr
                                     //running. Then it takes a rotation count.


 xb=MotorRotationCount(OUT_B)*(-1);  //this changes reverse rotation to fwd
 xc= MotorRotationCount(OUT_A)*(-1);

 tEXf=tEXf/100;          //change micr-sec to cent-secs

 xbc=xb;
 if (xb>xc) {xbc=xc;}
 Rtacx=((xb+xc)/20);    //change revs to 1/10 scale

 Rtac0=(((Rtacx)/tEXf));
 Ktac0=(pwr/15);         //Ktac0 is a variable that (by observation) estimates the
                         //RPM output for a given power range and chassis load
NumOut(35,LCD_LINE5,Rtac0); NumOut(45,LCD_LINE5,Ktac0);
```

Unit1 Mark5 Rover
III
INNOVATION

PROGRAMMING SENSORY FEED BACK

The robot **Unit1 Mark5 Rover** has been developed with simplicity of function. The programming method deals with event streams which have No Rhyme or Reason to the robot. In the case of an automaton, the signals which pass through its circuits are not acknowledged by the computing entity as significant or inherently meaningful. The computer is a device from which humans interpret and decode meaning. This is possible when it involves a machine with an ability to sort "meaning" from a stream of sensory signals.

I have included this chapter on programming theory to present some of the fundamentals of the code sequences (algorithms) that will be ever-present in the text to follow. The Unit1 Mark5 presentation represents years of designing and programming, all aimed at producing a responsive and cogent automaton. Short explanations will be offered for certain decisions which have determined the shape and/or nature of the Mark5 and its operation.

Understanding of the subject theory is not essential to implementation of the programming. You may skip this segment if you wish and go directly to Chapter IV, Programming. For a more elaborate description of the algorithms, Chapter VI, Technical Approach, is offered. Either way, the text is intended to supply you with programming strategies intended to improve your level of experience.

The Unit1 Mark5 Rover utilizes sensory feed back in a way that enables the robotic Rover to operate with many self reliant capabilities. These programming methods are tailored specifically for the sensory Lego™ devices. However the reasoning behind the coded sequences is applicable to many of the existing sensors currently on the market.

We start with the proposal that experience is merely a series of events without a reference to time. Any sensory signal can be experienced in any time or place and within any other sequence of events. Events which occur in a sequence, although unplanned and random, can be arranged on the basis of the (random) sequence alone. They can be characterized as **logical** summations, or in other words they can be added and subtracted. In addition, events are not considered controlled by known or previously recognized associations.

From this logical summation of random and unplanned events, the observer draws a conclusion about the series of events. This is referred to as an **Observed Outcome**, and must have an observer.

The programming associates awareness and perception as elements of a **structure.** Although structure is symbolic it expresses an event as a signal within the train or sequence of all the sensors that were polled in the same instant. These bundled segments of **past structures** enter the robot's stream of **present** observations. The robot can be considered in a state of "knowing" when past and present both combine in this way to form observed experience.

UNIVERSES OF POSSIBILITIES

Can computer driven robots take the form of thinking creatures, or are they merely a computational device? There is the notion that humans can be considered computational devices. Can we add sophistications to our already complex robot computers and make them more *like* us?

In the first place, how is it that lowly creatures (e.g. the ant) can take a stream of sensory impulses and make any kind of "sense" out of them? By this is meant creating a pattern of action/behavior that draws information from the stream of consciousness. The programming aim is to create a means where a simple set of switches (represented as gates) has the ability to build more switching ports, developing complexity.

The robot programming presented here directs a computer to construct a series, based upon the results of a disconnected, random input. Or given any position in the input stream, the programming directs the computer to find its way to any other randomly chosen position in the stream. This is accomplished by developing a reasoned set of arguments which describe an association of events and how they may be symbolically depicted. Let us say event is considered a discrete observation of a quality (e.g. light intensity) or state (e.g. radiation.) It then hypothesizes that an **observer** is associated with the event through qualities or states by developing groups of membership (where they belong) and influence (when they happened.)

SWITCHING

The event logic involves a circuit with a switching pattern that has four states, rather than two.

As a physical construct, where each boundary side represents a switching alternative with four possible states, the switching boundary would comprise four sides. These four sides link other possibilities of state to form cubical "structures."

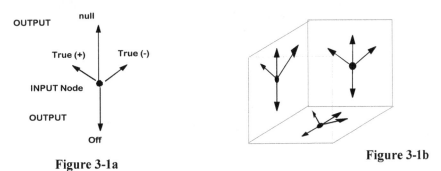

Figure 3-1a

Figure 3-1b

The symbolic logic of these postulates can be tested using a computer to sort, in an extremely disconnected frame of reference, all the events submitted to it, random or otherwise.

At the time I developed this approach, I was running my professional work on a Cray at Control Data in Minneapolis. I didn't need that power for this, so in 1985, I bought a Radio Shack TRS-80 desk top computer running at 4.2 MHz. The process to solve *equations of state* was initially coded in Fortran, later in Basic, QuickBasic, and C. This began as an elementary maze-like problem of random experiences. In no time it became much more complex.

THE ROBOT OBSERVES ITSELF

An *event* is an observed quality or state of an element. **Observational strategies** for an automaton are built upon layers of observations, each observation experiencing multiple events. Observations are expressed as

Real compound patterns. In other words they are all linked. Sensors acting as observers interact at this level of linking patterns. These interactions are for no reason other than initiating motor commands.

Motor responses are a necessary part of the Real universe experience. In the Real world, stimuli are evaluated within the framework of an imperative, which in our model is **Socialization,** and sponsors "activation." Just what is this activation? In the timeless and static layer of universes of the **Unit1 Mark5 Rover** possibilities of state lead to decisions.

WHAT IS A REAL EVENT?

History is built from sensory and feed back signals of actual sensory events Within the theory developed here, logical states are simple things that exist by themselves and are not considered related or inter-dependant but can be observed.

A group of events can be represented as a series with any order, called a ***battery***. A battery of sensors' events, or sensor qualities, can be arranged as rows and columns, representing *Members* of the group of events. This arrangement of qualities can be viewed as a pinball game where the Members' qualities represent the fixed studs upon a square table and the *Observed* events represent free flowing pin balls placed at the top of the table. When the balls are released and roll down each column of sensor qualities, any pinball (representing an observer) that hits a Member stud lights up the screen. This indicates that quality has been observed.

The screen lights up with an intensity that increases with more pinball hits. At a certain threshold, the intensity is great enough to initiate a Score. This is not dependant upon the sequence of the event experience, but upon the *density* of the events. In other words, it depends upon the number of pin balls hitting the studs in any given row of Member qualities. These experiences occur within the **Grid** of the of the *Members'* sensory group. They are *illuminated* by the pinball (observed) **events.**

Matrix Math

If you've gotten this far you probably are ready for some formal explanations about matrix expressions and linear solutions of multiple unknowns. The simple concept behind the proposal described in this text is that what we consider to be reality can be defined as a set of equations and can be solved in terms of logical states (+1,-1, 0,null.) I will show how to set up the equations of state and to define the variables. But first I want to offer for clarity information on the technique of the multiplication of matrix forms.

First let us define a set of unknown variables as a row. $A = (a1 \ \ a2 \ \ an)$

Next a set of known values we defined as a column.. $e = \begin{pmatrix} e1 \\ e2 \\ en \end{pmatrix}$

The *inner product* of **[A]x[e]** is the sum of the products of the corresponding components of the row matrix and the column matrix.

$$f[Q] = [A] \ x \ [e] \ = \ (a1 \ \ a2 \ \ an) \begin{pmatrix} e1 \\ e2 \\ en \end{pmatrix} = (a1e1 + a2e2 + an\text{-}en)$$

This is like changing the column matrix to a row and moving it directly over the row matrix. Then multiplying each element directly down in each column and adding the results in each row.

$$
\begin{array}{ll}
& (e1 \ \ e2 \ \ en) \quad \textbf{[e] is transposed to a row} \\
& \ x \ \ \ x \ \ \ x \qquad \textbf{e values are multiplied by each A value in the columns} \\
f[Q] = [A] \ x \ [e] \ = & (a1 \ \ a2 \ \ an)
\end{array}
$$

$$= \quad (a1e1 + a2e2 + an\text{-}en) \qquad \text{and the results are summed for each A row}$$

The set of unknown variables can be rows and columns as well, just as long as the rows and columns **A** and **e** are compatible. The number of columns of **A** must be equal to the number of rows of **e**.

For example a set of unknown variables **A** may be a square array represented as **[K]**

$$K = \begin{pmatrix} k11 & k12 & k13 \\ k21 & k22 & k23 \\ k31 & k32 & k33 \end{pmatrix}$$

If you know the row values **e** then you can solve for the column of values **[Q]**

$$e = \quad (e1 \quad e2 \quad en)$$

$$x$$

$$K = \begin{matrix} k11 & k12 & k13 \\ k21 & k22 & k23 \\ k31 & k32 & k33 \end{matrix} \quad [K] \times [e] = \begin{matrix} k11xe1 + k12xe2 + k13xen \\ k21xe1 + k22xe2 + k23xen \\ k31xe1 + k32xe2 + k33xen \end{matrix} \quad = \begin{pmatrix} Q1 \\ Q2 \\ Q3 \end{pmatrix}$$

The square matrix **[K]** will be called a logical **Grid.**

A **Grid** consists of a square matrix with coefficients representing unknown values. This **Grid** is intended to mirror reality as TRUE when values are either (+) converse or (-) adverse.

A Parallel Experiential GRID Exhibits:

Converse Focus. True Converse Reality (+1) is common to all observers. A Parallel universe function which involves discrete Observations forms identical event continua regardless of observer(s). Whether or not the observers interact, the event continua for the same converse matrix sets are identical. *True events are experienced by all observers.*

Adverse Diffusion. True Adversity (-1) is not shared between observers. A parallel universe function which involves discrete Observers forming different event continua involving adverse reality forms different continua. When the Observers do not interact, the event continua for the same adverse matrix sets are not similar. *True event outcomes are open to interpretation.*

So the simple description of this method, based solely upon experience (experiential,) is to arrange for the free flowing pinball Observations (whatever they may be) to fall through the fixed *Grid* of the Member sensory group that represents the sensors. In this *Grid* a universe (**Fig 3-2a**) has compound event qualities (or nodes) that form an *Experience.*

The system is complex where an event range (i.e. more than two,) symbolized by the column matrix **[e]**, multiplies coexisting sequences, symbolized by the square matrix as the *Universe of sensors* **[K]**, to form an *Observed Experience,* symbolized by the column matrix **[Q]**. In a TRUE **Grid** a known *Experience* **[Q]** can divide the coexisting sequences **[K]**$^{-1}$ to recreate the events of the original series **[e]**.

If [K] x [e] = [Q]   then   [e] = [K]$^{-1}$ x [Q]

This gives rise to the notion that the sequence of events involves an inherent causality. This notion is false, since the events are considered discrete elements. It is only the path (basically the *Experience*) followed that leads to an outcome that is predictable in terms of a TRUE observation.

It is much like following a road. Road side monuments describing the path, such as a house or tree, may not have caused each other to exist. Specific outcomes are a result of the path.

SORTING MULTIPLE SENSOR ACTIVITIES IN A REAL GRID

Perception Guides Awareness of Possibilities of State

If you don't like one possibility, then shift to another option. Well, what are the options? Attention to detail plays a significant part in an observed outcome of experiences and may change a landscape. The number and sophistication of sensors, or sensory capabilities, are the only tools through which possibilities of state are detected. These tools provide the details of the surrounding environment. The type and arrangement of sensors is equally important. Dual purpose sensors are quite useful in this regard. Infrared which measures both direction and intensity, and light which measures both intensity and color fit this category. Also sensors which can be arranged to provide a second function, through mounting and/or boundary design, such as sound sensors, can provide both direction and intensity. Motor commands, arising from the sensor matrix, must be designed to utilize the sensor array, as a form of feed back. Motor commands which are most useful in this regard are those which ***engage the event.*** Or in other words embody **curiosity.**

CREATING A FUNCTIONING OBSERVER WITH THE GRID EXPERIENCE

In order for the automaton to operate as an observer it must have an experiential framework for receiving and evaluating events. In an utterly simple observing unit, the operative distinction is entirely Real and without conjecture. **(Fig 3-2a)**

Simple Observation Structures

The primitive observer is functioning on a Grid, where the observations are complex or compound complex structures. The complete *Experience* is the sum of all the sensory elements within the *Observed* universe planes. Imagine a set of intersecting planes, each representing a universe of possible events. Then exaggerate the set where these planes all exist at the same time within the same space.

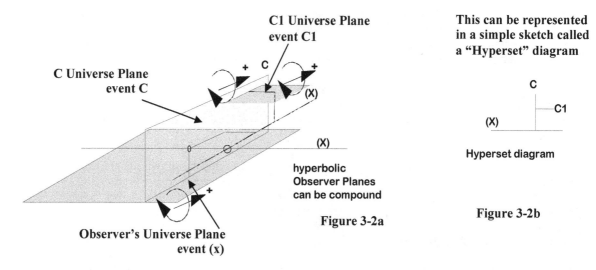

C1 Universe Plane
event C1

C Universe Plane
event C

(X)

hyperbolic
Observer Planes
can be compound

Observer's Universe Plane
event (x)

Figure 3-2a

This can be represented in a simple sketch called a "Hyperset" diagram

Hyperset diagram

Figure 3-2b

An Observer (x) is tied into to the set of planes which includes the functionality of sensor (x). For example, (x) may be a single sound sensor. [C] may be a second sound sensor and [C1] may be an ultrasound distance finder **(Fig 3-3a.)** The [C1] sensor is located on the observer plane of [C] (the ultrasound) because it is only observed if [C] has a quality of "contact" or is in a converse state. In a Grid environment, the [K] matrix would be:

Universe [K] Grid matrix of combined coexisting sequences

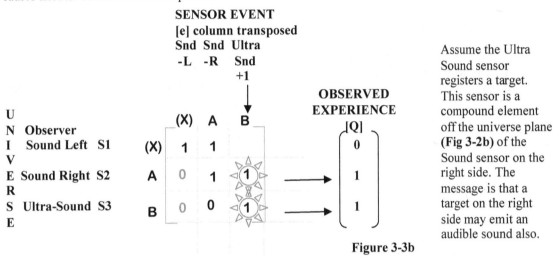

	(X)	A	B
(X)	1	1	
A	0	1	1
B	0	0	1
	[K]		

	Version 1		Version 2	Version 3	
Observer:	sensor1 sound-left	or	sensor2 or	sensor3	x
Sensor2	sound-right	or	sensor1	sensor1	A
Sensor3	ultrasound	or	sensor3	sensor2	B

Figure 3-3a

A member of the **[K] Grid** is "illuminated" if it receives a pin ball hit from a specific sensor registering a TRUE quality. For example, if in version 1, sensor 3 (ultra-sound) receives a "contact" signal, it is assigned a (+1) value (**Fig 3-3b.**) For each observer, the illumination of one or both of the other "observed" sensor causes another sensor to in turn equal +1

SENSOR EVENT
[e] column transposed

UNIVERSE	Observer		(X)	A	B	OBSERVED EXPERIENCE [Q]
	Sound Left S1	(X)	1	1		0
	Sound Right S2	A	0	1	(1)	1
	Ultra-Sound S3	B	0	0	(1)	1

Snd -L   Snd -R   Ultra Snd +1

Assume the Ultra Sound sensor registers a target. This sensor is a compound element off the universe plane (**Fig 3-2b**) of the Sound sensor on the right side. The message is that a target on the right side may emit an audible sound also.

Figure 3-3b

If the sound sensor on the right side also detects an audible sound, the Observed Experience from Universe **A** will increase in value. This increase is interpreted as *intensity*. Certain intensities may initiate actions.

For example, if only sensor1 is activated (illuminated), sensor2 fluoresces as observer.
As shown in the alternate configurations, versions 1 to 3, this **[K]** form also represents the two other sensors in question, where the observer plane (x) is shifted between the three sensors, as observers.

Matrix elements   **Hyperset Diagram**

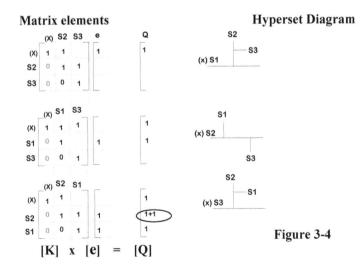

$$[K] \quad x \quad [e] \quad = \quad [Q]$$

The observer plane (x) is also a sensor function.

The sensor **battery** of S1, S2 & S3 can be represented in three possible states. S3 must always have membership with S2 because it is primarily observed by S2 and is actuated by it.

If sensors S1 & S2 are actuated (illuminated,) S3 is consequently "Lit Up" (fluoresces.) Observed experience Q2 is increased in intensity. This could prompt a head turn to the right.

Figure 3-4

Does this mean that Observed Experiences should cause a 'reaction' in some way? Essentially yes, although there may be pass through (null) options. An automatic reaction directing the Rover to seek out stimuli would activate some (motor) function, even causing the sensors to realign in a searching pattern.

Each battery of sensors could be linked to a sensor from other batteries. The batteries may look something like this:

Sensor1: sound_left	Sns3: ultrasound	Sns4:infra-red	Sns5: light
Sns2: sound_right	Sns4: infra-red	Sns5:light	Sns3: ultrasound_scan
Sns3: ultrasound	Sns5: light	Sns6: bump	Sns7: ultrasound_road

The pattern would be to illuminate as many (observing) Members as possible by motor commands causing the Rover to "look" in more places. Motor routines designed to focus attention and examine the landscape would be feeding sensor event information to the processing unit as an efficient strategy to utilize the sensor arrays.

COMPLEX SENSOR ACTIVITY

The battery of sensors shown above where each sensor sponsors a specific activity is considered a complex Grid system. The activity may consist of alerting another sensor to test the environment for significant stimuli. The switching pattern is the four pole arrangement shown in **Fig 3-1a.** The logic flow through the switches would be similar to the **Diagrams 3-5a through 3-5c.**

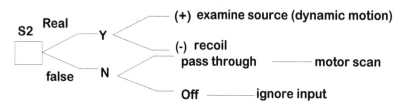

Switching Prerogatives within a Battery   Diagram 3-5a

A Real event triggers an observing sensor to examine other 'linked' sensors. When a given sensor is triggered, or "illuminated," programming gates check what other linked sensors are doing. If they maintain the status of merely observer, then a pass-through (unevaluated) would be appropriate. If the linked sensors register stimuli, then a more complicated reaction would be in store.

Each sensor is a *quadratic* (two to the second power or 4 pole) switch. If the inquisition signal returns a **True** (yes, we have an event) response, it can be either (+/-). If the inquisition is met with a **False** (no, we have not experienced an event) response, then the status can be either null (pass through to a neutral terminal) or Off (terminate or ignore the connection.) So in Version 1(**Fig 3-3a,**) where the observer is sensor1, the switching pattern would appear as:

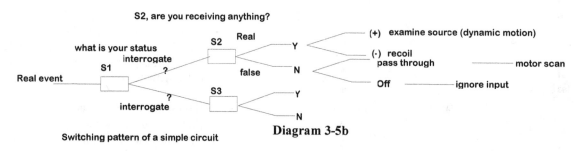

Diagram 3-5b

This can be expanded to include **Vers2**, where the observer is sensor2. With the addition of Observer Sensor2 to the array, the observational functions increase by a factor of 2. If Sensor2 actually observes an event, the observational functions increase by a factor of 4.

The options of *plus, minus, null & off* can also be labeled as **action** designations *Act1, Act2, Act3 & Act4*. This is a convenient method of labeling if the options are meant to lead to an activity. For example a sound signal may alert an infra-red sensor to test for direction of any heat emitting object. If such an object is found, another signal is sent to an ultra-sound sensor to scan for the distance of the object. If the distance is within a certain boundary, the Unit may physically react.

A matrix **Grid** can be developed for any combination of sensor readings and purposes. Merging sound and infra red readings can give important information on peripheral conditions, avoiding unnecessary Rover head turns. This type of observational chain or **manifold** is represented in the **Diagram 3-5c.**

The manifold could be arranged using sound (S2), infra red (S4) and ultra sound (S3) sensors actuating the head (M1) and tractor/body (M2) motors. This is shown in the accompanying hyperset drawings.

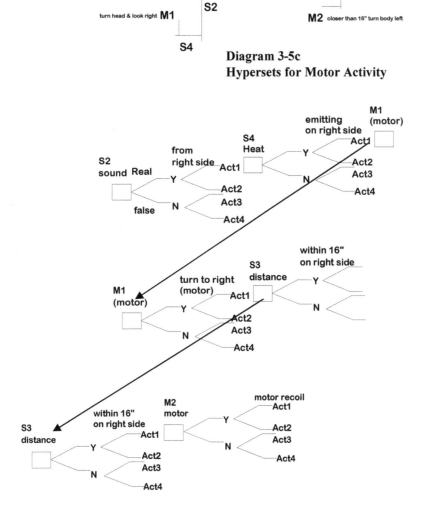

Diagram 3-5c
Hypersets for Motor Activity

Diagram 3-5d
Train of 4 pole switching Sequences for Peripheral vision

48

MOTOR EVENT COLUMN MATRIX

Representing event manifolds, such as the motor functions detailed above (**Diagrams 3-5c & 3-5d,**) usually begins with hyperset diagrams. These functions can then be assembled in matrix form according to a set of membership and influence rules (**Chapter VI**) to create a Universe **[K]**. The process begins by defining the event elements of the hypersets. The basic example of a **Grid** Membership matrix is shown in **Fig 3-6a** for simple complex sequences

Simple Complex

A single universe intersection on an observer plane offers significance when the universe exhibits a shift in the observer plane, creating a complexity. Using the simplex-complex format shown in **Fig 3-6a**, the respective hyperset diagrams and their associated matrix arrays are shown below.

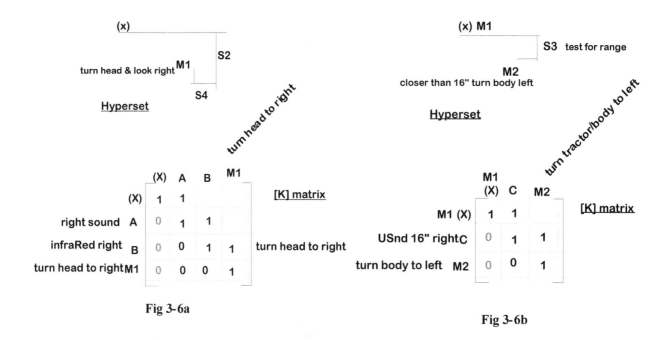

Fig 3-6a

Fig 3-6b

[K] Grid and Column [e] of Motor Events

Standard **Grid** formats, assembled from the hyperset **Diagrams 3-5c** are combined to form the complete sequenced array. This is the **[K]** matrix or the *Universe* **Grid.** It combines the observer's participation (witness of events) in the collection of events that are registering occurrences (or measurements.)

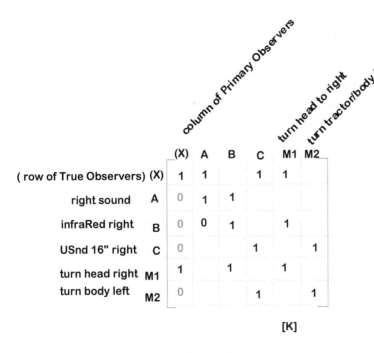

		(X)	A	B	C	M1	M2
(row of True Observers)	(X)	1	1		1	1	
right sound	A	0	1	1			
infraRed right	B	0	0	1		1	
USnd 16" right	C	0			1		1
turn head right	M1	1		1		1	
turn body left	M2	0			1		1

[K]

Figure 3-7

In combining the sequential Universe [K] matrices, certain elements must be preserved.

- The row of the Observer (x) must reflect all TRUE observers.
- The column of the Observer must show all primary observer platforms

All the event options are represented as TRUE (+1) in the matrix. This does not mean that all options will be *experienced*. Only those events which register a signal by the Observer will be illuminated by the [e] event matrix.

These observed events will in turn cause the *experience* to fluoresce or stand out as an Observed Outcome [Q].

Version 1: Episode 1
Observer (x)
Sensor1 sound-right
Sensor2 infraRed-right
Sensor3 USnd 16" right
Motor M1 head turn to right

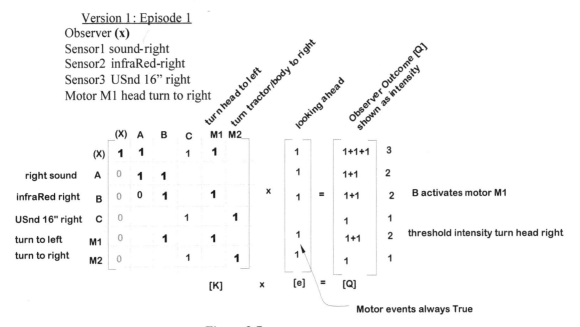

Figure 3-7a

In the **Fig 3-7a** the [K] values that are affected by the events [e] are shown in ***bold*** type face. These are the states that are illuminated by the events and contribute a cumulative significance or ***intensity*** to the observed outcome [Q]. The sequence displayed in the matrix follows the series that

- the observer notices a sound source;
- an infra red source increases intensity to the sound direction;
- a motor response is initiated to "check it out."

In constructing the matrix, the terminus of the polled events results is a motor action. The Motor row "turn left" is artificially populated with the infra red event that initiates action. This is merely a programming choice.

The column matrix of Observed Outcomes **[Q]** can also be represented in a *scalar* format (1,2,3 … etc.) This is done as a convenience, rather than the more real *cumulative* or analogue bulk format. Basically as a system of switches, the outcomes would vary in the size or power of the charge (+).

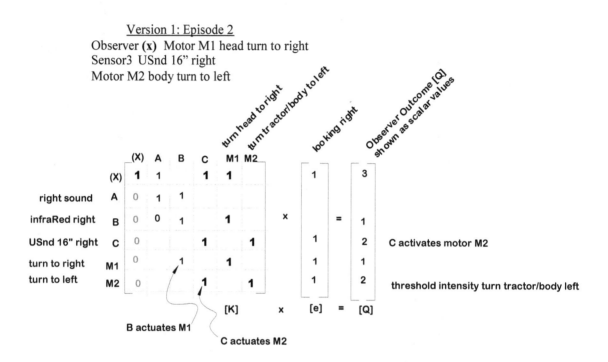

Figure 3-7b

THE MATRIX AS A RESOURCE

Fig 3-7 represents a typical matrix arrangement for a set number of events or sensor activities. This demonstrates typical Unit1 programming and deals with *multiple* inputs to arrive at a *single* output. The sensor polling methods used in the programming for **Unit1 Mark5 Rover** are developed along the lines shown in the examples and figures above but embody an added complexity. The sensor signals are divided into *properties* that the programmer decides are important or pivotal. In this arrangement there is only one primary observer **(x)** but many TRUE observers that are functions of the primary. This includes all the sensors being polled. The signals are outputs and contribute to the observed outcomes **[Q]**.

The benefit of this approach is the ability to include large blocks of peripheral information into the main stream of sensory data that is being gathered each time the sensor(s) is polled. It also builds information that can be used in other matrix sources, such as motor efficiency and stalled motion.

EVENTS ARE A FORMAL BASIS FOR BUILDING HISTORY AS A TRAIN OF EXPERIENCES

Once the polling of the sensors has provided a stream of events **[e]** the resulting outcomes **[Q]** that are their cumulative products can be used to augment and refine other event streams. This means that the outcomes can be used as a resource to fill in more event phenomenon for further analysis. A Past-Present matrix decision manifold would merge past events with the present sensate landscape.

SLAVE Event Matrix for Track1 file

Group	Sensor	Label	#	x (0)	hit_L (1)	hit_R (2)	hit_B (3)	Rtac0 (4)	Q11 (5)	Q19 (6)	Q17 (7)	Q21 (8)	Positx (9)	KEvent (10)	FMQ3 (11)	FMQ6 (12)	FM2Q8 (13)	Op1 (14)	Op2 (15)	Op3 (16)	Op4 (17)	Op5 (18)
		x	1	1					1	1	1	1	1									
Current Primary Slave Polling	Antenna_L	hit_L	2																			
	Antenna_R	hit_R	3																			
	Ant_bkwd	hit_B	4																			
	RPmS	Rtac0	5																			
Current Primary Master Polling	BackUpX	Q11	6						1													
	UltraBkUp	Q19	7							1												
	Algn_Right	Q17	8								1			-1	-1	1						
	Algn_Left	Q21	9									1		-1	-1	1						
Track1 Past Secondary Polling		Positx	10										1	1	1	1						
		KEvent	11						1				1	1				1				
	Fwd_err-Bk	FMQ3	12							1	1			1		1		1				
	Obst_err-Bk	FMQ6	13							1	1					1		1				
	Turn_err-L	FM2Q8	14							1	1						1			1		
Future Options	Suspend Q	Op1	15															1				
	BackUp_L	Op2	16																1			
	BackUp_R	Op3	17																	1		
	Act_antenna	Op4	18																		1	
	Scan_L&R	Op5	19																			1

Figure 3-8

Fig 3-8 displays a sample arrangement of event outputs including observed output from a main matrix labeled as **Q11, Q19, Q17** and **Q21,** and observed output from a motor response matrix labeled as **FMQ3, FMQ6** and **FM2Q8.** The identifier **Q** indicates a value from another *Observed Outcome.* Actions prompted by **Q** outcomes can also be treated as events and grouped in the category of **Future Options [Op_n].** This sample matrix is partially filled in with values identifying their *membership* and TRUE relationships. Some of the relationships are *adverse TRUE* or assigned a (-1). You will notice that these come into play when they are associated with some motor error outcomes. This is a sample programming strategy that disallows actions between **[Q] and [FMQ]** events in all *but* one action, in this case Act_antenna (actuate antenna).

This shows how properties of the Matrix can be tailored for specific combinations which prompt actions. Using the matrix to sort multiple sensor activities helps in regulating motor actions and responses. These resources are put to actual use in **Chapter IV Programming.**

ESTABLISHING POSITION

Perhaps the quality that receives the least attention in automaton design is the Rover's ability to recognize and remember where it is situated within a known frame of reference. Establishing the relationship and proximity of the landscape as well as alignment and position are important aspects in successful movement in straight line or in and around obstacles.

The first effort is to establish an initial frame of reference. This is an arbitrary reference and corresponds to the Rover's first impression of its situation in the environment. In a coordinate system, the Rover will be referred to as *looking* in a **specific** direction and *facing* in a **local** direction. Essentially the first impression is always *looking* **front** and *facing* forward. The Rover is **front** *facing* simply because it begins by specifically looking ahead. Its local position is arbitrarily facing forward (**Fig 3-9.**)

Functioning as an Observer, the Rover only initiates *Specific* coordinate changes. On the operational level of our Rover the notions of *Specific* and *Local* coordinates are easily defined.

When the automaton is turned on and the Rover program begins, alignment and position coordinates are set to the default *front* facing *forward*.

SPECIFIC COORDINATES

Specific notations keep track of where the Rover is **looking.** They are simply labeled :

- Front – F
- Right - R
- Left - L
- Back - ta

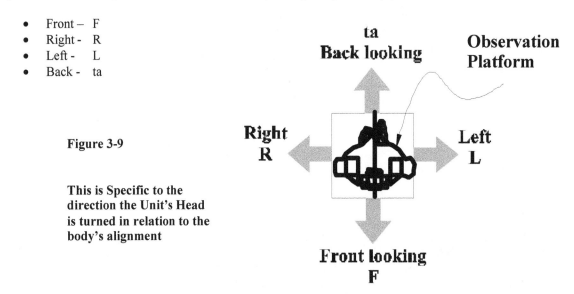

Figure 3-9

This is Specific to the direction the Unit's Head is turned in relation to the body's alignment

Specific coordinates are annotated with script designations. These indicate a **movement of the head** from the **front.**

LOCAL COORDINATES

A **local** system describes the immediate surroundings for the Unit's initial position within the landscape. It remains fixed for the observational period. Where *specific* coordinates can rotate and change with body and head movements, the local surroundings remain fixed. These are the local coordinate designations:

- Forward - 1
- Inward - 2
- Outward - 3
- Backward - 4

This is Local to the landscape itself, like the direction of North.

Figure 3-10

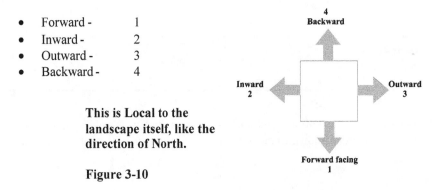

Local coordinates are annotated with number designations. These numbers combine in certain ways to indicate the direction of the Unit when it changes alignment. These are also used in the coding to determine the direction the Unit is looking. This specific script combines with local numbers to indicate the direction the Unit is looking. For example **R-3** indicates the Rover's center is aligned "Outward" and the head is turned to its "Right."

COMBINED SPECIFIC AND LOCAL COORDINATES

This combination creates the framework where the Rover observes and navigates. The Observational platform is different from navigation because local features are fixed, and the Rover head movements are specific to the Rover's body. In the Observational platform, the Unit may be *front* looking **Inward** and move ahead, but not gain ground in an **Forward** position (**Fig 3-11**.) In the same vein, the Rover can turn its head and look to the *right* and be scanning the **Backward** landscape (**Fig 3-12**.)

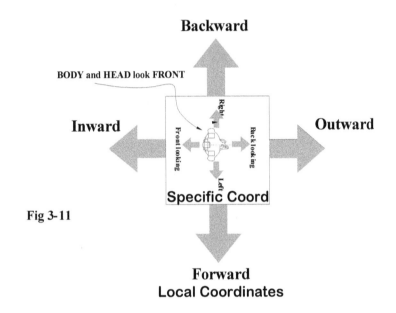

Fig 3-11

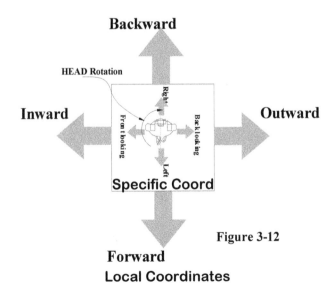

Figure 3-12

While the observational platform (or head) is turned to the right, the tractor may actually be making movement **Inward**. In fact it is common for the Unit to be looking right and left while it is moving in a direction to the front, where ever that might align with the local landscape.

With each specific movement or alignment, the appropriate local coordinate must be upgraded. Response to stimuli and all event actions are nonsense if coordinate locations are not maintained, or fall into error. To maintain operational focus, the initial function of any Rover operation is the calibration of the *Specific* and *Local* coordinates. Normally this involves a simple act of starting the Rover when it is front facing Forward.

With the Rover calibrated, changes in *Specific* alignment are recorded and automatically interpreted into *Local* alignment. For example in **Fig 3-12** where the Rover is facing **Inward**, if it turns its head *right,* its body is still ***Inward facing*** but the head looks locally **Backwards** (**Fig 3-5.**) If the Rover then bodily turns *left,* it is ***Forward facing*** and its head is looking *Inward.* These alignments are handled by subroutines which are accessed at every motor direction.

IV
PROGRAMMING the ROVER

BASIC PROGRAMMING GOALS

In **Chapter I** the Rover is described as an automaton which travels over landscapes observing features, obstructions and other notable characteristics. It is capable of decisions enabling a number of functions, such as:

- Reaching Locations Too Confined for Humans
- Entering Smoke Filled Spaces
- Examining Dangerous Items
- Mapping an Area

In performance of these functions, the Rover executes programming utilizing a method that develops analytical and interpretive sequences from observed output qualities **[Q].**

MASTER – SLAVE MULTIPLE MICROPROCESSORS

FUNCTION

The **Unit1 Mark5 Rover** utilizes 8 sensor ports and 3 motor ports. The program size required to operate and monitor these accessories exceeds the capacity of one Atmel microprocessors. As a consequence, two (and possibly more) are used in tandem to supply the needed capacity for code execution. The micros are divided in two categories, master and slave. The micro running the principal programming that controls and oversees the Rover's operation is used as the Master. The second micro (and possibly up to a third) is termed the Slave. The micros communicate with each other through a Bluetooth device that allows wireless data transfer.

MASTER PROGRAMMING

Programming code is bundled into discrete *tasks* that operate simultaneously. The set of tasks produce decisions that result in specific **subroutine** calls (**Chapter V**) for each actionable observed output quality **[Q]**.

These fundamental tasks deal specifically with**:**

1. path ahead
   a. Ultra sound range *Limit* (clearance ahead)
   b. Motor speed adjusted for clearance ahead
   c. braking
2. peripheral landscape
   a. objects to the side
   b. Ultra sound reflections
   c. dynamic scanning

3. accuracy of path keeping
   a. heading changes
   b. off center distance closing
4. physical obstructions and contacts
   a. touch sensors
   b. very close distance readings
   c. motor stalling
5. efficiency of motor actions
   a. effective turning
   b. motor revolutions
6. remedial actions
   a. execute matrix math process for Motor actions
   b. create motor output values **[MQ]**
   c. backing
   d. turning
   e. compound movement strategies
7. proximity of objects
   a. listening for echoes
   b. sensing heat/radiation
   c. stalled motor

SLAVE PROGRAMMING

Support for additional sensor outputs and processor capacity is provided by the Slave. These routines utilize a single task main () with subroutines and internal branches. They operate in sequence when called and branch from a central clearing area designated as [Listen:]. The Slave remains in the closed [Listen:] loop until it receives an interrogatory from the Master. The interrogatory is in the form of a code word (or *string)* that directs the Slave to a specific branch. This word comes through the Bluetooth receiver/sender system.

The Slave is designed to branch to separate operations when it receives a command from the Master. These operations are discrete (operate individually, not as a group) and either make a specific decision or obtain a specific sensor reading, interpret the input and send the result to the Master.

These discrete operations deal with:

1) Listen
   i) for Master's inquiries
   ii) branching to specific operations

2) Touch
   i) receiving touch signals from local sensors
   ii) interpreting the signal's direction
   iii) sending the message to Master

3) Qf_File
   i) receiving **[Q]** output values from Master
   ii) assigning values to Motor events
   iii) interpreting heading variations

4) Get_Mag
   i) read magnetic compass
   ii) jump to Correct
   iii) calibrate the Rover's heading as a "start" position
   iv) send magnetic reading to Master

5) Correct
   i) correct magnetic reading for deviation

ii) establish alignment headings (for current heading, change due to turn, etc.)

iii) send alignment info to Master

CONFIGURING EVENT STRUCTURES AS THREADED TASKS

An event structure is a matrix (Chapter III.) As a primary function, a Matrix is used to process feedback from sensory readings of the Rover's surroundings. **Unit1's** functions are located in specific areas developed as *tasks* all set up to run concurrently. This programming method is commonly referred to as *threading.* Each **task** will have a *local* set of variables that are used only within the task, and another *global* set that all the tasks share. The various tasks build, maintain and interpret the Matrix event structures of the Rover.

Execution begins with the **task main ( ).** But programming compilation begins with ancillary tasks all preceding the task main () and this is the way they are listed below with task main () last.

MASTER

1) task a_BTSignal ( )
   - i) Open Bluetooth communication channels
   - ii) Obtain **Magnetic** heading from Slave
   - iii) Register **Touch & Proximity** signals from Slave

2) task b_Evalpoll ( )
   - i) **Begin_Poll** routine to poll all sensors
   - ii) Initiate **Basic_Eval** routine to sort polling results
   - iii) Check for **Minor Obstructions**
   - iv) **Poll Sensors**
       - (a) Scan Left & Right
       - (b) Solve Sensory Event Matrix **[Q]**
       - (c) Evaluate Go-No-Go options
       - (d) Write Go decision

3) task c_Chk_FwdUSnd ( )
   - i) Constant Scan **USnd_Act** for eye level proximity
       - (a) Establish an Ultra Sound **[hit]**
       - (b) Set motor power levels **[pwr]**

4) task d_Motr_Feed ( )
   - i) **Motr_Monitor** checks for **stalled rotations**
       - (a) Stalled forward motion
       - (b) Stalled/incomplete turns
   - ii) **Solve** Motor Event Matrix **[MQ]**

5) task main( )
   - i) initiate arrays and text files, set timing clock, start threaded task elements
   - ii) Begin **Basic Evaluation** sequence
   - iii) Initiate **Basic Execution** actions
   - iv) Evaluate **MotorFeed** signals
   - v) Monitor **Alignment** with landscape and obstructions

SLAVE

1) task main()
   - i) maintain contact with Master
   - ii) execute branching to discrete operations
   - iii) build Motor universe matrix
   - iv) obtain touch sensor signals

Parallel threaded programs which are functionally codependent use common variables. Problems arise with these programs when the tasks run simultaneously. Threaded elements must cooperate and in some form synchronize their efforts to avoid stalling or confusing/corrupting the function.

LOGICAL GATES

Gate keys assign protocol and pass/no pass information. This method has been developed in lieu of "mutex" instructions because of the positive tracking applications. For example, task **a_Evalpoll** builds the sensory event matrix **[Q]**. From this matrix, decisions are made in task **main** which deal with monitoring the Rover's **Alignment** with landscape and obstructions. **a_Evalpoll** even monitors itself when a sudden STOP occurs from task **c_Chk_FwdUSnd**. When task **a_Evalpoll** forms **[Q]** and the segment "Alignment:" (within task **main**) reads **[Q]**, there must be a clear queue for motor events landscape, meaning no *STOP* actions or *Bump* signals can be in the action queue to corrupt **Q's** execution. To maintain an open queue, **Unit1** programming utilizes a "gate" to block competing actions.

Alignment gate [code word "GateA"]

The variable "GateA" is declared in the general common segment at the inception of the program. This value is then common to all the tasks
The applications are:

GateA== 1   Alignment decisions are not in effect. All gates are open and all motor actions are allowed.

== -1   Only Alignment decisions are working to align and position the unit1. No other tractor motor commands are allowed

== 0/null   No inquires on status

The protocol for action is determined by sequence. Task main acts on the decision to GO forward and performs a basic set of decisions to proceed. Within this period the Rover evaluates its alignment with the landscape. This gate delays action where the unit is out of alignment, (e.g. colliding with some peripheral object) and when the basic GO forward action may overlap or interfere with some local problem the unit is trying to solve. Also if the Alignment decisions are being performed, task b_Evalpoll does not write a GO forward clearance to be passed to the basic action in task main. Instead b_Evalpoll loops to the beginning of its cycle.

Head turning gate [code word "Gate"]

Head turning is actuated in a number of event situations, primarily to determine surrounding obstructions or influences. Many of these situations arise simultaneously driven by the concurrently threaded tasks.

Gate == -1   Allow only the head motor action in the task b_Evalpoll for subroutine calls
Cycle_ChkFwd
ScanL_R
About_Face

task main for subroutine calls

Cycle_ChkFwd (Stalled: and Fwd Obstruction:)
Power_TurnR/L

== 1   Reset to open gate allowing motor actions for head turning
            at start of task main
            after each subroutine call using a head turn

Motor Gate [code word "Motr"]

This is a local variable. It is generated within each threaded task and not shared in a common declaration. To keep the variable local, it is written to a file. The file is read by each task when appropriate. "Motr" designates the availability of the tractor. This availability is sporadic because of sudden *STOP* commands, avoidance operations that are in progress and other general operations that take place even while the threaded elements are receiving sensory data and performing evaluations.

task main() sets the Motr and writes the file. This
controls the motor usage and releases it to the robot.

Motr==-1   keeps the motor in stasis AND keeps *STOP* (hit==1) in the action queue.
                task b_Evalpoll sets motor availability
                        Poll_Eval execution:
                task c_Chk_FwdUSnd sets motor at *STOP* when a forward obstruction is
                registered.
                As long as Motr==-1, no new hit value is written to the FwdAct file
                Motr is kept at -1 until Motr=1 is read from file MotrAct

                task Chk_FwdUSnd() sets the *STOP* value and writes the file "FwdAct.txt"
                SensorFile("FwdAct.txt") stores the current logical state

== 1   Reads Motr flag from main()
                If main() sends a Motrx==1, this causes the task to reset its readings and
                release the *STOP* [hit==1] setting that it previously locked in

Go Forward Gate [code word "QGOgate"]

This logical gate signals when the Unit1 has completed an evaluation of the sensory input. If an evaluation has resulted in a set of instruction, to be read in task main, then the gate is actuated.

QGOgate == 1   task b_Evalpoll has written instructions for the **Unit1** to proceed.
                        and sets QGOgate at [End_pEval:]
                Once the gate is set, it will not allow an instruction over write.
                Recycle to [Poll_Finish:]
                task main is now cleared to read the procedural instructions

== 0   This is a setting made by task main indicating it has read the latest set of
                instructions and has executed those instructions.

Motor Stall gate [code word "Stallgate"]

Poor motor performance or no rpm's (revolution per minute) when the motor should be turning are both indicators of some problem in traction. Stallgate is the execution flag for a Stall.

Stallgate ==1   For a specific timed period, when an actual motor rpm doesn't equal
                         the minimum value for the applied power (pwr) [Rtac0<Ktac0] in
                         Motr_Feed, set Stallgate.

Read MQ[ ] in main() at [Motr_feed:]

Stallgate== 0

Alert unit1 that motor rpm lags performance and set at time of reading. Exit the motor evaluation {goto Out_MQ;}

== -1

Suppress Stall actions while GateA & Gate are closed (-1). These are Head action gates, but also signals when motr actions may halt task Motr_Feed() [if((GateA!="1")||(Gate!="1")){goto Stall_Out;}]

== 11

This is a null or disconnect reading signaling a bypass.

//Programming Notes::
        Create complex Stallgate flags {1,0,-1 & 11}
        set pwr changes for Stallgate==1 -> OK set at 40
        correct [Motr_Feed()] sequence & logic for Stallgate flag
        if(RunTx>=8000) Allow wait time
        Use increase wait time to 8sec
        Add time click to Stall point(s)

        Open Track1c file for Motr_Feed notations
        In task Motr_Feed, relocate[Stallcnt=QGOcnts;] where Stallgate is set to 1
        main() Aligment:: If an Align takes place then reset [Stallgate=0]
        Increase Stallgate pwr to 50:: [if(Stallgate==1) {pwr= 50*Pwr1/60;]
        Relocate all Bump motr matrix solutions to task Motr_Feed() & use as
            a Stall signal. If HitBmp==-1 then Stallgate=1.
        Use task main() Motrfeed:: stall routine to sort hitBmp motr actions
        This approach removes hitBmp from any conflict w/ Stall

Motor Stall Timing Queue [code word "Tstgate_b"]

Stallgate is activated by a measured time sequence.

Tstgate_b == 1

if Stallgate == 1, set "Tstgate" and begin timed sequence for period during which stall is apparent

Controlling Motor Action [code word "MQAct"]

Motor action can experience serial repetitions if they are not blocked after the execution of each action. This prevents over corrections, halting movements and loss of heading

MQAct=="-1"

blocks a repeat use of the Back Up/Forward options

```
if((MQ[11]>2)||(MQ[7]>2))
        {
        TextOut(0,LCD_LINE1,"Back Up  ");
Posit1c=" Back Up";
        OnFwdSync(OUT_AB,85,OUT_REGMODE_SPEED);
        Wait(1200);Off(OUT_AB);
        MQAct="-1";Stallgate=0;
        hitBmp=1;                          //hitBmp must be initialized after
                                           //execution if it doesn't jump to
```

goto Out_MQ;
}

WRITING KEY VARIABLES TO A FILE

Preserve the action variable, even while the contributing sensor(s) continues generating output. There are a number of design features that keep threaded programs from colliding and crashing.

- allocate one thread for each specific variable (sensory) reading
- keep specific actions localized
- once an action is mapped, allow it to be completed regardless of a current conflicting variable
- use the same variable code word throughout the threads

The threads are designed to take readings throughout their local cycle, or recurring loop. A reading may trigger and event notation [e] and in turn an observed outcome [Q]. This may initiate a motor action. As the action is taking place, causing the reading to change, the event itself could suffer revision. If this is allowed the logic path of the action could be interrupted, resulting in confusion and crashing. The Rover's method of dealing with this possible conflict is to assign a variable name that is specific to a motor action. This name is then written to a file, if the file is "empty." The motor logic reads the file. If the file is *true* then action may be initiated. In the mean time the sensor activity is not abbreviated and any consequent readings do not pervert the *true* motor reading.

```
Acquire (FileAcc);
// hit=current; hitz=previous . Compare the old hitz with the newly generated hit.
//If they are not the same and Motr has been reset to [1] then re-evaluate the
//settings

if ((hit!=hitz)&&(Motr!=-1))
                //if the local flag Motrx is not closed (-1) then record
                //the current hit value if it is different
{
                if (hit==1){
                Acquire (Fwd_Motr);         //Acquire control only
                Off(OUT_AB);                //when the hit==1 is
                Release (Fwd_Motr);         //first encountered
                        }                   //after a period of
                                            //hit==0
                DeleteFile ("FwdAct.txt");
//write the new hit=0 or 1 & pwr=0 or nn
                Write_FwdAct(hit,pwr);
}
//if  Motr==-1, meaning no new Motr command from main(), set the new hit to the
//old hitz [locking it in]
                else {hit=hitz;
                Write_FwdAct(hit,pwr);}
                if (hit==1) {Motr=-1;}
//as long as Motr==-1, no new hit value is written to the FwdAct file
//Motr is kept at -1 until Motr=1 is read from file MotrAct
//NumOut(75,LCD_LINE3,hit);
                Release (FileAcc);
```

LINKING MULTIPLE SENSORS

In the programming language of *C*, individual *tasks* perform specific functions while maintaining contact with the entire group of sensors and motors. This requires a complex arrangement of traffic control (sorting techniques) to prevent jamming and crashing the program. This traffic control is also a function of the matrix **[Q].**

THE AUTOMATON UNIT 1 OBSERVES ITSELF

Observational strategies for a Rover are built upon layers of observing elements, experiencing multiple events both internal and external. Observations are expressed as multiple compound Real patterns. Sensor observers may initiate motor commands to augment sensor activity (e.g look to the left to measure heat.)

Perception Guides the Observed Outcome

The number and sophistication of sensors, or sensory capabilities, are the only tools through which possibilities of state are detected, eventually leading to an Observed Outcome. These tools provide the details of the surrounding environment. The type and arrangement of sensors are important. Dual purpose sensors are preferred. Infrared which measures both direction and intensity, and light which measures both intensity and color fit this category. Sensors which can be arranged to provide a second function, through mounting and/or boundary design, such as sound sensors, can provide both direction and intensity. Motor commands, arising from the sensor matrix, should be designed to optimize the sensor array, and commands which are most useful are those which *engage the event,* acting out of **curiosity.**

Developing Sensor Input

First arrange a group (battery) of sensor readings according to predetermined (programmer selected) amplitudes or intensities of senor output (**Chapter III.**) These readings correspond to the column matrix **[e]** and are also arranged as the column headings in the **[K]** experience matrix, representing the Rover's universe. This model utilizes numbered rows, beginning with zero and up to 26. Column (0) represents the observer. The sensory/input designations for the events **[e]** are:

[e]   single
Column 1

Row		input	possibility of state (e) based upon Amplitude	array symbol for Amplitude modulation (AM)
0	(x) as	observer	present/absent	x
1		left sound bud	on/null	S1
2		left sound	e <30db	S1.A1_30
3		"	30> e <50db	S1.A1_50
4		"	e>50db	S1.A1_80
5		right snd bud	on/null	S2
6		right snd	e<30db	S2.A1_30
7		"	30> e <50db	S2.A1_50
8		"	e>50db	S2.A1_80
9	distance	UltraSound	on/null	S3
10		"	<18 in	S3.A1_18
11		"	<40 in	S3.A1_40
12		"	>40 in	S3.A1_+40
13		"	>48 in (quarter point head turn)	S3.AQP_48
14	Infra red	intensity/dir.	on/null	S4
15	IR right side most intense		medium	S4.A1_R
16		"	high	S4.A1.1_R
17	IR ahead most intense		medium	S4.A1_F
18		"	high	S4.A1.1_F
19	IR left side most intense		medium	S4.A1_L
20		"	high	S4.A1.1_L
21		drive motors	on/null	MX_F
22	head turn right		on/ active	M1_R
23	head turn left		on/	M1_L
24	drive motor right turn		on/	M2_R
25	drive motor left turn		on/	M2_L
26	drive motors reverse		on/	M3_FR

Example 4-1a

As each sensor state is interrogated, its logical state (output signal) is recorded in the file array as
a) True converse (+1)   conforms to the membership
b) True adverse (-1)   does not conform (e.g. head turned to the side not looking forward)
c) False zero (0)   no reading (sensor is OFF or there is no output)
d) False disconnect (n)   null (pass through: output is not registered or is overwritten)

Sensor input is retrieved within each designated task or by a subroutine. Readings are stored as current updates in an "event" file array. The text of the polling subroutine is reproduced in **Chapter V, poll_sensors**. Results from the subroutine might look something like the Example 9-b

[e]   Column 1

Row	input		possibility of state (e)	array symbol	Logical State	
0	(x) as	observer	present/absent	x	1	Observer is present
1		left sound bud	on/null	S1	n	left side pass thru
2		left sound	e <30db	S1.A1_30		
3		"	30> e <50db	S1.A1_50		
4		"	e>50db	S1.A1_80	n	
5		right snd bud	on/null	S2	1	Right Snd is strongest
6		right snd	e<30db	S2.A1_30		
7		"	30> e <50db	S2.A1_50		
8		"	e>50db	S2.A1_80	1	50db echo
9	distance	UltraSound	on/null	S3	1	USnd is on
10		"	<18 in	S3.A1_18		
11		"	<40 in	S3.A1_40		
12		"	>40 in	S3.A1_+40	1	Dist ahead +40in
13		"	>48 in (quarter point head turn)	S3.AQP_48		
14	Infra red intensity/dir.		on/null	S4	1	IR is on
15	IR right side most intense		medium	S4.A1_R	1	right signal
16	"		high	S4.A1.1_R	1	strong right signal
17	IR ahead most intense		medium	S4.A1_F	n	front is pass thru
18	"		high	S4.A1.1_F		
19	IR left side most intense		medium	S4.A1_L	n	left is pass thru
20	"		high	S4.A1.1_L		
21		drive motors	on/active	MX_F	1	Logical state
22	head turn right		on/	M1_R	1	for All motors
23	head turn left		on/	M1_L	1	is On and
24	drive motor right turn		on/	M2_R	1	Active
25	drive motor left turn		on/	M2_L	1	
26	drive motors reverse		on/	M3_FR	1	

Example 4-1b

In this example, all the sensors are reading and providing output, none are Off. Specific levels of sensory output (e.g. S1.A1_30 denoting audio to the left in decibels) may be over written, thereby creating a null. The null is treated the same as a zero (False) in mathematical terms.

DEVELOPING THE EXPERIENCE MATRIX [K]

Given the fact that the automaton model is gauging input from 26 event states plus 1 observer, the membership and influence matrices will be 27x27 with row & column designations identical to the **(e)** detailed above. Because in a **Grid** events do not affect signals beyond their own universe, the influence matrix is a simple diagonal. Membership is limited to the observer's hyperbolic (intersecting) plane and is open for possibilities between other events. Multiplying influence by simple membership results in a diagonal matrix for **[K].** However observer planes can be compound, enabling one observed universe to act as an observer to another.

This is called a Simple Complex Membership where the observer becomes the observed

A single universe intersection on an observer plane offers significance when the universe exhibits a shift in the observer plane, creating a complexity.

Simple Complex

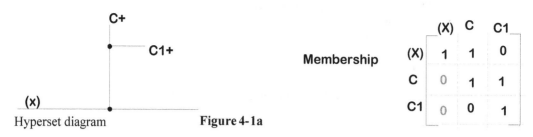

Hyperset diagram   **Figure 4-1a**

Membership

(X)	C	C1
(X)	1	1	0
C	0	1	1
C1	0	0	1

Figure 4-1b

For example, the 4 sensor states (on/off) plus the one observer (x) are members of (x's) parallel universes. The actual logical state of the sensor reading is a member of the sensor's universe, not the observer's.

In addition, other sensory output (or signals) can share boundaries. Membership in this case becomes compound complex. This is where the Unit observers itself.

This is called a Compound Complex Membership where there are many cross observations.

So even though in a Grid where events do not influence each other, they can be members of a compound observation. The compound observation will have a specific observed outcome **[Q].** The compound complex attribute of membership builds a consensus of sensory input that enables the use of many unrelated sensors in monitoring and guiding automaton decisions.

COMPOUND COMPLEX

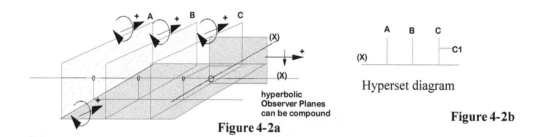

Figure 4-2a

Hyperset diagram

Figure 4-2b

Universe diagram

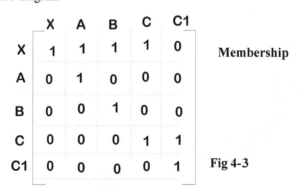

	X	A	B	C	C1
X	1	1	1	1	0
A	0	1	0	0	0
B	0	0	1	0	0
C	0	0	0	1	1
C1	0	0	0	0	1

Membership

Fig 4-3

For the current model of Unit1 Mark5 Rover, the **[K]** matrix has already been constructed from compound complex event memberships where the Unit1 is programmed to observer itself in all sensor formats. To explain these formats would require diving into the divisions of **Grid** development, and there is no space for that in this presentation.

65

This presentation includes the compound complex associations of a working **Grid** matrix **[K]** shown in Example 9-b, that will be used for the Unit1 Mark5 Rover acting as an observer. The support program (**Chapter IV**) "BasicWrite_Kmtx" creates the **[K]** matrix used in the model presented. This is a file array stored in memory as "K_Mtx.txt."

SOLVING FOR THE OBSERVED OUTCOME [Q] AND ITS INTERPRETATION

The observed outcome matrix **[Q]** is solved by multiplying **(e)** by **[K].** This outcome informs the automaton what it has observed and represents the "solution" to the otherwise puzzling array of sensory readings.

This results in a column matrix **[Q]** (like the **(e)** matrix) where the outcomes are expressed as cumulative values arising from the contributions of any number of independent sensor or feed back signals.

When specific sensors **[e]** receive stimuli (illuminated logical states Example 9-b,) they cause Observed Outcomes **[Q]** to exhibit a True (+/- 1) state (fluoresce.) Decoding the pattern of True outcomes is a matter of examining each row (where an event fluoresces) for a predetermined value, called a threshold. When the threshold is reached or exceeded, then an action or chain of actions is initiated.

For the purpose of example, a column matrix **[e]** will be created with hypothetical illuminated logical states (Example 9-b) and multiplied by the **[K]** matrix (Example 9-c.) These logical states **[e]** will be established by the reading of the respective sensors (sound, infra red or Ultra Sound) and will simply consist of 1, -1, or 0.

The example supposes that an object is positioned to the *Right* of the Unit1. The readings of logical states would be similar to those shown in the Example.

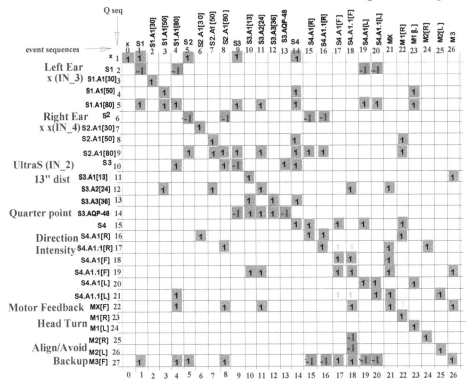

Looking FRONT Switches4a
(Revision: Oct 17, 2012)
Advanced Sensor Matrix [Q] U4_Fb2x
w/ Distance Variations - Motor Feedback & Signal Clustering

Example 4-1c

The next operation is to multiply [e] by [K].

$$[K] [e_n] = [Q_n]$$

This is an operation that multiplies the variables in the column (e) by the variables in each row of [K], sums the products for each row and expresses this as a value in the row of column [Q]. This is a common procedure, as shown in **Chapter III**, and is reproduced as the subroutine "Matrix_Math()" in **Chapter V**.

So basically executing this operation by hand, multiplying the column [e] by the first row of [K], we have:

Expressed in a $[K_{Row,Column} (e_{Row}) ....]$ format

[note: because of the convention used in the model, the first Row of the [e] column is designated as zero (0)]

$K1,1(e0) + K1,2(e1) + K1,3(e2) .... = Q1 =$ **scalar 4** (Imagine your hand in a glove with fingers.) Or restated as an analogue pressure of (++++) ones. (Imagine your hand in a mitten.)

$K2,1(e0) + K2,2(e1) ..... = Q2 = 0$

And so on for the remaining 25 rows of [K].

[Q] Column 1

Row #	Action	Action Threshold	Pattern	Pattern Threshold	Row	(Scalar) Observed Outcome
1					1	4
2					2	0
3					3	0
4	Look Left w/ simple pivot	>2			4	2
5	Look Left w/ distance pivot	>3	Q[5] open frame struct	>4	5	3
6					6	-4
7					7	0
8	Look Right w/ simple pivot	>2			8	2
9	Look Right w/ distance pivot	>3	Q[9] open frame struct	>4	9	7
10	(e[9]= -1)		Q[10] doorway portal	<2	10	2
11					11	1
12					12	1
13					13	1
14	clear to go forward	>1	Q[14] quarter portal clear	>1	14	-1
15					15	3
16	obstruct on right/ veer to left	>2			16	3
17	obstruct on right/ turn left	>3			17	4
18					18	1
19	obstruct ahead/ back up	>3			19	2
20	obstruct on left/ veer right	>2			20	1
21	obstruct on left/ turn right	>3			21	2
22	back up	>3	Q[22] motor feed back	>3	22	4
23					23	1
24	_____				24	1
25	**detected on the Right**		**Obstructing**	>1	25	1
26	**detected on the Left**		**Object or**		26	1
27	**detected Ahead**		**Mass**		27	1

Example 4-1d

Decoding the Observed Outcome

After the observed outcome **[Q]** has been solved the decision making segment of the program will compare the results to the action thresholds. The first characteristic to notice is the complexity and strength of the signal. By complexity it is meant the number of events that comprise the Observed Outcome. The greater the number of mutually observed (and related) events, the greater the significance of the outcome. Essentially this is a way the automaton has for deciding if the specific outcome is something to cause a reaction. It is also a means by which the automaton can project a probable outcome.

In the example of sensory input (events) presented a preponderance of output indicates
1. a looming obstruction to the right of the Unit1; **Q[9] > 4**
2. an open structure (clustered objects) rather than solid. **Q[16] >2 , Q[17] >3**
3. Backup **Q[22]** and left turn **Q[17]**

The output of the model has been designed (by the programmer) to initiate motor action causing the Unit1 to turn away to the left from the current path. In the model each of the actionable outcomes **[Q]** has been reviewed on the basis of complexity and logically assigned a threshold value. This is of course open to interpretation. The current threshold value on actionable items may be changed, depending on insight or just plain curiosity. The Unit1 in this model has no input on the actionable thresholds.

EXECUTING MOTOR ACTIONS

Actions are determined for each Observed Outcome **[Q]** by summing the product of multiplication of **(e)** by the matrix **[K]**. These motor actions fall into categories that reflect the nature of the observed outcome. The motor actions are listed below in order of least significance to most compelling. The column to the right shows the row number from **Example 9-c.**

1. **MX** - Measure quality (distance, intensity)   **Row (19)** -
2. **M1** – Head turn towards a source   **Row (16 or 20)** –
3. **M1(L-Algn)** – Minor alignment from a left source   **Row (5)** -
4. **M1(R-Algn)** – Minor alignment from a right source   **Row (9)** -
5. **M1[C]** - Turn away from a left source   **Row (4 or 5)** -
6. **M1[C]** - Turn away from a right source   **Row (8 or 9)** –
7. **M2** - Major realignment away from a right side influence   **Row (17)** – right onstr
8. **M2** - Major realignment away from a left side influence   **Row (21)** – left obstr
9. **M3** – Backup   **Row (11)** -
10. **Recoil**   **Row (11, 19, 22, 27)**

Any motor action row where the sum of its events is greater than a given threshold value initiates an action. In **Example 9-d,** the rows are numbered on the left and motor actions with their scalar quantities are listed on the right.

BUILD THE SENSOR UNIVERSE MATRIX [K_MTX]
PROGRAM:: BASIC_WRITE_KMTX

Function

The universe matrix **[K]** interprets and sorts the main sensor groups (batteries.) The following code writes the matrix to the text file "**K_Mtx[n].**" This file is then accessed by the threadede tasks in program **U1_MK5_MODC5.**

```
#define FILE_LINES 29
#define MB_LINES 12
#define M2_LINES 15
```

```
// ******* Basic_Write_KMtx  12/05/2012  *********
// ******* Unit1 Observer Master*********


// *****source ObsAdv_U4_Fb3b ******
//


task main()
{
int MB_Mtx[196], Mevent[14], Act;
int MT_Mtx[289], Tevent[17] ;
int Array[28];
 int xcnt, fcnt, GOcnt, CAct,MQset, execCnt;

  int MQ[14], Qout[29],MTQ[17], Qf[27];

//  build_MBK(12, MB_Mtx);

{
int K_Mtx[784]   ; //this is a 28x28 matrix
          //read row by row, across
int event[31], FEvent[31], LEvent[31], REvent[31];
int Q[28],LQ[28],RQ[28];
int Dirx[5];
string row  ;
string Trackx1, Trackx2, Trackx3,Trackx4, Posit0, Posit1, Posit2, PositM;
string TkHead, Track1a, Track1b, Track1c,Track1d ;
string FName, Pout, Pin, pollx,tends;
string Deg0s,DegM0s, FCE0s,hit0;
string val, SMV, Local, Lk, TruHdn, NOgo, Eps, ClrHdn, LkQP;
string Hdn="Heading";
string Quad, Instr, QAction, OutCom;
int InstrX, execCnt;
string NOgoF,NOgoL,NOgoR, Port;
 int xdx, hit,hitx, ShmyA, X0;
int cnx,cnt,Rc,Rb,Rtac,Rtac0,Rtacx,Rtaxx, Rtaz,Rpwr,Motr;

int poll, R_L;
int Q1, Deg0,DegM0,DegZ, DegRef,DegMx,dM0,DegM02,DegM03,DegZx;

poll=1;
//DeleteFile("Posit.txt");
DeleteFile ("Track1.txt");
DeleteFile ("FwdAct.txt");
byte Posit, Trk1, Qf1, handle, Fwd1,MQ1, Mtx1;
int bytesWritten;
int fsize2=30*28*10, fsize3=100 , fsize4=100, fsize5=100;
bool eof=false;
int fsize=FILE_LINES*5;
int Mfsize=MB_LINES*5;
int cntr, xd;

int opnxL, opnxR, opnxD,opnxqD;
string buf;

ArrayInit(Tevent,0,17); ArrayInit(MTQ,0,17);
```

```
ArrayInit(Mevent,0,14);ArrayInit(MQ,0,14);
ArrayInit(FEvent,0,28);ArrayInit(Q,0,28);

if(CreateFile("Track1.txt",fsize2,Trk1)==NO_ERR)
{CloseFile(Trk1);}
Trackx1="xx";Trackx2="xx2";Trackx3="xx3"; Trackx4="xx4";
Posit1="xx3"; Posit2="xx4";

if(CreateFile("K_Mtx.txt",2500,Mtx1)==NO_ERR)
{CloseFile(Mtx1);}

do
{ cnt=cnt+1;
xdx=((cnt-1)*27) ;
row = NumToStr (cnt);

if (cnt<2)
{
//ClearScreen();
//NumOut(0,LCD_LINE3,cnt);
K_Mtx[0]=1;K_Mtx[1]=1;K_Mtx[5]=1;K_Mtx[9]=1;K_Mtx[14]=1;
}
else if (cnt<3)
{

K_Mtx[(xdx+1)]=-1;K_Mtx[(xdx+2)]=0;K_Mtx[(xdx+3)]=0;K_Mtx[(xdx+4)]=-1;
K_Mtx[(xdx+19)]=-1;K_Mtx[(xdx+20)]=-1;


}
else if (cnt<4)
{ K_Mtx[(xdx+2)]=1;  //K_Mtx[(xdx+3)]=1;K_Mtx[(xdx+4)]=1;K_Mtx[(xdx+9)]=1;
}
 else if (cnt<5)
{ K_Mtx[(xdx+3)]=1;K_Mtx[(xdx+14)]=1;K_Mtx[(xdx+23)]=1; }
else if (cnt<6)
{
K_Mtx[(xdx+1)]=1;K_Mtx[(xdx+3)]=1;K_Mtx[(xdx+4)]=1;K_Mtx[(xdx+9)]=1;K_Mtx[(xd
x+11)]=1;K_Mtx[(xdx+14)]=1;
K_Mtx[(xdx+19)]=1; K_Mtx[(xdx+20)]=1; K_Mtx[(xdx+21)]=0;K_Mtx[(xdx+23)]=1; }
else if (cnt<7)
{ K_Mtx[(xdx+5)]=-1;K_Mtx[(xdx+6)]=0;K_Mtx[(xdx+7)]=0;K_Mtx[(xdx+8)]=-1;
K_Mtx[(xdx+15)]=-1;K_Mtx[(xdx+16)]=-1;}
else if (cnt<8)
{ K_Mtx[(xdx+6)]=1;  //K_Mtx[(xdx+7)]=1;K_Mtx[(xdx+8)]=1;K_Mtx[(xdx+17)]=1;
}
else if (cnt<9)
{ K_Mtx[(xdx+7)]=1;K_Mtx[(xdx+14)]=1;K_Mtx[(xdx+22)]=1; }
else if (cnt<10)
{
K_Mtx[(xdx+5)]=1;K_Mtx[(xdx+7)]=1;K_Mtx[(xdx+8)]=1;K_Mtx[(xdx+9)]=1;K_Mtx[(xd
x+11)]=1;K_Mtx[(xdx+14)]=1;
K_Mtx[(xdx+15)]=1;K_Mtx[(xdx+16)]=1;K_Mtx[(xdx+21)]=0;K_Mtx[(xdx+22)]=1; }

else if (cnt<11)
{                                K_Mtx[(xdx+4)]=1;K_Mtx[(xdx+8)]=1;K_Mtx[(xdx+9)]=-
1;K_Mtx[(xdx+10)]=0;K_Mtx[(xdx+11)]=0;K_Mtx[(xdx+12)]=1;
K_Mtx[(xdx+13)]=0;K_Mtx[(xdx+14)]=1;
//K_Mtx[(xdx+26)]=1;
```

```
}

// [3] new rows must be added These are the rows that reflect varying distance
else if (cnt<12)
{ K_Mtx[(xdx+10)]=1;K_Mtx[(xdx+26)]=1;}
else if (cnt<13)
{
K_Mtx[(xdx+3)]=1;K_Mtx[(xdx+7)]=1;K_Mtx[(xdx+11)]=1;K_Mtx[(xdx+18)]=1;K_Mtx[(
xdx+21)]=1;}
else if (cnt<14)
{                                                              K_Mtx[(xdx+9)]=   -
1;K_Mtx[(xdx+10)]=1;K_Mtx[(xdx+11)]=1;K_Mtx[(xdx+12)]=1;K_Mtx[(xdx+14)]=1;}

//this marks the revision rows
else if (cnt<15)
{ K_Mtx[(xdx+9)]=-1;K_Mtx[(xdx+10)]=0;K_Mtx[(xdx+11)]=0;K_Mtx[(xdx+12)]=0;
K_Mtx[(xdx+13)]=-1;  //K_Mtx[(xdx+25)]=1;
}
else if (cnt<16)
{ K_Mtx[(xdx+14)]=1;K_Mtx[(xdx+15)]=1;K_Mtx[(xdx+17)]=1; K_Mtx[(xdx+19)]=1;
K_Mtx[(xdx+22)]=1; }
else if (cnt<17)
{
K_Mtx[(xdx+6)]=1;K_Mtx[(xdx+15)]=1;K_Mtx[(xdx+16)]=1;K_Mtx[(xdx+22)]=1;K_Mtx
[(xdx+22)]=1; }
else if (cnt<18)
{
K_Mtx[(xdx+4)]=0;K_Mtx[(xdx+8)]=1;K_Mtx[(xdx+16)]=1;K_Mtx[(xdx+21)]=1;K_Mtx[(
xdx+24)]=1;}
else if (cnt<19)
{ K_Mtx[(xdx+17)]=1;K_Mtx[(xdx+18)]=1;K_Mtx[(xdx+21)]=1; }
else if (cnt<20)
{
K_Mtx[(xdx+10)]=1;K_Mtx[(xdx+11)]=1;K_Mtx[(xdx+17)]=1;K_Mtx[(xdx+18)]=1;K_Mt
x[(xdx+21)]=1;K_Mtx[(xdx+26)]=1; }
else if (cnt<21)
{
K_Mtx[(xdx+2)]=0;K_Mtx[(xdx+19)]=1;K_Mtx[(xdx+20)]=1;K_Mtx[(xdx+23)]=1;K_Mtx
[(xdx+21)]=0; }
else if (cnt<22)
{
K_Mtx[(xdx+4)]=1;K_Mtx[(xdx+8)]=0;K_Mtx[(xdx+20)]=1;K_Mtx[(xdx+21)]=1;K_Mtx[(
xdx+25)]=1; }

else if (cnt<23) //this is motor feedback, row 22
{K_Mtx[(xdx+4)]=1;   K_Mtx[(xdx+8)]=1;   K_Mtx[(xdx+11)]=1;   K_Mtx[(xdx+18)]=1;
K_Mtx[(xdx+21)]=1;K_Mtx[(xdx+26)]=1;
}
else if (cnt<24)
{ K_Mtx[(xdx+22)]=1;}
else if (cnt<25)
{ K_Mtx[(xdx+23)]=1; }
else if (cnt<26) //align to a right obstruction row 25
{ K_Mtx[(xdx+18)]=-1;K_Mtx[(xdx+18)]=-1;K_Mtx[(xdx+24)]=1;}
else if (cnt<27) //align to a left obstruction row 26
{ K_Mtx[(xdx+18)]=-1;K_Mtx[(xdx+18)]=-1;K_Mtx[(xdx+25)]=1;}
else if (cnt<28)
```

```
{K_Mtx[(xdx+1)]=1;K_Mtx[(xdx+4)]=1;          K_Mtx[(xdx+5)]=1;K_Mtx[(xdx+8)]=1;
K_Mtx[(xdx+15)]=-1;
K_Mtx[(xdx+16)]=-1; K_Mtx[(xdx+17)]=1;K_Mtx[(xdx+18)]=1; K_Mtx[(xdx+19)]=-1;
K_Mtx[(xdx+20)]=-1;K_Mtx[(xdx+26)]=1; }

}
while (cnt<28);

//TEST SEQUENCE GOES HERE >>>>>>>>>>>>>>>>>>>>>>>>>>>>>>>>>>>

{
int FMtx;
byte Mtx1;
int zcnt=xcnt+1;
string FMtxs;
int xcnt;
string MtxName="K_Mtx.txt";
int fsizez=1500;

TextOut(0,LCD_LINE2,"Into Write File  ");
cnt=0;
xcnt=27;
OpenFileAppend(MtxName,fsizez,Mtx1)  //==NO_ERR)
{ ClearScreen();
  do
  {cnt=cnt+1 ;
 cntr=0;
  xdx=((cnt-1)*xcnt);
              TextOut(0,LCD_LINE4,NumToStr(xdx));
              do
              { xd=xdx+cntr;
              FMtx= K_Mtx[xd];  //this recalls each row value
              FMtxs=NumToStr(FMtx);
              NumOut(0,LCD_LINE5,xd);TextOut(30,LCD_LINE5,FMtxs);
              //Wait(SEC_1);
              WriteLnString(Mtx1,FMtxs,bytesWritten);
              cntr=cntr+1  ;
              }
              while (cntr<(xcnt+0));
                   //Mtx[] is arranged starting from [0], not [1].
                   //(cnt) is the real Mtx array column #
                   //displayed as a column, not row
                   //remember- the first element in a
                   //row is "0"
  FMtx=0;cntr=0;
  }
  while (cnt<(xcnt+0));
  cnt=0 ;
  CloseFile(Mtx1);
  TextOut(0,LCD_LINE7,"End of File");
}
}

goto Read_File2;

Read_File1:
if(OpenFileRead("K_Mtx.txt", fsize,Mtx1) == NO_ERR)
{
```

```
TextOut(0,LCD_LINE7,"Reading K_Mtx     ");
cnx=0;
until (eof == true)
    { // read the text file till the end
if(ReadLnString(Mtx1,buf)!= NO_ERR) eof = true;
K_Mtx[cnx]=StrToNum(buf);
NumOut(0,LCD_LINE6,cnx);NumOut(30,LCD_LINE6,K_Mtx[cnx]);
cnx=cnx+1;
    }
}
CloseFile(Mtx1);

Read_File2:
{
 int FMtx;
byte Mtx1;
int zcnt=xcnt+1;
string FMtxs;
int xcnt;
string MtxName="K_Mtx.txt";
int fsizez=1500;


if (OpenFileRead(MtxName, fsize,Mtx1)==NO_ERR)
{  ClearScreen();
TextOut(0,LCD_LINE7,"Reading K_Mtx     ");
xcnt=27;
cnt=0;
  do
  {cnt=cnt+1 ;
 cntr=0;
  xdx=((cnt-1)*xcnt);
            TextOut(0,LCD_LINE4,NumToStr(xdx));
            //Wait(SEC_1);
            do
            { xd=xdx+cntr;

            //Wait(SEC_1);
            ReadLnString(Mtx1,buf);
            K_Mtx[xd]=StrToNum(buf);
            NumOut(0,LCD_LINE6,xd);NumOut(30,LCD_LINE6,K_Mtx[xd]);
             cntr=cntr+1  ;
            //Wait(SEC_1);
            }
            while (cntr<(xcnt+0));
                //Mtx[] is arranged starting from [0], not [1].
                //(cnt) is the real Mtx array column #
                //displayed as a column, not row
                //remember- the first element in a
                //row is "0"
  cntr=0;
  }
  while (cnt<(xcnt+0));
  cnt=0 ;
  CloseFile(Mtx1);
  TextOut(0,LCD_LINE7,"End of File");
}
}
```

```
    Wait(SEC_10);
    //TEST SEQUENCE ENDS HERE <<<<<<<<<<<<<<<<<<<<<<<<<<<<<<<<<<<<
    }
}
```

MOTOR FEED BACK [MQ]

When the motors are activated, it is intended that movement is sustained for the duration of the activation. This is not always the case. Motors are stalled or movement is somehow attenuated. The processing unit must be alerted to times when this happens. This is accomplished through feed back sensors and position algorithms evaluated as a Motor Matrix **[MQ]**.

The execution of a command is expected to change the environment, as registered by sensory polling. Before the Rover can be expected to operate satisfactorily, it must be able to detect whether or not an action has been properly executed. But it is more important that the Rover observes the local conditions regardless of alignment or bearings. This brings up an approach proposing that precision of movement and precision of placement are functionally unnecessary, and at best low in priority.

As long as the Rover, functioning as an observer, can locate features of the landscape and conforms its movements to the imperative, the introduction of precision would not alter the basic observer response.

INTERNAL ERRORS

There may be some reason an action is not falling within the boundaries of execution, and the Rover is loosing effectiveness in its placements. If there is a need for precision, such as passing through a doorway, this often creates a barrier to effective function.

Since the Rover is capable of observing (a) itself, (b) its internal functions and (c) the observational process, it should be able to detect the imbedded error. This involves including the functioning events of the action, namely all the sensate impulses which bring about the action, the motor signals and the action itself, in the event matrix. The working theory here is if you know the extent and nature of the error, the *travel position* can be mitigated by applying this knowledge. As will be seen, this builds a very sophisticated matrix of member event states **[K]**.

There are certain Motor (related) Events that develop and reflect fields of error.

1. Voltage
2. Power
3. Command profile
4. Revolutions
5. Tachometer

Voltage

The voltage available to the motors varies from a peak (9 volts for Mindstorms ^{TM}) to a basin (appx. 6v) where operation of the **Unit** falters. As long as the voltage level is between 7.4v and 8.4v, the **Unit1**^{TM} systems seems to operate satisfactorily. The available voltage can be represented in factors of (.25v) units for the working **Unit.**

Power

Motor power is specified in the program that directs motor activity. During operation, the motor may not be getting this specified power. A system call allows the motor to be polled for the power (percentage) that is actually being used. This is to be compared to what is called. Each motor action must be associated with a

power range. These can be grouped in decimal metrics (factored groups of 10) representing the percent of available power assigned to the motor action. In the Mindstorms ^{TM} NXT, servo and motor power are expressed as a percentage of available power. If voltage drops, so does supplied power. Even though the command is for a factor of [100], this is merely a percentage of available power.
Set the volage and power parameters.

(Ref: task main ( ); [SkipX:])

```
zxxa=BatteryLevel();          // the current voltage level
Bx=(7800/zxxa);               // the ratio of current to design level (7.8v)
Bxx=Bx*100;                   // the ratio in percentile
Pwr1= 60*Bxx/100;             //This sets the motor power for reliable
                              //operation at the design level
```

Command Profile

The series of commands which direct and activate the motor activity must be established as events. This would include the motor combinations (for example: OUT_ABC,) their durations and rotational directions. Each command issued to the motors originates in the polling results of the tactile and digital sensors. These commands are represented by the observed event matrix **[Q]** and designated as **Q[n]**, where *n* is the respective row number. If motor action does not change the command profile (essentially changing the observed landscape,) then action can be considered incomplete. An incomplete motor action also can be analyzed using power, revolutions and tachometer readings.

(Ref: task d_Motr_Feed ( ); [Motr_Monitor:])
Bundled outcomes **[Q]** are treated as single motor events

```
Motr_Monitor:
if(Resettask=="Yes") {goto Reset_c;}
Rtaz=0;
Rtac0=0;
Rtaxx=0;

tEXs=CurrentTick();
ResetRotationCount(OUT_AB);

        // tac*
ArrayInit(Mevent,0,14);

ctickx:
 tEXf=CurrentTick()-tEXs;
 if (tEXf<2300) {goto ctickx;}      //this must allow 23000ms to elapse w/ motr
                                    //running. Then it takes a rotation count.

xb=MotorRotationCount(OUT_B)*(-1);
xc= MotorRotationCount(OUT_A)*(-1);

tEXf=tEXf/100;      //change micr-sec to cent-secs

xbc=xb;
if (xb>xc) {xbc=xc;}
 Rtacx=((xb+xc)/20);    //change revs to 1/10 scale

Rtac0=(((Rtacx)/tEXf));
Ktac0=(pwr/15);        // this is an empirical value indicating the tachometer
                       // reading that should be produced at the power level
                       // (pwr) specified
```

```
//NumOut(35,LCD_LINE5,Rtac0); NumOut(45,LCD_LINE5,Ktac0);
//diagnostic printout

DegM0=StrToNum(DegM0s);    //this is the current heading in degrees
                          //DegRef is the reference heading
                          //before the operation

DeltaDeg=(DegM0-DegRef);   //if(DeltaDeg<=3) {Mevent[6]=-1;}
                          //this is optional, signaling no operation

        if (Q[11]>1) { Mevent[1]=1;}
        if (Q[19]>2) { Mevent[7]=1;}
        if (Q[17]>2) { Mevent[8]=1;}   //right obstr
        if (Q[21]>2) { Mevent[9]=1;}   //left obstr
```

EXTERNAL ERRORS

In spite of voltage and power variations, most motor functions resulting in the event errors listed above are caused directly by run-ins with external obstructions or stress. These would affect the motor in the same way as internally created difficulties, but would most likely exhibit a physical signature detected by the sensors. External errors fall into categories.

1. Sensor group (battery) prompting the action
2. Change in terrain composition
3. Serial events which cause confusion

Sensor Group (*Battery)* Prompting the Action

As shown in **Chapter III, Fig 3-4**, sensors are grouped into *batteries* which define conditions surrounding certain actions. Sensor batteries can also be represented by a primary sense (e.g. sound.) After the motor action has completed, the sensor battery is polled again to detect changes. Since the battery profile initiated the action in the first place, it is important to check if the conditions have changed. If not, there is reason to believe that execution has been unsuccessful.

(Ref: task a_Evalpoll ( ); [Cycle_ChkFwd:])

```
//>>>>>>>>>>>>>> Cycle Check for Minor Obstr >>>>>>>>>>>>>>>>>>>>>
if((Gate=="-1")||(GateA=="-1")) {goto Begin_Poll;}
                              // no Basic_Eval while
                              //Alignment: is working
                              //or Head is turning

Gate="-1";
Cycle_ChkFwd( hit, Motr, Lk, GFwd,xyL,xyR);        //this checks clearance
                                                  //to the left and right
Gate="1";
if((GFwd==1)&&(hitTch==0)) {goto End_pEval;}
//" Fwd Obstr "

        if (xyL>xyR)
          {
          //before Unit can execute a left turn, it must make sure
          //the backside can clear a swing.
          //don't use a Head_RightC sub, its too long and complicated
          if(xyR<41) {
                  TShmy_Right();
```

```
                    OnFwdReg(OUT_AB,85,OUT_REGMODE_SYNC);
                    Wait(1200);        //new chassis requires 13" back up
                    Float(OUT_AB);
                    //This is the complex motr series for a clear swing
                    //1.) TShmy_Right
                    //2.) Backup and then
                    //3.) Dyno_ShmyL(). This will
                    //provide clearance for the rear to swing in a clear arc.
                    //this is a simple pivot to the left
                    }

            Dyno_ShmyL(Seek);
            bku=0;trn=trn+1;
            //" Veer Left ";
            goto Shmy_OutEv;
            }
            if (xyR>xyL)
            {
            if(xyL<41) {
                    TShmy_Left();
                    OnFwdReg(OUT_AB,85,OUT_REGMODE_SYNC);
                    Wait(1200);
                                        //new chassis requires 13" back up
                    Float(OUT_AB);
                    //This is the complex motr series for a clear swing
                    //1.) TShmy_Left
                    //2.) Backup and then
                    //3.) Dyno_ShmyR(). This will
                    //provide clearance for the rear to swing in a clear arc.
                    //this is a simple pivot to the left
                    }
            Dyno_ShmyR(Seek);
            bku=0;trn=trn-1 ;
            //" Veer Right ";
            goto Shmy_OutEv;
            }
        Shmy_OutEv:
        hitTch=0;
        Lk="N";     //this is a last snap-shot look at clearance
        Cycle_ChkFwd( hit, Motr, Lk, GFwd,xyL,xyR); //*G4x6b3
        Lk="F";
{int dummy1,dummy2,dummy3;
dummy1=-1;
                //this is a turn to the left & a return to center the head
Lk="L";Lk_D( Lk,dummy1, dummy2, dummy3);
Lk="LR";Lk_D( Lk,dummy1, dummy2, dummy3);
 }
        if(GFwd==1) {
                //no action taken and clear
                goto End_pEval;
                }
        else {//Veered clear of obstr}
```

//<<<<<<<<<<<<< END of Cycle Check <<<<<<<<<<<<<<<<<<<<<<<<<<<<

Change in Terrain Composition

If certain physical components, such as sounds or Infrared (IR) images, arise and persist at the time of an external error then the terrain is probably involved in the motor error. If an internal function error is detected in association with an external sensory battery alert signal, the Unit should commence extrication exercises. These arise when the motor feed back matrix **[MQ]** registers threshold values for backout functions MQ12 & MQ13. These functions are heavilt influenced by infrared and *Stop* events.

(Ref: task main ( ); [MotrFeed:] [Stalled:])

```
{
Stalled:
Read_DegHd(DegRef);
DegX1=DegRef;
DegZ=100;
Read_FwdTch( hitx);
        //MQAct:: this is the motor array MQ action event gate.
        //If MQAct==1 then the gate is open
        //and action is allowed as motor events.

        if ((MQAct=="1"))
        //this indicates that nothing
        //has been done for a stall yet
        {
        GateA="-1";        // ::must set Align Gate to -1 if Stall is actuated

if((MQ[12]>2)||(hitx==-1))
        {
        if(MQ[12]>=MQ[13])
                {
                //"BackUp R_face_L "
        OnFwdSync(OUT_AB,100,OUT_REGMODE_SPEED);Wait(1200);
                OnFwdSync(OUT_AB,85,-40);
                Wait(1200); Off(OUT_AB);
                Wait(2000);    //00b
                goto Chk_MQ;
                }
        }

if((MQ[13]>2)||(hitx==1))
                {
        //"Back Up L_face_R "
OnFwdSync(OUT_AB,100,OUT_REGMODE_SPEED);Wait(1200);
        OnFwdSync(OUT_AB,85,40);
        Wait(1200); Off(OUT_AB);
        Wait(2000);    //00b
        goto Chk_MQ;
                }

if((MQ[11]>2)||(MQ[7]>2))
                {
        //"Back Up "
 OnFwdSync(OUT_AB,85,OUT_REGMODE_SPEED);
        Wait(1200);Off(OUT_AB);
        MQAct="-1";Stallgate=0;
                                //MQAct=="-1" blocks a repeat use of
                                //the Back Up option
        hitBmp=1;               //hitBmp must be initialized after
                                //execution if it doesn't jump to
                                //Chk_MQ
```

```
                goto Out_MQ;
                }
```

Serial Events Cause Confusion

Events which happen in a series (leading up to some seminal point that triggers a motor action) may cause a premature action that result in duplication or multiple self-canceling efforts. These over-reactions on the part of the automaton can cause exaggerations of travel and develop inaccurate heading directions. If something happanes too frequently, one remedy is to simply back up and reassess the landscape.

(Ref: task b_Evalpoll, [Cycle_End:])

```
Read_FwdTch( hitx);
    Posit1=StrCat(NumToStr(hit),NumToStr(hitx));
              Rep_episode(SeqBK, EpsBK, SeqC);
              //EpsBK must be [1] before significance can be attributed
    if (EpsBK>0) {BUC[EpsBK]=ClrHdn;} //DegM0;
              //Back_Up Cntr:: (3) (EpsBK) (BUC[EpsBK]) (ClrHdn)


  if (EpsBK>0){
          Epsbk=EpsBK-1;
          if ((Epsbk>0)&&(BUC[Epsbk]==BUC[EpsBK]))
          //if Unit is on the same quadrant too long, it needs to back up
          {
          //:Boxed in: Back_Up()
          // sub call
          //Boxed in: Back Out

          Back_Up(FCE,Dirx,DegRef);
           Instr="BkO";EpsBK=0;
           ArrayInit(BUC,0,5);
//no action executions in this task Polling()
//Instr "Bk0" should be written to the output file
          }
//This should prompt a Back_Up() Action
//this means there is no hitx L or R
// and it starts a fwd action
```

REGULATING MOTOR ACTIONS AND RESPONSES USING A REAL GRID

As the **Unit1** responds to actionable outcomes, changes its alignment or initiates motion, motor errors are bound to exist. Slight position changes can cause significant errors where the terrain and landscape vary (e.g. the Unit1Rover is operating amongst open furniture structures and textured floor covering.) Generally these errors fall into categories.
1. Random errors and creep
2. Frictional slip (the wheels/tracks don't grip well)
3. Change in terrain composition
4. Directional instability (e.g. left turn is easier than right.)
5. Realignment causes perceptional variations

In some situations, these errors can be kept to a minimum or even rendered negligible if motion functions are properly controlled.

DEVELOPING THE MOTOR FEED BACK MATRIX [MQ]

Motor events can be represented in the same type of matrix used for the global sensory *experience* matrix **[K]**. According to membership and influence (**Chapter VI,**) motor events would be arranged as possibilities of state, depending upon the "observer." They are applied to a Universe in which the observer registers events **[e]** as well as *observed experiences [Q]*.

Establishing Alignment

As the automaton maneuvers through the landscape and activates motors, there is the presumption (on the part of the automaton) that such actions are successfully executed. If a sensory impression is static and cannot be dispelled through continued action, the automaton assuming success just continues to bump into the same wall over and over. One of the first chores of the course keeping, performed as background, is to maintain a record of current heading. For the Unit1, compass readings are constantly taken by the **Slave** and evaluated in terms of quadrant and heading variation. In this sense:

    a) Quadrant location is important because it alerts the Unit1 to large scale deviations in heading. Using a magnetic compass introduces a sizable error over the course of an excursion. As the Unit1 wanders around an obstacle, changing its relative heading to a different quadrant would raise a significant alert.

    b) Heading variation is second in importance since it can alert the Unit1 to static or near static turning or motion conditions. These would infer no action or poor executed action.

    c) Touching an obstacle in association with heading variation would assist in deciding alternate actions intended to change alignment.

Motor Feed Back

If the automaton is stuck, pressed against a wall or otherwise blocked from movement motor action calls may be completely ineffective. In these cases it is likely that the drive surface (wheel or track) may be slipping.

    a) Motor activity measured in revolutions (RPmS) is used to gage the actual motor response against the intended response. This is done through an algorithm that monitors motor activity whenever the Unit1 is driving. If the motor RPmS (revolutions per micro-second) fall off from a sustained average, then this is considered an event.

    b) Motor activity during turning and directional change, not when the Unit1 is driving, is an important aspect of execution and operation. In this case variations in RPmS during a commanded turn sequence and a small or near zero alignment change would further alert the Unit1 to a significant event.

    c) Motor feed back can be arrayed to reflect failure in terms of a serial event (happening over and over.)

These activity indicators can be defined in terms of *Forward action* and *Turning*. The best approach would be to combine the common features of each activity into one *Advanced function*.

Advanced Motor Events

The basic sensory Experience matrix provides important information about the landscape. But as discussed, this is limited to the number and type of sensors. One way to increase the effectiveness of the basic experience is to include certain observed outcomes **[Q]** in evaluating motor feed back. For example, if the Rover senses infrared signals of an obstruction ahead, but not close enough to cause an ultrasound Stop, the Outcome **Q[19]** would signal something ahead. If it is associated with a touch event it could alert the Rover to a specific movement, involving a back out or other unique action. The touch event would be a signal detected by the **Slave** and sent to the **Master.** The processing of the information would take place in a specific Advanced forward action matrix.

a) Motor feed back and touch events and Observed Outcome **Q[19]** of an obstruction ahead can alert the Rover to sophisticated avoidance actions before a complete Stop occurs. The range and complexity of the sensor array(s) requires interpretation. This is accomplisher by combining a variety of seemingly unrelated evens which leads to a more nearly complete outlook.

b) Observed Outcome **Q[11]** stop, back up and alignment **Q[19]**, **Q[17]** & **Q[21]** actions contribute to the Rover's decisions.

Advanced Turning Events

Sensor events and Observed Outcome are particularly useful in decisions involving direction and heading. These Outcomes from the main **[Q]** observations are:

a) **Q[17]** for turn left due to a right obstruction

b) **Q[21]** for a turn right due to a left obstruction

Motor Actions

Motor response actions designed by the programmer are the result of an understanding (or lack thereof) of the automaton's predicament and/or tactic for extracting from a stalled situation. Basically the automaton has no idea what it is doing. The hardware must be integrated with the software in a manner that appears seamless (like the automaton does know what it is doing.) The programmer sets up logical task situations that are decided by threshold Outcomes **[Q].** The actions are subroutines called by the task main() when an action threshold is met or exceeded. (Ref: Chapter V Intergrating Hardware with Software, Motor Events.)

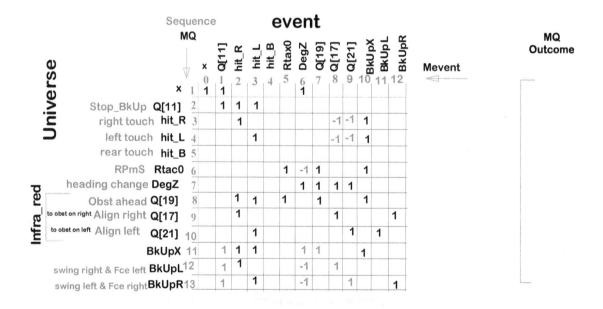

Fig 4-4

Figure 9-4 details a matrix constructed as compound, since other Universe elements are included, that defines the observed outcome **[MQ]**.

81

In the included events there are instances where **Infrared** signals may be detected at the front (Q[19]), left (Q[21]) or right (Q[17]). The backup (BkUpX) action is initiated when a complex series of events creates a row sum larger than [2]. Where the degree heading does not change (DegZ) this signal operates as adverse. Front IR receptions (Q19) are significant.

SOLVING FOR THE MOTOR FEEDBACK OBSERVED OUTCOME [MQ] AND IT'S INTERPRETATION

The observed outcome matrix **(Fig 9-4)** is solved by the familiar process of multiplying **(Me)** by **[MBK].** This outcome is now open to interpretation. This process begins in the task c_Motr_Feed(), where the **[Q]** outcomes 11, 17, 19 & 21 are assigned motor event possibilities of state.

```
if (Q[11]>1) { Mevent[1]=1;}
if (Q[19]>2) { Mevent[7]=1;}
if (Q[17]>2) { Mevent[8]=1;}    //right obstr
if (Q[21]>2) { Mevent[9]=1;}    //left obstr
```

Touch events are also attributed to Mevent states. The completed event column is then multiplied by the motor feed back **[MB-K]** matrix, solving for **[MQ]** outcomes. This approach enables a comparison between peripheral objects and motor malfunctions, such as poor RPmS. Specific **[MQ]** outcomes are evaluated in the task main() in the internal routine "MotrFeed:" for stalled conditions and directional (right/left) extraction solutions.

```
if ((MQAct=="1"))
            //this indicates that nothing
            //has been done for a stall yet
            {
            GateA="-1";        // ::must set Align Gate to -1 if Stall is actuated

if((MQ[12]>2)||(hitx==-1))
        {
        if(MQ[12]>=MQ[13])
                    {TextOut(0,LCD_LINE1,"BackUp R_face_L ");
Posit1c=" Back Up R_face_L ";
OnFwdSync(OUT_AB,100,OUT_REGMODE_SPEED);Wait(1200);
                    OnFwdSync(OUT_AB,85,-40);
                    // backup Left turn "OnFwdSync(OUT_AB,Pwr1,-50);"
                    Wait(1200); Off(OUT_AB);
                    Wait(2000);    //00b
                    goto Chk_MQ;
                    }
        }
    }
}
```

BUILD THE MOTOR UNIVERSE MATRIX [MB_MTX]
PROGRAM:: BASIC_WRITE_MBMTX

Function

The motor universe matrix **[K]** interprets and sorts the motor functions and feed back issues The following code writes the matrix to the text file "**MB_Mtx[n].**" This file is then accessed by the threadede tasks in program **U1_MK5_MODC5.**

```
#define FILE_LINES 29
#define MB_LINES 12
#define M2_LINES 15
#define BT_Cnx 1          //  12/05/2012


task main()
//sub build_MBK(int xcnt, int &MB_Mtx[])
//this is the subroutine to create the ** FORWARD ACTION *** matrix
//xcnt is the ROW count - start the count at (1) not (0)
//Version 2 [SLV] is the advanced matrix reflecting motor corrections
//determined by Slave and sent to Master

{
int MB_Mtx[225];  //this is a matrix
            //read row by row, across
int xcnt;
 int xdx;
int cnt;          //xcnt=13
int bytesWritten;
string row;
int FMtx;
byte Mtx1;
xcnt=13;
//ClearScreen(); TextOut(0,LCD_LINE2,"MB_Mtx Matrix");
//NumOut(0,LCD_LINE2,xcnt);
if(CreateFile("MB_Mtx.txt",800,Mtx1)==NO_ERR)
{CloseFile(Mtx1);}


do
{ cnt=cnt+1;
xdx=((cnt-1)*xcnt) ;
row = NumToStr (cnt);

//NumOut(0,LCD_LINE3,cnt);NumOut(20,LCD_LINE3,xdx);
//Wait(SEC_2);
if (cnt<2)
{

MB_Mtx[0]=1;MB_Mtx[1]=1;MB_Mtx[5]=1;MB_Mtx[6]=-1;
}
else if (cnt<3)
{
MB_Mtx[(xdx+1)]=1;MB_Mtx[(xdx+2)]=1;MB_Mtx[(xdx+3)]=1;MB_Mtx[(xdx+10)]=1;
}
else if (cnt<4)
{ MB_Mtx[(xdx+2)]=1;MB_Mtx[(xdx+5)]=0;MB_Mtx[(xdx+6)]=0;MB_Mtx[(xdx+8)]=-1;
MB_Mtx[(xdx+9)]=-1;MB_Mtx[(xdx+10)]=1;}
 else if (cnt<5)
{ MB_Mtx[(xdx+3)]=1;MB_Mtx[(xdx+5)]=0;MB_Mtx[(xdx+8)]=-1;MB_Mtx[(xdx+9)]=-1;
MB_Mtx[(xdx+10)]=1; }

else if (cnt<6)
```

```
{ MB_Mtx[(xdx+4)]=1;}

else if (cnt<7)
{                                                    MB_Mtx[(xdx+5)]=1;MB_Mtx[(xdx+6)]=-
1;MB_Mtx[(xdx+7)]=1;MB_Mtx[(xdx+7)]=0;MB_Mtx[(xdx+8)]=0;
MB_Mtx[(xdx+10)]=1; }
else if (cnt<8)
{MB_Mtx[(xdx+6)]=1;MB_Mtx[(xdx+7)]=1;MB_Mtx[(xdx+8)]=1; MB_Mtx[(xdx+9)]=1; }
else if (cnt<9)
{
MB_Mtx[(xdx+2)]=1;MB_Mtx[(xdx+3)]=1;MB_Mtx[(xdx+5)]=1;MB_Mtx[(xdx+7)]=1;MB
_Mtx[(xdx+10)]=1; }
else if (cnt<10)
{  MB_Mtx[(xdx+2)]=1;MB_Mtx[(xdx+3)]=0;MB_Mtx[(xdx+8)]=1;MB_Mtx[(xdx+12)]=1;
}
else if (cnt<11)
{  MB_Mtx[(xdx+2)]=0;MB_Mtx[(xdx+3)]=1;MB_Mtx[(xdx+9)]=1;MB_Mtx[(xdx+11)]=1;
}
else if (cnt<12)
{
MB_Mtx[(xdx+1)]=1;MB_Mtx[(xdx+2)]=1;MB_Mtx[(xdx+3)]=1;MB_Mtx[(xdx+5)]=1;MB
_Mtx[(xdx+6)]=-1;
MB_Mtx[(xdx+7)]=1;MB_Mtx[(xdx+10)]=1; }
else if (cnt<13)
{                                               MB_Mtx[(xdx+1)]=0;MB_Mtx[(xdx+2)]=1;
MB_Mtx[(xdx+5)]=1;MB_Mtx[(xdx+6)]=+1;MB_Mtx[(xdx+8)]=1;MB_Mtx[(xdx+11)]=1;}

else if (cnt<14)
{
MB_Mtx[(xdx+1)]=0;MB_Mtx[(xdx+3)]=1;MB_Mtx[(xdx+5)]=1;MB_Mtx[(xdx+6)]=+1;M
B_Mtx[(xdx+9)]=1;MB_Mtx[(xdx+12)]=1; }
//else if (cnt<15)
//{ MB_Mtx[(xdx+14)]=1;}
//else if (cnt<16)
//{ MB_Mtx[(xdx+15)]=1;}
}
while (cnt<14);

// sub Write_MtxQ(string MtxName, int xcnt, int fsize2, int &Mtxin[] )
//Write_MtxQ( MtxName, xcnt, fsize2, Mtxin);
{

int zcnt=xcnt+1;
string FMtxs;
int xcnt,cntr;
string MtxName="MB_Mtx.txt";
int fsizez=800;
int xd;
TextOut(0,LCD_LINE2," Write MB_Mtx.txt ");
Wait(SEC_1);
cnt=0;
xcnt=13;
//goto Read_File2;
//if(
OpenFileAppend(MtxName,fsizez,Mtx1)  //==NO_ERR)
{ ClearScreen();
  do
  {cnt=cnt+1 ;
```

```
        cntr=0;
    xdx=((cnt-1)*xcnt);
              TextOut(0,LCD_LINE4,NumToStr(xdx));
              do
              { xd=xdx+cntr;
              FMtx= MB_Mtx[xd];  //this recalls each row value
              FMtxs=NumToStr(FMtx);
              NumOut(0,LCD_LINE5,xd);TextOut(30,LCD_LINE5,FMtxs);
              //Wait(SEC_1);
              WriteLnString(Mtx1,FMtxs,bytesWritten);
              cntr=cntr+1  ;
              }
              while (cntr<(xcnt+0));
                  //Mtx[] is arranged starting from [0], not [1].
                  //(cnt) is the real Mtx array column #
                  //displayed as a column, not row
                  //remember- the first element in a
                  //row is "0"
    FMtx=0;cntr=0;
    }
    while (cnt<(xcnt+0));
    cnt=0 ;
    CloseFile(Mtx1);
    TextOut(0,LCD_LINE7,"End of File");
}

Read_File2:
//sub Read_MtxQ(string MtxName, int xcnt, int fsize, int &Mtxin[] )
//Write_MtxQ( MtxName, xcnt, fsize, Mtxin);
{
 int FMtx;
byte Mtx1;
int zcnt=xcnt+1;
string FMtxs;
int xcnt;
string MtxName="MB_Mtx.txt";
string buf;
int fsizez=800;


if (OpenFileRead(MtxName, fsizez,Mtx1)==NO_ERR)
{  ClearScreen();
TextOut(0,LCD_LINE7,"Reading MB_Mtx    ");
//Wait(SEC_2);
xcnt=13;
cnt=0;
  do
  {cnt=cnt+1 ;
 cntr=0;
   xdx=((cnt-1)*xcnt);
              TextOut(0,LCD_LINE4,NumToStr(xdx));
              //Wait(SEC_1);
              do
              { xd=xdx+cntr;

              //Wait(SEC_1);
              ReadLnString(Mtx1,buf);
              MB_Mtx[xd]=StrToNum(buf);
```

```
                   TextOut(0,LCD_LINE6,"              ");
                   NumOut(0,LCD_LINE6,xd);NumOut(30,LCD_LINE6,MB_Mtx[xd]);
                   cntr=cntr+1  ;
                   Wait(SEC_1);
                   }
                   while (cntr<(xcnt+0));
                           //Mtx[] is arranged starting from [0], not [1].
                           //(cnt) is the real Mtx array column #
                           //displayed as a column, not row
                           //remember- the first element in a
                           //row is "0"
            cntr=0;
            }
            while (cnt<(xcnt+0));
            cnt=0 ;
            CloseFile(Mtx1);
            TextOut(0,LCD_LINE7,"End of File");
         }
         }

         }
         }
```

PROGRAM SET UP FOR THE MASTER PROCESSOR
PROGRAM NAME:: U1_MK5_MODC5

The coded elements of the complete chain are detailed in the subsequent headings. They are listed in the required sequence and are to be assembled and compiled as shown. The text may be copied and pasted directly to the Bricx Command Center working page (**Chapter II, Example 2-7.**)

Set up the Bricx Operating System

The Mindstorms NXT OS 3.1 is used in this Unit1 application. This version can be downloaded from the LEGO Mindstorms web site and installed on the NXT. After installation, the default programs should be trimmed away to make space for the **U1_Mk5_modC5**^{TM} version of the Rover software. After trimming the default system programs, the operating queue should look like this:

> ! Click.rso
> ! Startup.rso
> RPGReader.sys
> NVConfig.sys

These system files will serve the purpose of the Rover.

Set up the Rover Reference Files

After installing the Bricx operating system, reference files which contain matrix Universe states must be written and installed in flash memory. This must take place each time the operating system is updated or replaced. To write the matrix files **K_Mtx.txt** and **MQ_Mtx.txt** the two execution files must be compiled and loaded onto the Bricx. These files are listed above as

> **Basic_Write_KMtx.nxc**
> **Basic_Write_MBMtx.nxc**

When these files are compiled and loaded, execute them on the Bricx. They will create and write the appropriated **.txt** files onto the flash drive of the microprocessor. After the **.txt** files have been written, remove the execution **.nxc** files to make room for the Rover executable files.

Set up the UNIT1 Executable files

The listed files with the block headings **Master** or **Slave** should now be compiled and loaded onto the microprocessor(s) as executable files. This involves following the directions and procedures outlined in the Bricx Command Center operations manual that is available for download (**Chapter II, ref: Source Forge Web Site.**)

From the NXT Bricx Command Center NeXT Explorer, the contents of the Bricx flash memory should appear with these contents:

Sound effects

> ! Click.rso
> ! Startup.rso

System files

> RPGReader.sys
> NVConfig.sys

Text

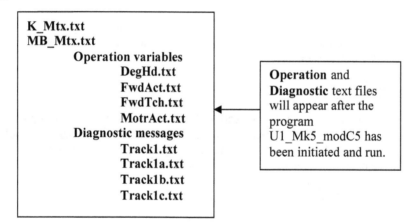

> **K_Mtx.txt**
> **MB_Mtx.txt**
> **Operation variables**
> **DegHd.txt**
> **FwdAct.txt**
> **FwdTch.txt**
> **MotrAct.txt**
> **Diagnostic messages**
> **Track1.txt**
> **Track1a.txt**
> **Track1b.txt**
> **Track1c.txt**

Operation and **Diagnostic** text files will appear after the program U1_Mk5_modC5 has been initiated and run.

Program

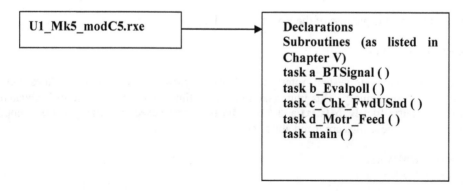

> **U1_Mk5_modC5.rxe**

> **Declarations**
> **Subroutines (as listed in Chapter V)**
> **task a_BTSignal ( )**
> **task b_Evalpoll ( )**
> **task c_Chk_FwdUSnd ( )**
> **task d_Motr_Feed ( )**
> **task main ( )**

The threaded tasks are started automatically in the sequence established in "main ( )." There are provisions in task main( ) for testing subroutines. When this window is opened, tasks b_ and c_ are to be suppressed using comment slashes that are identified with double slashes followed by an asterisk "//*."

MASTER:

DECLARATIONS

FUNCTION

Initial declarations establish constant values of expressions and assignments that will be used frequently in the code.

```
//Unit1_Mk5_modC5
//   Use WrkngSLAVE_00y1

                        //Front Wheel Drive  ::: Head Fwd
                        //2.6:1 gear box
                        //Located over drive wheels
                        //LimiT==45
#define SNX4 IN_3
          //aft (at the casters) looking fwd towards the
                        //drive wheels, Motor desigantions are:
          //A is Left Motor
          //B is Right Motor
          //C is Head Moter
#define IRSEEKER IN_3
#define SND1 SENSOR_4    //left ear
#define SND2 SENSOR_1    //right ear
#define LimiT 50 //cm
          //"Limit" is the distanced traveled during the time
                //it takes to poll the sensors
          //FrontWheelDrive Fat Tire requires 50cm fwd of USnd
                //due size and rotation speed of 2.5in tires
                //and to placement of Oculus
#define FILE_LINES 29
#define MB_LINES 14
#define BT_Cnx 1
#define INBOX 1
#define INBOX0 2
#define INBOX1 6
#define OUTBOX0 3
#define OUTBOX1 5
#define OUTBOX2 4
#define OUTBOX3 7
          //Motor commands (AB) corrected for geared drives
                //Fwd is now Rev for Front Wheel Drive, Rev is now Fwd
                //Head movement (C) corrected for reverse position on drive
mutex Fwd_Motr;
mutex FileAcc;
mutex FileAcc1;
mutex FileAcc2;
mutex FileAcc3;          //Track1.txt
mutex USndAcc;
```

```
//>>>>>>>>>>>>>>>>>>>>>>>>>DECLARE VARIABLES <<<<<<<<<<<<<
int MB_Mtx[196], Mevent[14], Act;
int MT_Mtx[289], Tevent[17] ;
int Array[28], BUC[5];              //BUC is the Back_Up Cntr array
 int xcnt, fcnt, GOcnt, CAct,MQset, execCnt;

int MQ[14], Qout[29],MTQ[17], Qf[27];

int K_Mtx[784];  //this is a 28x28 matrix
          //read row by row, across
int event[31], FEvent[31], LEvent[31], REvent[31];
int Q[29],LQ[29],RQ[29];
int Dirx[5];
string row  ;
string Trackx1, Trackx2, Trackx3,Trackx4, Posit0, Posit1, Posit2, PositM;
string TkHead, Track1a, Track1b, Track1c,Track1d ;
string FName, Pout, Pin, pollx,tends;
string Deg0s,DegM0s, FCE0s,hit0;
string val, SMV, Local, Lk, TruHdn, NOgo, Eps, ClrHdn, LkQP;
string Hdn="Heading";
string Quad, Instr, QAction, OutCom;
string NOgoF,NOgoL,NOgoR, Port;
 int xdx, hit,hitx, ShmyA, X0;
int cnx,cnt,Rc,Rb,Rtac,Rtac0,Rtacx,Rtaxx, Rtaz,Rpwr;
int MTac;  //Motrx;  //6Ce_a

int poll, R_L;
int Q1, Deg0,DegM0,DegZ, DegRef,DegMx,dM0,DegM02,DegM03,DegZx,DegNX;
int x,x1,x2,y,HR, HL,SLR,BK,xa,xb;
int FCE0, FCEx, FCE, FCEa, Trvl, Dix, Fa, FCENX;
int SeqC, SeqQS, SeqN, Eps16, Eps18, Eps14, Eps13,Eps11, Eps17,AlgR, AlgL ;
int Eps4,Eps5, Eps8,Eps9, Eps24, EpsBK, Epsbk, Eps59;
int EpsM3,SeqM3,SeqBK ;
int                                              SeqN24,SeqN4,SeqN5,
SeqN8,SeqN9,SeqN11,SeqN16,SeqN18,SeqN14,SeqN13,SeqN17;
int SeqN19,SeqN20, SeqN21, SeqN22, SeqN23,Seqhx ;
int Eps19, Eps20, Eps21,Epshx;
int SeqM212, EpsM212, SeqM210, EpsM210,SeqM214, EpsM214;
int  SeqM5,EpsM5,SeqM6,EpsM6,SeqM7,EpsM7,SeqM8,EpsM8,SeqM9,EpsM9;
int SeqM11,EpsM11;
int BKS,GFwd,Runx;
long tx ,pwr;
long txx;
long ts,tend,tendx,tendLast,TmeClk,tmNG;
int tEXs,tEXf;
long tp, tpoll;
long deltaT;
float Ratio,xxx,Rsqpwr, xxa, tendSeg;
int dir, se1, se2, se3, se4, se5, result,IRcntr;
int se1x ,se2x ,se3x ,se4x ,se5x ;
byte Posit, Trk1, Qf1, handle, Fwd1,MQ1, QA1, QxV, QuE;
int bytesWritten,bytes2;
int fsize2=30*28*10, fsize3=100 , fsize4=100, fsize5=100;
int fsizex=30*28*20, fsizex2=30*28*2;
bool eof=false;
int fsize=FILE_LINES*5;
int Mfsize=MB_LINES*5;
```

89

```
int cntr, xd,Keyx,eLines;

int opnxL, opnxR, opnxD,opnxqD;
string buf,fname, Key, Key0;
int lines,jumpx,QGOcnt,keyx,key0,xyL,xyR,trn,bku;
int keyx0;
//&&&&&&&&&&&&&&&&&&&&&&&&&&&&&&&&&&&&&&&&&&&&&&&&&&&&&&&&
string Gate,GateA;
//&&&&&&&&&&&&&&&&&&&&&&&&&&&&&&&&&&&&&&&&&&&&&&&&&&&&&&&&
int InstrX;
string QGOcnts,AReps,Stallcnt;

int QGOgate,Stallgate;
byte Trk1a,Trk1b,Trk1c;
int QGOcntx,ARep;
int hitTch,hitBmp;
int Bxx,zxxa,Pwr1;
float Bratio,Bx;
string Dx,Seek,Dxkey;
string DegRefs,MQAct;
int DeltaDeg;
string Resettask;
int ResetX;
int QGOLast, QGOClk;
int DegX1,DegX2;
//********* THESE ARE THE COMMON VARIABLES USED BY ALL task(s) **********
```

MASTER

TASK A_BTSIGNAL ( )

FUNCTION

UNIT1 uses two microprocessors. It communicates between the two using a Bluetooth modem. The two micros are always on line and checking each other for queries and responses.

```
task a_BTSignal ( )
{
ClearScreen();
string MagCalls;
MagCalls="Calib";
//>>>>>>>>>>>>>>>>>>>>>>>>>>>>>>>>>
                   Mag_Data:
if(Resettask=="Yes") {goto Reset_a;}
SendRemoteString(BT_Cnx,OUTBOX1,MagCalls);
Check_Pin0:
ReceiveRemoteString(BT_Cnx,INBOX,Pin);

DegRef=StrToNum(Pin);

if (Deg0==0) {Deg0=DegRef;DegM0s=NumToStr(Deg0);}
        //DegRef is the initial compass heading
if (DegRef!=0) {
  goto Cont1;}
  else goto Check_Pin0;
```

```
Cont1:
NumOut(80,LCD_LINE3,DegRef);
Write_DegHd(DegRef);
//>>>>>>>>>>>>>>>>>>>>>>>>>>>>>>>>>>
                    BT_Talk:
int pcnt;
string Pin, pinx,Positb;
Pin="";pcnt=0;
if(hitBmp==1)
{
 hitx=100;hitTch=0;    //relocate initialzing hitx & hitBmp
SendRemoteString(BT_Cnx,OUTBOX1,"Tch"); Wait(800);   //box 5 to Slave

Chk_PinTch33:
{ReceiveRemoteString(BT_Cnx,INBOX,Pin);Wait(300);}    //box 1 from Slave
if (Pin=="") {pcnt=pcnt+1;
        if (pcnt<10) {goto Chk_PinTch33;}
        else goto Tch_Out33;
        }

TextOut(0,LCD_LINE4,Pin);
if(Pin!="Nx") { Off(OUT_AB);
        if (Pin=="L") {hitx=1;hitBmp=-1;}
        if (Pin=="R") {hitx=-1;hitBmp=-1;}
                //This uses a USnd in SLAVE fwd sensor
        if (Pin=="FN") {hitx=-10;hitBmp=-1;hitTch=10;}
        if (Pin=="FL") {hitx=-9;hitBmp=-1;hitTch=11;}
        if (Pin=="FR") {hitx=-11;hitBmp=-1;hitTch=9;}
                if(hitBmp==-1)
                {
            tend=CurrentTick()-ts;tends=NumToStr(tend);
            Positb=StrCat("BUMP! ",NumToStr(hitx)," ",tends);
            Write_Positb(Positb);
                }
        }
 }
Tch_Out33:
 Write_FwdTch(hitx);
MagCalls="Mag";
goto Mag_Data;
Reset_a:
}
```

MASTER	
	TASK B_EVALPOLL ( )

FUNCTION

This task calls subroutine "poll_sensors()" to run concurrently w/ the task main(). It writes the [e] to a file that is accessed

```
task b_Evalpoll( )
{
int Motr,Tstgate_a,Tstgate_b,hitx;
```

91

```
string Posita;

Trackx1="xx";Trackx2="xx2";Trackx3="xx3"; Trackx4="xx4"; //5b2a2

QGOcnt=0;
Tstgate_a=0;Tstgate_b=0;
Read_MtxQ( "K_Mtx.txt", 27, fsize, K_Mtx);    //This reads in the K_Mtx
//>>>>>>>>>>>>>>>>>>>>>>>>>>>>>>>>>>>>>>>>>>>>>>>>>>>
Begin_Poll:
if(Resettask=="Yes") {goto Reset_a1;}

Trackx1="xx";Trackx2="xx2";Trackx3="xx3"; Trackx4="xx4";
//>>>>>>>>>>>>>>>>>>>>>>>>>>>>>>>>>Test Polling Gate >>>>>>>>>>>>>>>>>>>>
if ((GateA=="-1")||(QGOgate==1))             //||(Gate=="-1")) this confuses the loop
        {
        if(Tstgate_b=0)
        {
        tend=CurrentTick()-ts;tends=NumToStr(tend);
Posita=StrCat(NumToStr(ResetX),"  p:Eval   Gate   closed:  = ",Gate," ",tends,"
",GateA);
         Tstgate_b=1;
        }
        goto Poll_finish;
        }                //this avoids multiple observations
                         //of the same issue, once GateA has
                         //been declared

//>>>>>>>>>>>>>>>>>>>>>>>>>>>>>>>>>>>>>>  end Test Polling gate >>>>>>>>>>>>>>>

tend=CurrentTick()-ts;tends=NumToStr(tend);

if (Tstgate_a==0) {
                    Lk="F";
        poll_sensors( event , Mevent , Ratio, Lk, Posit0, Posit1, Motr);
        Keyx=Keyx+1;
        NumOut(0,LCD_LINE2,event[1]);NumOut(20,LCD_LINE2,event[5]);
        xcnt=27;
        Matrix_Math( 27, event , K_Mtx , Q  );


        Q[0]=Keyx;        //Keyx allows a check on the most current
                          //version of Qxx.txt

        } //use one print, otherwise it hogs the write sub

//>>>>>>>>>>>>>>>>>>>>>>>>>>>>>>>>>>>>>>>>>>>>>
if(QGOgate==0) {QGOcnt=QGOcnt+1; } //6Cc3  //6Cc4a
QGOcnts=NumToStr(QGOcnt);
tend=CurrentTick()-ts;tends=NumToStr(tend);
Posita= StrCat("p:OK->Start Basic_Eval for ",QGOcnts," ",tends);
    Tstgate_a=0;Tstgate_b=0;
     Write_Posita(Posita);


//<<<<<<<<<<<<<<<<<<<<<<<<<<<<<<<<<<<<<<<<<<<<<

//This begins the evaluation of the sensed landscape
//from the function call "poll_sensors"
```

```
//*********************************************

Basic_Eval:
cnt=0;

QAction="NOStop";
NOgoF="Opn";
NOgo="clear";
Port="F";

//Read in the controlling variables

Read_FwdAct( hit,pwr);
if (ARep>1) {            //If an alignment is stuck ARep>1 set hit=1
       hit=1;
         }
if (hit==1)
     {QAction="QStop";
       }
             //hitx==-10 is a direct hit fwd. This is like hit==1
             //hitx==1 or -1 already has an action. It does not need
             //a boost.
             //Do NOT respond in Evalpoll to a side hitx

if ((hitTch==10))   //this is a touch fwd
         {   //suppress Qhitx
           }
if ((hitTch==11)||(hitTch==9))
               //hitTch==11 is Left, ==9 is Right
                {QAction="QStopx";  }                       }

Posita= StrCat("p:",QAction," ",NumToStr(hit));
     Write_Posita(Posita);


//*************** start of Poll_Eval execution **************

SeqC=SeqC+1;
         //This is the sequence rep cntr for a given cycle of polling
           //It is not the QGO cntr that synchronizes input/output

//Poll_Eval must have a parameter [hit or hitx] to enter this gate


if(QAction!="NOStop")
{
  {
  tend=CurrentTick()-ts;tends=NumToStr(tend);
Posita= StrCat( " p:Obstr Ahead Q11 ",NumToStr(Q[11])," ",Gate,GateA," ",tends);
    Write_Posita(Posita);
                     //Q11 is a Stop reaction to a
                     //fwd hit
 Motr=-1;Write_MotrAct(Motr,Lk);
  }

  if(QAction=="Qhitx")   // this is only fo hitx==-10
  {
```

```
        }                               //  this is only a Fwd hitx and
                                        //should be associated w/ a
                                        //second sensor

//hitx values must be inserted here

if ((QAction=="Qhitx")||(QAction=="QStopx"))
{ Posita=StrCat(Trackx2,"p: hitx Back_Up");
         Write_Posita(Posita);
         Back_Up(FCE,Dirx,DegRef);  //*6b4-by-bz Only for hitx
//Set up the MQ[] value immediately- Don't wait for the matrix math
//The back up should be considered as clearing the Tch obstr

                    //"if (abs(hitx==10))":: keep the obstr ahead even w/ a back up
                    //assign Mevent on the basis of hitTch 9 or 11
                    //hitTch==11 is Left, ==9 is Right
   {
     if(hitTch==11) {Mevent[3]=1;}
     if(hitTch==9) {Mevent[2]=1;}
      MQ[5]=1;                //MQ[5] signals a Fwd obstr
           if((Q[19]>=3)&&(Q[11]>1))
              {
                MQ[11]=3;  //MQ[11] is a BackUp command
              } //3zY Q[19]>=3 shows Fwd Obstr
   }
}
  {
                    //This sets the count for repeated obstr on the same heading
                    //the string "ClrHdn" from Veri_Head is the quadrant code (1 to 4) of
                    //the current heading.
                    //"FCE0" is the code (1 to 4) for the formal intended
                    //SMV due to programmed turns and moves [sub position2()].

//>>>>>>  Cycle Check for Minor Obstr >>>>>>>>>>>>>>>>>>>>>

if((Gate=="-1")||(GateA=="-1")) {goto Begin_Poll;}
                                //no Basic_Eval while
                                //Alignment: is working
                                //or Head is turning
Gate="-1";
Cycle_ChkFwd( hit, Motr, Lk, GFwd,xyL,xyR);
Gate="1";
if((GFwd==1)&&(hitTch==0)) {goto End_pEval;}
Posita=" Fwd Obstr ";

        if (xyL>xyR)
          {
          //before Unit can execute a left turn, it must make sure
          //the backside can clear a swing.
          //don't use a Head_RightC sub, its too long and complicated

          if(xyR<41) {
                 TShmy_Right();
                 OnFwdReg(OUT_AB,85,OUT_REGMODE_SYNC);
                 Wait(1200);      //new chassis requires 13" back up
                 Float(OUT_AB);
```

94

```
                              //This is the complex motr series for a clear swing
                              //1.) TShmy_Right
                              //2.) Backup and then
                              //3.) Dyno_ShmyL(). This will
                              //provide clearance for the rear to swing in a clear arc.
                              //this is a simple pivot to the left
                              }

                    Dyno_ShmyL(Seek);
                    bku=0;trn=trn+1;
                    Posita=" Veer Left ";
                    goto Shmy_OutEv;
                    }
                    if (xyR>xyL)
                    {
                    if(xyL<41) {
                              TShmy_Left();
                              OnFwdReg(OUT_AB,85,OUT_REGMODE_SYNC);
                              Wait(1200);        //new chassis requires 13" back up
                              Float(OUT_AB);

                              //This is the complex motr series for a clear swing
                              //1.) TShmy_Left
                              //2.) Backup and then
                              //3.) Dyno_ShmyR(). This will
                              //provide clearance for the rear to swing in a clear arc.
                              //this is a simple pivot to the left
                              }
                    Dyno_ShmyR(Seek);
                    bku=0;trn=trn-1 ;
                    Posita=" Veer Right ";
                    goto Shmy_OutEv;
                    }
               Shmy_OutEv:


       hitTch=0;
       Lk="N";      //this is a last snap-shot look at clearance
       Cycle_ChkFwd( hit, Motr, Lk, GFwd,xyL,xyR); //*G4x6b3
       Lk="F";
{int dummy1,dummy2,dummy3;
dummy1=-1;
                    //this is a turn to the left & a return
                    //to center the head
Lk="L";Lk_D( Lk,dummy1, dummy2, dummy3);
Lk="LR";Lk_D( Lk,dummy1, dummy2, dummy3);
 }
       if(GFwd==1) { Posita=StrCat(Posita," and clear ");
              Write_Posita(Posita);
              goto End_pEval;
              }
       else {Write_Posita(Posita);}

//<<<<<<<<<< END of Cycle Check <<<<<<<<<<<<<<<<<<<<<<<<<<<<<
Cycle_END:   //6Cc4a
Trackx1="p:Through Cycle Chk ";
Lk="F";
poll_sensors( event , Mevent , Ratio, Lk, Posit0, Posit1, Motr);
```

```
        Matrix_Math(27,event,K_Mtx,Q) ;
        //this recalcs K_Mtx to account
        //for any new FEvent[ ] values
    Read_FwdTch( hitx);
    Posit1=StrCat(NumToStr(hit),NumToStr(hitx));
            Rep_episode(SeqBK, EpsBK, SeqC);
            //EpsBK must be [1] before significance can be attributed
            if (EpsBK>0) {BUC[EpsBK]=ClrHdn;} //DegM0;
        Posita=StrCat(Posit1,"          p:Back_Up          Cntr          ",NumToStr(3),"
        ",NumToStr(EpsBK)," ",NumToStr(BUC[EpsBK])," ",NumToStr(ClrHdn));
            Write_Posita(Posita);
  if (EpsBK>0){
        Epsbk=EpsBK-1;
        if ((Epsbk>0)&&(BUC[Epsbk]==BUC[EpsBK]))
        //if Unit is on the same quadrant too long, it needs to back up
        {
        Trackx1=StrCat(Trackx1,"p:Boxed in: Back_Up() ");
        Trackx2=StrCat(Trackx2," sub call ");
        TextOut(0,LCD_LINE5,"Boxed in: Back Out ");

        Back_Up(FCE,Dirx,DegRef);  //*6b4
         Instr="BkO";EpsBK=0;
         ArrayInit(BUC,0,5);
//no action executions in this task Polling()
//Instr "Bk0" should be written to the output file
        }
        }

        //This should prompt a Back_Up() Action
        //this means there is no hitx L or R
        // and it starts a fwd action
  }

tend=CurrentTick()-ts;tends=NumToStr(tend);
TkHead="p:GOnoGO impressions ";

Lk="F";

//Use Posit0 as a carrier for QAction prompting a side adjustment during
//a polling side scan
Posit0=QAction;
Test_Gate:
if (Gate=="-1") {goto Begin_Poll;}
Gate="-1";


Ratio=0.5;        //this is for a single look to the Right or Left scan only
                  //it does not include a quarter point look
                  //Ratio=1.0; → this allows a quarter point scan for clearances
                  //It might be preferred to a single point side scan
      {
      if (Motr==1) {Float(OUT_AB);   // Motr doesn't equal 1
      } //turn off motors and fwd chk while scanning L/R
      Posita=StrCat("p:Scan - L/R ");
            Write_Posita(Posita);

ScanL_R(LEvent, REvent,  Mevent,Dirx, DegRef, FCE,Lk, Ratio, Posit0, Posit1);
Gate="1";
```

```
}

Ratio=1;
int x1,x2,X0;
ArrayInit(LQ,0,28);
ArrayInit(RQ,0,28);

Posita=StrCat("p:Solving Q- L/R ");

              Write_Posita(Posita);

 Matrix_Math(27,LEvent,K_Mtx,LQ) ;
 Matrix_Math(27,REvent,K_Mtx,RQ) ;

 Keyx=Keyx+1;

 Q[0]=Keyx;          //* Keyx allows a check on the most current
                          //version of Qxx.txt

 ArrayInit(LEvent,0,28);
 ArrayInit(REvent,0,28);

 string NOgoR, NOgoL;
 NOgoR="Nr";NOgoL="Nl"; Port="^";

Fwd_Eval:
NOgoF="xa";
 xa=Q[5];xb=Q[9];
              //NOgoF is placed alone as a "Fwd_Eval"
GOcnt=xa-xb;

{
if (GOcnt>0) {NOgoF="L";}
 if (GOcnt<0) {NOgoF="R"; }
 if (Q[19]==4) {NOgoF="F";}   //this uses motor feedback MQ event[21]
 if (Q[11]==2) {NOgoF="F";}
 if ((Q[10]==2)&&(hit==0)) {NOgoF="Opn";}

Posita=StrCat("p:Test     Q19,11&10     ",NumToStr(Q[19])," ",NumToStr(Q[11]),"
",NumToStr(Q[10]));
Write_Posita(Posita);
}
 Eval_GOnoGO( NOgoF, NOgoR, NOgoL, NOgo, LQ , RQ , Q );

//Use the touch matrix MQ[ ] to avoid conflict with the USnd events.
//The Unit may not "see" what it runs into.
                    //Mevent[ ] will rule NOgoF
                    //don't use this, use event[10]
Posita=StrCat("p:Test MQ3&4 ",NumToStr(MQ[3])," ",NumToStr(MQ[4]));
Write_Posita(Posita);  //*6b4-bz
 if (MQ[4]<2) {if  (NOgoL=="Opn") {Port="L";} }
 if (MQ[3]<2)  {if (NOgoR=="Opn") {Port="R";} }
 if ((MQ[2]<2)&&(MQ[5]==0)) {if (NOgoF=="Opn") {Port="F";}  }
        //Fwd is last because it is favored as a "clear" route

Posita=StrCat("p:Test R_LQ13 ",NumToStr(RQ[13])," ",NumToStr(LQ[13]));
Write_Posita(Posita);  //*6b4-bz
 if (Mevent[2]==1) {NOgoF="R";}
```

```
if (Mevent[3]==1) {NOgoF="L";}
if (event[10]==1) {NOgoF="F";}
if (abs(hitx)==10) {NOgoF="F";}
if ((LQ[13]>1)&&(MQ[4]<2)) {Port="L";}
if ((RQ[13]>1)&&(MQ[3]<2)) {Port="R";}
if (Q[14]>1) {Port="QPL";}  //create LkQP=="R/L" for a direction flag
if (Q[14]>1) {Port="QPR";}
if ((MQ[3]<2)&&(MQ[4]<2))   //if there is no QStopx
{
if ((NOgoF=="Opn")&&(NOgo!="F")) {Port="F";}
if ((NOgo=="clear")&&(NOgoF!="F")) {Port="F";}
}

//if there are no instructions, NOgoF must be set to "xa" a null
string EvalOut=StrCat(" ",NOgoF," ",NOgo," ",Port," ");

tend=CurrentTick()-ts;tends=NumToStr(tend);
Posita=StrCat(">Polling:GOnoGO Eval ",EvalOut," ",GateA," ",tends);

Write_Posita(Posita);


}
//************ end of Poll_Eval execution **************

End_pEval:

if(Port=="^")
    {tend=CurrentTick()-ts;tends=NumToStr(tend);
    Posita=StrCat("p:[PORT== ^] closes HdGate @ QGO ",tends);
    Write_Posita(Posita);

    if(Gate=="-1") {goto Begin_Poll;}
   Gate="-1";
    Instr="x_a";
    About_Face(FCE0,FCE,Dirx,DegRef,Deg0, DegM0, DegZ,Instr, ShmyA);
   Gate="1";  //3v2a?
   tend=CurrentTick()-ts;tends=NumToStr(tend);
   Posita=StrCat(NumToStr(ShmyA)," p:About Face out ",GateA," ",tends);
    Write_Posita(Posita);
   Motr=1;Lk="F";
   Write_MotrAct(Motr,Lk);     //Motr reset
    goto Begin_Poll;
    }

string Key;
if(Gate=="-1") {goto Begin_Poll;}
                    //this keeps Evalpoll from over writing
                    //the actions of Alignment
                    //and before QGOgate is set to 1 and
                    //QGOcnt is incremented
tend=CurrentTick()-ts;tends=NumToStr(tend);

QGOgate=1;
MQAct="1";
        //Reset MQAct after each polling for QGO. This opens the stall gate
        //and allows stalled action
Posita=StrCat("Polling:write QGO   "," ",NOgoF," ",NOgo," ",Port,"
",NumToStr(QGOcnt)," ",GateA," ",tends);
```

```
Write_Posita(Posita);
        //GateA is set in task main() and should be Common to task Evalpoll()

TextOut(0,LCD_LINE3,StrCat("-> QGO ",QGOcnts));
Wait(500);           //insert a [wait] to allow main() to sync time
Poll_finish:

goto Begin_Poll;
//****************************************
//This ends the "QAction - QStop" Evaluation, before Eval Actions
//The variables developed in the BASIC elements are

goto Begin_Poll;
Reset_a1:
}
```

<table>
<tr><td>MASTER</td></tr>
<tr><td align="center">TASK C_CHK_FWDUSND( )</td></tr>
</table>

FUNCTION

This task sets all the major FWD action calls that originate from the Main task. Action is always based upon the Rover looking forward (Lk=="F",) UltraSound (USnd) clearance ahead, Motor actions (Motr). All variables used in this thread/task are common.

```
task c_Chk_FwdUsnd ( )
{
int xa;
int hit, hitz,hitx, Motr,bytesWritten;
int Motrx,pwr;     //6Ce_a
int x2a=250;
string Action0, Hdng0, Lk;     //Action0 is the Motr ==0 or 1
string Positb;
int Pwrx;

SetSensorLowspeed(IN_2);

byte Fwd1;
int fsize4;
string buf, hit0;
bool eof = false;
        //SensorFile("FwdAct.txt",FILE_LINES);
        //**task Chk_FwdUSnd() sets the hit value
        //and writes the file "FwdAct.txt"
        //**task main() sets the Motr and writes the file. This
        //controls the motor usage and releases it to the robot.
        //Motr==-1 keeps the motor in stasis AND keeps hit==1
        //in the action queue

USnd_Act:
if(Resettask=="Yes") {goto Reset_b;}
Read_MotrAct(Motrx, Lk);
```

```
                    //Reads Motr flag from main()
                    //If main() sends a Motrx==1, this causes
                    //the task to reset its readings and
                    //release the [hit==1] setting that it
                    //previously locked in


zxxa=BatteryLevel();

        //Pwr1= 60*Bxx/100;
        //power output equivalent to 4680 mv (4.68v)
        //Pwrx=pctx*Bxx/100;
MTac=0;
if ((Motr==-1)&&(Motrx==1)) {Motr=1;}
else if (Motr!=-1) {Motr=Motrx;}
    //Motr is the local Motr value from main()

 MTac=Motr;    //6Ce_a use a separate common variable to take to Motr_Fwd
//*********************** This is the Fwd Scan Sequence *****************
if (Motr==1)
{
        //Isolate the Fwd scan by bracketing the entire
        //scan sequence for [if(Motr==1)
        // from: [{Lk="F"; ...to: NumOut(); } Read_FwdTch..]
        //Suspend the scan sequence when (Motr!=1) and
        //other functions are using the USnd scanner

Lk="F";
DegM0s=DegRefs;
}
x2a=250;

hitz=hit;
                //hitz is the hit value from the last pass
zxxa=BatteryLevel();
Bx=(7800/zxxa);
Bxx=Bx*100;
Pwr1= 60*Bxx/100;

hit=0; //Gate="1";
                //hitx=100;  →do not initialize hitx; it is written to  FwdTch
MQ[4]=0;MQ[3]=0; //3zY        //Start out w/ hit=0

int xGaChk,cntrGa,GasxxL,Gazxa;
GasxxL=0;
repeat(3)               //do a repeat for the USnd
                        //this takes 644ms to accomplish
        {
xGaChk= (SensorUS(IN_2))
cntrGa=cntrGa+1;
GasxxL=GasxxL+xGaChk;
        }
Gazxa=GasxxL/cntrGa;        // use averaging for FwdUSnd

TextOut(0,LCD_LINE1,"      ");NumOut(5,LCD_LINE1,Gazxa);
 cntrGa=0;

x2a=Gazxa;
```

```
NumOut(87,LCD_LINE1,Stallgate);
if (Stallgate==-1) {
            goto EndPwr;
            }
if (x2a>120) {pwr=Pwr1;}
if ((x2a>60)&&(x2a<121)) {pwr=25*Pwr1/60;}
if ((x2a>44)&&(x2a<61)) {pwr= 15*Pwr1/60;}

if(Stallgate==1) {pwr= 25*Pwr1/60;
            Stallgate=-1;}
EndPwr:

if ((x2a<45)&&(Lk=="F"))
{ pwr=0;
 hit=1;
          //if an obstr, then [1] is the new hit value
 DegM0s=DegRefs;
                                    }
       if((pwr<45)&&(Motr==1)) {
              // suppress
              // Write_FwdAct(hit,pwr);
              // Forward( FCE, Dirx, DegRef, Motr,pwr);
               }
NumOut(80,LCD_LINE5,pwr);
Mevent[2]=0;Mevent[3]=0;Mevent[4]=0;

             //hitBmp=1:: this is general common
             //Do not release hitBmp until main() Motr_feed: has been read
goto XXX;

XXX:
 //end of if(Motr==1) action
//****************************This is the End of the Fwd Scan Sequence *******

Acquire (FileAcc);
          // hit=current; hitz=previous . Compare the old hitz
          //with the newly generated hit.
          //If they are not the same and Motr has been reset to [1]
          //then re-evaluate the settings

if ((hit!=hitz)&&(Motr!=-1))
                //if the local flag Motrx is not closed (-1) then record
                //the current hit value if it is different
{
                if (hit==1){
                Acquire (Fwd_Motr);          //Acquire control only
                Off(OUT_AB);                 //when the hit==1 is
                Release (Fwd_Motr);          //first encountered
                     }                //after a period of
                                      //hit==0
             DeleteFile ("FwdAct.txt");
//write the new hit=0 or 1 & pwr=0 or nn
             Write_FwdAct(hit,pwr);
}
        //if  Motr==-1, meaning no new Motr command
        //from main(), set the new hit to the
        //old hitz [locking it in]
             else {hit=hitz;
```

```
            Write_FwdAct(hit,pwr);}
            if (hit==1) {Motr=-1;}
        //as long as Motr==-1, no new hit value is written to the FwdAct file
        //Motr is kept at -1 until Motr=1 is read from file MotrAct
Release (FileAcc);
goto USnd_Act;

hit_Outx:
Write_FwdAct(hit,pwr);
        //this should send a message that the USnd is closed
Reset_b:
}
```

MASTER
                    TASK D_MOTR_FEED( )

FUNCTION

This is a motor feed back task. This [is a threaded task that] reads "F" motor RPmS when called [all the time.] Differences in readings are assessed by conditions of [Motr] set in the main( ) and recorded in the variable Runx [file Motr_Act.txt] [Output from the task is recorded in the file ["MQ_tac.txt"] which is opened and read in [main()]]

```
task d_Motr_Feed ( )
{
int Rtac,Rtaz,Rtaxx,tEXs,tEXf,deltaC,deltaB,xb,xc,xbc;
int hit;
int  Runx0,Ktac0;
int Motr;
int Tac0fz=100;
int Tac0bytes;
int RunT, RunTx;
string MQAct,Positc;

MQAct="1";

Motr_Monitor:
if(Resettask=="Yes") {goto Reset_c;}
Rtaz=0;
Rtac0=0;
Rtaxx=0;

tEXs=CurrentTick();
ResetRotationCount(OUT_AB);

TextOut(0,LCD_LINE5," tac*          ");
NumOut(60,LCD_LINE5,hitBmp);
ctickx:
 tEXf=CurrentTick()-tEXs;
if  (tEXf<2300) {goto ctickx;}
                //this must allow 23000ms to elapse w/ motr
                //running. Then it takes a rotation count.

 xb=MotorRotationCount(OUT_B)*(-1);
```

```
xc= MotorRotationCount(OUT_A)*(-1);

tEXf=tEXf/100;          //change micr-sec to cent-secs

xbc=xb;
if (xb>xc) {xbc=xc;}
 Rtacx=((xb+xc)/20);    //change revs to 1/10 scale

 Rtac0=(((Rtacx)/tEXf));
 Ktac0=(pwr/15);
NumOut(35,LCD_LINE5,Rtac0); NumOut(45,LCD_LINE5,Ktac0);

DegM0=StrToNum(DegM0s);
DeltaDeg=(DegM0-DegRef); //if(DeltaDeg<=3) {Mevent[6]=-1;}

            if (Q[11]>1) { Mevent[1]=1;}
            if (Q[19]>2) { Mevent[7]=1;}
            if (Q[17]>2) { Mevent[8]=1;}    //right obstr
            if (Q[21]>2) { Mevent[9]=1;}    //left obstr

if ((pwr!=0)&&(hitBmp==-1))
  {
            if(DeltaDeg<=3) {Mevent[6]=-1;}
   Read_FwdTch( hitx);
   Mevent[1]=1;Mevent[5]=1;
   if ((hitx==1)||(hitx==-9))
        {
                        //left Tch -> turn Right
         Mevent[3]=1;
         Mevent[9]=1;         // this inhances a left touch
        }
 if ((hitx==-1)||(hitx==-11))
        {
                        //right Tch → turn Left
         Mevent[2]=1;
         Mevent[8]=1;         // this inhances a right touch
        }
 if (hitx==-10)
        {
                        //fwd Tch → BackUp
         Mevent[4]=1;
         Mevent[7]=1; //Q[19]
        }
                    // hitx=100; do not  reset hitx for all hitx's incl Fwd hitx==-10
                    // Write_FwdTch(hitx);
        Stallgate=1;
                        Stallcnt=QGOcnts;    //G5_02a2 //relocate C4ay1
   tendx=CurrentTick()-ts;tends=NumToStr(tendx);
   Positc=StrCat("c1         Stall         ",QGOcnts,"          ",NumToStr(Stallgate)," ",NumToStr(RunTx)," ",tends);
   if(Stallcnt!=QGOcnts) {Write_Positc(Positc);}
   Stallcnt=QGOcnts;
   TextOut(0,LCD_LINE1,StrCat("c1_Stall ",QGOcnts," ",Stallcnt));
        goto Stall_Out;
 }
NumOut(87,LCD_LINE1,Stallgate);

if(QGOcnts!="0")
```

```
{
if ((pwr!=0)&&(hitBmp==1))
 { if(QGOcnts=="0") { goto Stall_Out;}
    Runx=1;

            if (Rtac0>Ktac0)
                    {
                    Stallgate=0;RunT=0;

                     TextOut(0,LCD_LINE1,"No Stall     ");
                     goto Stall_Out;
                     }
//Fwd Motr is on, Unit1 should be moving Fwd
            if(QGOcnt!=0) {
                    if ((Rtac0==0)&&(QGOgate==1))
                    {TextOut(0,LCD_LINE1,"OK to Runx ");}
                    //if both motors are stalled Runx is still converse
                    }

            if ((Rtac0<=Ktac0)&&(Runx==1))
                 {   TextOut(0,LCD_LINE1,"Stall        ");

                    if(Stallgate==0){RunT=CurrentTick();
                            Stallgate=11;      //disconnect
                            }            //00b


                    {
                    //if the Gates are closed, reset RunT
if((GateA!="1")||(Gate!="1"))
                            {RunT=CurrentTick();Stallgate=0;}
                    //if QStop is active, reset Stallgate
                     if (QAction!="NOStop")
                            {RunT=CurrentTick();Stallgate=0;}

            RunTx=CurrentTick()-RunT;
            NumOut(60,LCD_LINE1,RunTx);
                if ((RunTx>=3500)) //&&(Stallgate==11))
                //Allow wait time
                //increase wait time to 8sec
                    {
                    Mevent[4]=1;Mevent[5]=1;event[21]=1;
                    Stallgate=1;
                    Stallcnt=QGOcnts;    //G5_02a2
    tendx=CurrentTick()-ts;tends=NumToStr(tendx);
    Positc=StrCat("c2        Stall        ",QGOcnts,"            ",NumToStr(Stallgate),"
",NumToStr(RunTx)," ",tends);
    Write_Positc(Positc);

    TextOut(0,LCD_LINE1,StrCat("c2_Stall ",QGOcnts," ",Stallcnt));
                        }
                    }
                }
    }
                //if Ktac0>=1 then pwr is on. If Runx==0 then
                //Fwd Motr is off and a turn is
                //being executed
    else Runx=0;        //this should be [Runx=0;] OK, done
```

```
}
 Stall_Out:
//>>>>>>>>>>>>>>>> this is Motr response for a turn >>>>>>>>>>>
            ///If there is a tachometer reading Rtac0>=1 and pwr==0
            //then the Unit1 is turning. This measures if a turn
            //is actually executed
//Stalls on a turn should be handled during the turning action and sub call
//This segment should be removed from the Motr_Feed() Stall feature

goto Stall_turn;

    if(pwr==0)
    {
        if ((Rtac0>=1)&&(Runx==0))
                {
                if(DeltaDeg==0)
                        {
                        //TextOut(0,LCD_LINE4,"No angle        ");
                        //NumOut(60,LCD_LINE4,DeltaDeg);
                        }
                //Dxkey="Y";        //this forces a turn on Dyno_Shmy
                Mevent[6]=-1;   //this would cause a Backup MQ[11]>1
                }
        else {Dxkey="N";}
    }

 Stall_turn:

if (pwr==0) {
if (Rtac0==0)
{Runx=0;}
  goto End_Monitor;
        }

if (Runx0!=Runx)
{ Runx0=Runx;}
End_Monitor:
Mevent[0]=1;Mevent[10]=1;Mevent[11]=1;Mevent[12]=1; //set up motor actions


//>>>>>>>>>>>>>>>>>>>>>>>>. beginning of matrix math >>>>>>>>>>>
//        matrix is calc only when Motr action should be engaged
if (pwr!=0)
{ xcnt=13;
 int zcnt=xcnt+1;
 ArrayInit(Qout,0,zcnt);

 int cnt, cntr, xdx,Q1, xd,Q2;
 cnt=0;  //6Ce_b1_x
 math:
 {cnt=cnt+1 ;
cntr=0;
 xdx=((cnt-1)*13);
 do
 { xd=xdx+cntr;
 //event[n] always starts from EvntIn[0]
 Q1= MB_Mtx[(xdx+cntr)]*Mevent[cntr] + Q1;  //this calculates each row value
 cntr=cntr+1;
```

```
    }
    while (cntr<(13+0));
                        //Qout[] is arranged starting from [1], not [0]
                        //Not (cnt-1). (cnt) is the real Q array #
                        //displayed as a column, not row
                        //remember- the first element in a
                        //row is "0"
  MQ[(cnt)]=Q1;
   Q1=0  ;cntr=0;
   }
     if(cnt<(13+0)) {goto math;}
   cnt=0 ;
   //>TextOut(20,LCD_LINE6,"End MQ[]");
   }
   NumOut(0,LCD_LINE8,MQ[1]);NumOut(20,LCD_LINE8,MQ[7]);
NumOut(40,LCD_LINE8,MQ[11]);
NumOut(60,LCD_LINE8,MQ[12]); NumOut(80,LCD_LINE8,MQ[13]);
//>>>>>>>>>>>>>>>>> end of matrix math >>>>>>>>>>>>>>>>>>>>
            if(MQ[1]<=1)   //this means motr options are Open; clear out arrays
            {MQAct="1";
            ArrayInit(Mevent,1,14);     //initialize Mevent with 1's; not 0's
            ArrayInit(MQ,0,14);
            }
//MQAct=="-1" means a motr option has been assigned
goto Motr_Monitor;
Reset_c:
}
```

FUNCTION

This is the heart of the program where major decisions are made and stalls or misalignments are corrected. Information provided by other logic systems that are threaded into the program is sorted in the main task. This task also opens the user files, builds the experience matrix [K] and initiates the various task threads.

```
task main ( )
{
int Motr,Pwrx;
string Positc,Posit1c;
ResetX=-1;

ts=CurrentTick();
//Retain timeing stream-thread

Resetmain:        // reset files too.
                    //Use the Reset to keep a current
                    //record of the actions
ResetX=ResetX+1;
DeleteFile ("Track1.txt");
```

```
DeleteFile ("Track1a.txt");
DeleteFile ("Track1b.txt");
DeleteFile ("Track1c.txt");
DeleteFile ("FwdAct.txt");

if(CreateFile("Track1.txt",fsizex,Trk1)==NO_ERR)
{CloseFile(Trk1);}
if(CreateFile("Track1a.txt",fsize2,Trk1a)==NO_ERR)
{CloseFile(Trk1a);}
if(CreateFile("Track1b.txt",fsizex2,Trk1b)==NO_ERR)
{CloseFile(Trk1b);}
if(CreateFile("Track1c.txt",fsizex2,Trk1c)==NO_ERR)
{CloseFile(Trk1c);}

//Retain timeing stream-thread
tend=CurrentTick()-ts;tends=NumToStr(tend);
tendLast=1;
QGOLast=tend;
//Resetmain:
ClearScreen();
Posit0=StrCat("  RESET ",NumToStr(ResetX)," ",tends);
Write_Posit0(Posit0);
{

ArrayInit(Tevent,0,17); ArrayInit(MTQ,0,17);
ArrayInit(Mevent,1,14);ArrayInit(MQ,0,14);
ArrayInit(FEvent,0,28);
ArrayInit(event,0,28);ArrayInit(Q,0,28);

Keyx=0;
hitTch=0;
eLines=28;
Q[0]=Keyx;
fname="Qxx.txt";

Trackx1="xx";Trackx2="xx2";Trackx3="xx3"; Trackx4="xx4";
Posit1="xx3"; Posit2="xx4";
jumpx=0;
QGOcnt=0;keyx=0;Stallgate=0;
QGOgate=0;    //00b3y_2b
QGOcnts="0";

DegMx=0;TmeClk=0;dM0=0;
hit=0;Motr=1;Lk="F",pwr=60,hitBmp=1;
Write_FwdAct(hit,pwr);
Write_MotrAct(Motr,Lk);
Resettask="No";

//*
       StartTask( a_BTSignal);

//*
       StartTask( c_Chk_FwdUSnd);  //*suppress for testing seq.

   //this task reads the USnd values and
   //writes current running values to file FwdAct.txt

goto skipX;
```

```
skipX:

 zxxa=BatteryLevel();
Bx=(7800/zxxa);
Bxx=Bx*100;
Pwr1= 60*Bxx/100;


Read_MtxQ("MB_Mtx.txt",13,fsize,MB_Mtx);    //This reads in the MB_Mtx
QGOcnt=0;QGOcnts="0";  //3v
Gate="1";      //3v2a?
Dx="N";
Seek="Y";      //Use [Yes] as the default for a Dyno_ShmyL/R Stall turn

SetSensorLowspeed (IN_2);
SetSensorLowspeed(IRSEEKER);
ReadSensorHTIRSeeker2AC(IRSEEKER, dir, se1x, se2x, se3x, se4x, se5x);


//ts=CurrentTick();
//do not reset [ts] Keep it as an ongoing thread
Lk="F";
//*
     StartTask(b_Evalpoll);    //*suppress for testing seq
//*
     StartTask(d_Motr_Feed);

Read_DegHd(DegRef);dM0=abs(DegRef-DegMx);
 FCE0=1; SMV="F";FCE=1;      //calibrate position front (F) facing forward (1)
 SeqQS=0;
 Instr="0";
 hit=0;
 DegM0=DegRef;           //set current mag heading DegM0
 DegMx=DegM0;            //set "last" reference mag heading DegMx
 SMV="F";
//Action Test Window SEQUENCE GOES HERE >>>>>>>>>>>>>>>>>>>>>>>>>
//*
                    Seq_Start:
//int M2event[28];
//int DegX1,DegX2;
//Pwrx=90;
//Lk="F";
//sample test entries follow::
               //Read_DegHd(DegRef);
               //DegX1=DegRef;
               //StallTurnL();
               //StallTurnR();
               //Read_DegHd(DegRef);
               //DegX2=DegRef;    DegZ=abs(DegX1-DegX2);    if(DegZ<12)    {goto
               Seq_Start;}

               //Ratio=0.5;
               //ScanL_R(LEvent,REvent,Mevent,Dirx,DegRef,FCE,Lk,Ratio,Posit0,
               Posit1);

               //poll_sensors( event , Mevent , Ratio, Lk, Posit0, Posit1, Motr);
               //Seek="Y";
               //Dyno_ShmyR(Seek);
               //Head_LeftC( opnxL,LEvent,Mevent,Lk,Ratio,Posit0,Posit1);
```

```
                //Head_RightC(opnxR,REvent,Mevent,Lk,Ratio,Posit0,Posit1);
                //Instr="L";
                //Power_TurnR(FCE0, FCE,Dirx,   Deg0, DegM0, DegZ, M2event,
                Instr, opnxL, SMV);
                //Wait(SEC_7);
                //goto Seq_Start;
//**when testing is finished, activate this command →      goto Seq_End;
//*********************************************
BASIC_Eval:
        // beginning of "QAction - QStop" Actions
        //Mevent[3 or 2] carries the hitx values into Back_UpX
        //BASIC_Eval begins by reading the obsv outcome
        //file Q[] from task Evalpoll()

cnt=0;          //At this point the output file from BASIC_Eval is read
xcnt=0;

Read_QGOx:
//TextOut(0,LCD_LINE3,StrCat(" * ",QGOcnts," ",NumToStr(pwr)));
jumpx=0;
tend=CurrentTick()-ts;tends=NumToStr(tend);

//>>>>>>>>>>>>> Stalled Program:: No Action Eval [QGO] Change >>>>>>>>>
                if((Gate=="-1")||(GateA=="-1"))
                {tendLast=QGOcnt; //goto BASIC_Exe;
                        //QGOcnt is a count not a time tic
                }

                if(Stallgate==-1)
                {tendLast=QGOcnt; //goto BASIC_Exe;
                }
        //If there has been NO movement, indicated by a NO change in QGOcnt, for
        //an extended period, a reset should be initiated.
        //QGOClk marks the time tic between QGOcnt points
QGOClk=tend-QGOLast;
//NumOut(0,LCD_LINE6,QGOClk);NumOut(50,LCD_LINE6,dM0);
                if (QGOClk>=60000)       //00b3y_3
                {QGOLast=tend; //QGOLast is the time marker for the
                        //Last time a Polling Action occurred
                        //this triggers a Reset if the Action hasn't
                        //changed in 60 seconds
                 goto Reset;
                }

                // if(QGOcnt>=24) {goto Reset;}
//>>>>>>>>>>>>>>>>>>>>>>>>>>>>>>>>>>>>>>>>>>>>>>>>>>>>>>>>>>>>>>>>>>>>>>

    if (QGOgate==0)    //this goes fwd if QGO==1
        {       //sometimes QGO vectors overlap. This [if] chooses
                //the most current
            if(QGOcnts!="0") {Wait(500);
                        goto BASIC_Eval;
                        }
        else {goto Cont7;}
        //recycle if QGOgate==0::
        //this means that the latest instruction hasn't been written
        }
```

```
if (QGOcnts!="0")
{ARep=0;
}   //3v1                          //The Key is the imbedded sequence from

{
//>>>>>>>>>>>>>>  Stalled Program :: No Heading Change >>>>>>>>>>>>>>>
Read_DegHd(DegRef);dM0=abs(DegRef-DegMx);
TmeClk=QGOcnt-tendLast;
NumOut(0,LCD_LINE6,TmeClk);NumOut(50,LCD_LINE6,dM0);
 if (TmeClk>=60)
            {//tendLast=QGOcnt;    //tendLast is the time marker for the
                    //Last time a heading check was made
            //DegMx=DegRef;
                    //this triggers a Reset if the Heading hasn't
                    //changed in 20 seconds
            // if(dM0<8)
            {goto Reset;}
            }
//>>>>>>>>>>>>>>>>>>>>>>>>>>>>>>>>>>>>>>>>>>>>>>>>>>>>
//>>>>>>>>>>>>>>>  Reset Program :: Track1 files Full >>>>>>>>>>>>>>>

 if (QGOcnt>=60)
            {
            {goto Reset;}
            }
//>>>>>>>>>>>>>>>>>>>>>>>>>>>>>>>>>>>>>>>>>>>>>>>>>>>>>>>>>>>>>
>>>>>

Positc=StrCat(NumToStr(ResetX)," main:  Read  ",NumToStr(QGOcnt)," ",tends);
Positc=StrCat(Positc,">QGO Eval ", NOgoF,"/",NOgo," ",Port,QAction," ",GateA);
Write_Posit0(Positc);

                // DO NOT ->Set [GateA="-1"] in task Evalpoll()
                //Evalpoll actions use GateA and prevent BASIC_Exe or
                //Alignment from over riding QGO action demands
                //set QGOLast as a time marker
goto BASIC_Exe; }

//****************************************
//This ends the "QAction - QStop" Evaluation, before Eval Actions
//The variables developed in the BASIC elements are

BASIC_Exe:
InstrX=0;

{
    Eval_In:

if (Port=="F") {
  SMV="F";Instr="x_a";
  Positc=StrCat(" Going Fwd ",NumToStr(Motr)," ",NumToStr(pwr));
  Write_Posit0(Positc);
  //this action may need a delay before execution
  Forward( FCE, Dirx, DegRef, Motr,pwr);
  TextOut(60,LCD_LINE3," Go    ");
  Instr="Clear ahead ";
  InstrX=0;GFwd=1; //Stallgate=0;
```

110

```
        GateA="1";if(MQ[1]<=1) {MQAct="1";}
        goto Eval_Out;
                }
                        //should this have a side move too for no action?
    Skip4:
     GateA="-1";
    Motr=-1;Write_MotrAct(Motr,Lk);   //*6b4
    if (Port=="L") {SMV="L"; Instr="x_a";
    Power_TurnL(FCE0, FCE,Dirx,  Deg0, DegM0, DegZ, Mevent,Instr, ShmyA, SMV);
    InstrX=1;goto Eval_Out;}
    else if (Port=="R") {SMV="R"; Instr="x_a";
    Power_TurnR(FCE0, FCE,Dirx,  Deg0, DegM0, DegZ, Mevent,Instr, ShmyA, SMV);
    InstrX=1;
    goto Eval_Out;}
    else if (Port=="QPL") {SMV="QL";Instr="x_a";
    repeat(1) {TShmy_Left();}
    Instr="QL Portal";
    InstrX=1;goto Eval_Out;}
    else if (Port=="QPR") {SMV="QR";Instr="x_a";
    repeat(1) {TShmy_Right();}
    Instr="QR Portal";InstrX=1;goto Eval_Out;}


    //When NOgoF, NOgo & Port come through Evalpoll, each action is filled.
    //Port is either L, R or F. Unfilled Port is handled in Evalpoll with [^]
    //and an About_Face

    if ((Port!="R")&&(Port!="L"))
        {
    if ((Port!="F")&&(NOgo!="ta")) {
        Instr="x_a";
        SMV="ta";
        Instr="About xFace-ta";InstrX=1;
        Posit0="main:This is opening Gate after ta-2 ";
        Write_Posit0(Posit0);
        Gate="1";  //3v2a?
        goto Eval_Out;
                        }
        }

     {
     if (NOgoF=="L") { SMV="R";
     Power_TurnR(FCE0, FCE,Dirx,  Deg0, DegM0, DegZ, Mevent,Instr, ShmyA, SMV);
     Instr="Choice R";}
      else {SMV="L";Power_TurnL(FCE0, FCE,Dirx,   Deg0, DegM0, DegZ, Mevent,Instr,
    ShmyA, SMV);}
     }

     {
      if (NOgoF=="R") { SMV="L";
     Power_TurnL(FCE0, FCE,Dirx,  Deg0, DegM0, DegZ, Mevent,Instr, ShmyA, SMV);
      Instr="Choice L";}
      else {SMV="R";Power_TurnR(FCE0, FCE,Dirx,  Deg0, DegM0, DegZ, Mevent,Instr,
    ShmyA, SMV);}
     }
    //a position2() call should be placed here to relocated the Local alignment
```

```
        Eval_Out:


  TkHead=StrCat("This is Eval_Out ",NumToStr(Motr)," ",NumToStr(pwr));
  tend=CurrentTick()-ts;tends=NumToStr(tend);
    Trackx1=StrCat(Posit1,"        main:Executed        ",    Instr,"    QGOcnt
",NumToStr(QGOcnt)," ",tends);
  Write_Track1(Lk, TkHead, Trackx1,Trackx2, Trackx3, Trackx4); //00b3y_3a

 Chk_Results:
 if (InstrX==1)
 {    Positc=StrCat("Start Cycle Chk after  ",Instr);
        Write_Posit0(Positc);

  Gate="-1";  //6Cd
  Cycle_ChkFwd( hit, Motr, Lk, GFwd,xyL,xyR);
  Gate="1";
Shmy:
if (GFwd==1) {goto Shmy_Outx;}

        Positc=StrCat("Apply GFwd correct " ); //*G4x6b3
        Write_Posit0(Positc);
        if (xyL>xyR)
          {
          TShmy_Left();
          bku=0;trn=trn+1;
          goto Shmy_Outx;
          }
          if (xyR>xyL)
          {
          //TextOut(0,LCD_LINE3," Right        ");
          //NumOut(50,LCD_LINE3,xyR);
          TShmy_Right();
          bku=0;trn=trn-1 ;
          goto Shmy_Outx;
          }
          if (xyL==xyR) {
                  //suppress GFwd back up when xyL==xyR
        if(xyL>(LimiT+10))
            if(SMV=="R") {TShmy_Right();bku=0;trn=trn-1;}
            if(SMV=="L") {TShmy_Left();bku=0;trn=trn+1;}
                  }


        else {
            OnFwdReg(OUT_AB,80,OUT_REGMODE_SYNC);
            Wait(1200);       //FWDrv FatTires chassis requires 18" back up
            Float(OUT_AB);
            bku=bku+1;
            }
        Shmy_Outx:

    Lk="N";    //this is a last snap-shot look at clearance
        Cycle_ChkFwd( hit, Motr, Lk, GFwd,xyL,xyR);
        Lk="F";
```

```
Shmy_Out:                    //try the action one more time //BASIC_Eval;
        if (GFwd==0) {goto BASIC_Eval;
                {if(cnt==0)
                {cnt=cnt+1;goto Chk_Results;} //BASIC_Exe;}
                else {cnt=0;goto BASIC_Eval;}
                }
            }

        if (GFwd==1) {Instr="Clear ahead ";
          Motr=1;Write_MotrAct(Motr,Lk);   //*6b4
          GateA="1";
          // if QGO actions are met, main can reset GateA to open
              }
        //Track values & progress
        Positc=StrCat("Eval_Out @ GFwd= ",NumToStr(GFwd)," ",Instr);
        Write_Posit0(Positc);
}
//************* end of Chk_Results: *************

tend=CurrentTick()-ts;tends=NumToStr(tend);


TkHead=StrCat(" Finishing BASIC Action ",QGOcnts," ",tends);
Trackx1=" This is opening GateA & goto Cont7  ";
Trackx2=" Local Awareness Cycle: ";   //00b3y_2a
Lk="F";
Write_Track1(Lk, TkHead, Trackx1,Trackx2, Trackx3, Trackx4);
  goto Cont7;
    }


Cont7:
        // GateA: YES ->[IS NEUTRAL] at BASIC_Eval.
        //Otherwise Alignment could cause
        //an over run of corrections
if ((GateA=="-1")&&(QGOgate==1)) {
Positc=StrCat("main:Reset GateA @ Cont7 -return to BASIC_Eval ");
    Write_Posit0(Positc);
                GateA="1";  //open GateA if QGO actions are finished
                QGOgate=0;
                goto BASIC_Eval;
                }


//>>>>>>>>>>>>>>>>>>>>>>>>>>> Motr Feedback Actions >>>>>>>>>>>>>>
MotrFeed:
//NumOut(60,LCD_LINE8,MQ[12]); NumOut(80,LCD_LINE8,MQ[13]);
Positc="null";
Posit1c=" No ReAction " ;
NumOut(87,LCD_LINE1,Stallgate);
if(MQ[1]<=1) {MQAct="1";}     // reinstall at beginning of MotrFeed
if((Stallgate!=-1)||(Stallgate==11))  {goto Out_MQ;}

TextOut(0,LCD_LINE1,"              ");
TextOut(0,LCD_LINE4,"              ");
TextOut(0,LCD_LINE5,"              ");
//Stallgate=0;
TextOut(0,LCD_LINE5,"MotrFeed ");
Positc="MotrFeed ";
```

```
if (hitBmp==-1){goto Stalled;}
if ((MQ[1]<=1)||(Q[9]*Q[5]==0)) {Stallgate=0;goto Out_MQ;}

TextOut(0,LCD_LINE1,StrCat("Eval Stall ",QGOcnts," ",Stallcnt));

{
Stalled:
Read_DegHd(DegRef);
DegX1=DegRef;
NumOut(30,LCD_LINE4,DegX1);
DegZ=100;
Read_FwdTch( hitx);
Positc=StrCat("m:Stall    ",MQAct,"    ",NumToStr(hitBmp),"    ",NumToStr(hitx),"
",NumToStr(Stallgate)," ",NumToStr(DegX1));
hitBmp=1;
        //MQAct:: this is the motor array MQ action event gate.
        //If MQAct==1 then the gate is open
        //and action is allowed as motor events.

          if ((MQAct=="1"))
          //this indicates that nothing
          //has been done for a stall yet
          {
          GateA="-1";        // ::must set Align Gate to -1 if Stall is actuated

if((MQ[12]>2)||(hitx==-1))
      {
      if(MQ[12]>=MQ[13])
                  {TextOut(0,LCD_LINE1,"BackUp R_face_L ");
Posit1c=" Back Up R_face_L ";
OnFwdSync(OUT_AB,100,OUT_REGMODE_SPEED);Wait(1200);
                OnFwdSync(OUT_AB,85,-40);
                Wait(1200); Off(OUT_AB);
                Wait(2000);    //00b
                goto Chk_MQ;
                }
      }

if((MQ[13]>2)||(hitx==1))
      {
      TextOut(0,LCD_LINE1,"Back Up L_face_R ");
Posit1c=" Back Up L_face_R ";
OnFwdSync(OUT_AB,100,OUT_REGMODE_SPEED);Wait(1200);
      OnFwdSync(OUT_AB,85,40);
      Wait(1200); Off(OUT_AB);
      Wait(2000);    //00b
      goto Chk_MQ;
      }

if((MQ[11]>2)||(MQ[7]>2))
      {
      TextOut(0,LCD_LINE1,"Back Up ");
Posit1c=" Back Up";
      OnFwdSync(OUT_AB,85,OUT_REGMODE_SPEED);
      Wait(1200);Off(OUT_AB);
      MQAct="-1";Stallgate=0;
                          //MQAct=="-1" blocks a repeat use of
                          //the Back Up option
```

```
            hitBmp=1;                    //hitBmp must be initialized after
                                         //execution if it doesn't jump to
                                         //Chk_MQ
            goto Out_MQ;
            }
Chk_MQ:
Read_DegHd(DegRef);
DegX2=DegRef;
NumOut(65,LCD_LINE4,DegX2);
DegZ=abs(DegX1-DegX2);
        MQAct="-1";Stallgate=0;hitBmp=1;
        if(DegZ<3)
        {
            if(MQ[13]>MQ[12])
{StallTurnR();Positc=StrCat(Posit1c," StallTurnR");Posit1c=" ";}
            if(MQ[12]>MQ[13])
{StallTurnL();Positc=StrCat(Posit1c," StallTurnL");Posit1c=" ";}
                        //Erase Posit1c after executing StallTurnR/L

//If MQ[7]==3, then DegZ>0 and the front & sides are obstructed
//This requires a backout wobble
            if (MQ[7]==3) {
                    Posit1c=StrCat(Posit1c," StallTurnL_R");
                     StallTurnL_R();
                     Read_DegHd(DegRef);
                     DegX1=DegRef;
                     DegZ=abs(DegX1-DegX2);
                     }
        }

goto End_StallEval;
//>>>>>>>>>>>>>>>>>>>>>>>>>>>>>>>>>>>>>>>>>>>>>>>>>>>>>>>>>>>>>>>..
Gate="-1";
 Cycle_ChkFwd( hit, Motr, Lk, GFwd,xyL,xyR);
 Gate="1";
 if(GFwd==1) {goto End_StallEval;}
 Positc=" Fwd Obstr ";

        if (xyL>xyR)
          {
          if(xyR<41) {
                TShmy_Right();
                OnFwdReg(OUT_AB,85,OUT_REGMODE_SYNC);
                Wait(1200);     //new chassis requires 18" back up
                Float(OUT_AB);
                }

          Dyno_ShmyL(Seek);
          bku=0;trn=trn+1;
          Positc=" Veer Left ";
          goto Stall_OutEv;
          }
          if (xyR>xyL)
          {
          if(xyL<41) {
                TShmy_Left();
                OnFwdReg(OUT_AB,85,OUT_REGMODE_SYNC);
                Wait(1200);     //new chassis requires 18" back up
```

```
                    Float(OUT_AB);
                    }
            Dyno_ShmyR(Seek);
            bku=0;trn=trn-1 ;
            Positc=" Veer Right ";
            goto Stall_OutEv;
            }

        Stall_OutEv:
    Lk="N";    //this is a last snap-shot look at clearance
    Cycle_ChkFwd( hit, Motr, Lk, GFwd,xyL,xyR); //*G4x6b3
    Lk="F";
{int dummy1,dummy2,dummy3;
dummy1=-1;
                        //this is a turn to the left & a return
                        //to center the head
Lk="L";Lk_D( Lk,dummy1, dummy2, dummy3);
Lk="LR";Lk_D( Lk,dummy1, dummy2, dummy3);
 }
        if(GFwd==1) { Positc=StrCat(Positc," and clear ");
                Write_Posit0(Positc);
                goto End_StallEval;
                }
        else {Write_Posit0(Positc);}
//>>>>>>>>>>>>>>>>>>>>>>>>>>>>>>>>>>>>>>>>>>>>>>>>>>>>>>>>>>>>>
            }

End_StallEval:
hitBmp=1; //C4ay1 initialize hitBmp after motr stall execution, not at Out_MQ
}
Out_MQ:
if(Positc!="null") {

tendx=CurrentTick()-ts;tends=NumToStr(tendx);
Posit1c=StrCat(Positc,Posit1c,"              ",tends,"           ",NumToStr(DegX1),"
",NumToStr(DegX2)," ",NumToStr(DegZ));
Write_Posit0(Posit1c);
ArrayInit(MQ,0,14);
TextOut(0,LCD_LINE1,StrCat(" executed ",NumToStr(DegZ)));
                GateA="1";     //00b1
            }
//>>>>>>>>>>>> END of Motr Feedback Actions >>>>>>>>>>>>>>>>>>

QGOgate=0;
GateA="-1";
Alignment:

if((pwr*1)==0) {pwr=0;}
TextOut(0,LCD_LINE7,"              ");
NumOut(0,LCD_LINE7,Q[5]);NumOut(30,LCD_LINE7,Q[9]);
if((pwr>15)||(pwr==0)) {GateA="1"; goto BASIC_Eval;}
            //this is less than 60cm clearance
            //45cm clearance is the stop point

//*********************FWD OBSTRUCTION*****************************
//
```

```
{
Float(OUT_AB);
ARep=ARep+1;AReps=NumToStr(ARep);
                                        //  AlignRepeat [ARep] is used to
if (ARep>1)  {goto BASIC_Eval;}         //force an exit from Alignment when a stuck
                                        //repetition is encountered
if (Gate=="-1") {goto Out_0b;}          //or during a Head turn  //6Cd

GateA="-1";     //this is the Alignment & Action GateA
Gate="-1";      //this is the head turn Gate
                //set this before the align action
tendx=CurrentTick()-ts;tends=NumToStr(tendx);
Positc=StrCat(QGOcnts,AReps," Align:Chk  Front  avoidance    ",NumToStr(pwr),"
",Gate,GateA," ",tends);
Write_Posit0(Positc);
Posit2=" NO Side Obstr ";
Instr="Chk";
if((Q[5]+Q[9])<7) {goto Best_FWD;}

     Float(OUT_AB);
     if ((Q[5]-Q[9])>2) {Instr="L";        //the Instr is used to force an initial
                                           //turn away from the obstruction
     Power_TurnR(FCE0, FCE,Dirx,Deg0, DegM0,DegZ, Mevent,Instr,ShmyA, SMV);
             HL=1; ARep=0;  //3v2a_3zZ
             Gate="1";
             Stallgate=0;     // if an alignment, then reset Stallgate
             Posit2=StrCat(" Left Obstr ",Instr);
             GFwd=1;
             goto Out_0b;
             }
     if ((Q[9]-Q[5])>2) {Instr="R";        //force a turn away from the "R"
     Power_TurnL(FCE0,FCE,Dirx,Deg0,DegM0, DegZ, Mevent,Instr, ShmyA, SMV);
             HR=1; ARep=0;
              Gate="1";
                               // NEW reset Head after align action
              Stallgate=0;
              Posit2=StrCat(" Right Obstr ",Instr);
              GFwd=1;  //6Cd
              goto Out_0b;
              }
   Best_FWD:
         if (Instr=="Chk")
         {
         Ratio=1;
         Dx="N";
         Seek="Y";
              if (Q[9]>Q[5])   //right obstr
              { Posit2=" Right proximity ";
         Head_LeftC(opnxL,LEvent,Mevent,Lk,Ratio,Posit0,Posit1);
         if(opnxL>=41) { Posit2=StrCat(Posit2," Shift Left ");}
              else {Cycle_ChkFwd( hit, Motr, Lk, GFwd,xyL,xyR);
              if(GFwd==0){
         if(xyL>xyR) {Dyno_ShmyL(Seek);}
         else {Dyno_ShmyR(Seek);}
                     }
                 }
          Dx="N";Seek="N"; Gate="1"; GFwd=1;
          goto Out_0b;
```

```
                    }
            if (Q[5]>=Q[9])        //right obstr
             { Posit2=" Left proximity ";
        Head_RightC(opnxR,REvent,Mevent,Lk,Ratio,Posit0,Posit1);
        if(opnxR>=41) {Posit2=StrCat(Posit2," Shift Right ");} //6Cc4b1
            else {Cycle_ChkFwd( hit, Motr, Lk, GFwd,xyL,xyR);
             if(GFwd==0){
        if(xyR>xyL) {Dyno_ShmyR(Seek);}
        else {Dyno_ShmyL(Seek);}
                   }
                 }
        Dx="N"; Seek="N"; Gate="1";GFwd=1;
                        //6&7; NEW
        goto Out_0b;
                 }
             }

        goto Out_0b;
}


Out_0b:
{int dummy1,dummy2,dummy3;
dummy1=-1;                    //this is a turn to the left & a return
Lk="L";Lk_D( Lk,dummy1, dummy2, dummy3);        //to center the head
Lk="LR";Lk_D( Lk,dummy1, dummy2, dummy3);
 }
GateA="1";
tendx=CurrentTick()-ts;tends=NumToStr(tendx);
Positc=StrCat(QGOcnts," Q Align ",Posit2," ",Gate,GateA," ",tends);
{Write_Posit0(Positc);}
Wait(800);   // add: this is a wait period for Head & Power_Turn to execute

 if(GFwd==1)
{SMV="F";Instr="x_a
  Positc=StrCat(NumToStr(ResetX)," Going    Fwd    Align    ",NumToStr(Motr)," ",NumToStr(pwr)," ",NumToStr(Stallgate));
  Write_Posit0(Positc);
  //this action may need a delay before execution
   Motr=1;Write_MotrAct(Motr,Lk);
   Forward( FCE, Dirx, DegRef, Motr,pwr);
   Instr="Clear ahead ";
   InstrX=0;//GFwd=1;
   }

goto BASIC_Eval;

goto Q_Listens;

Q_Listens:

tendx=CurrentTick()-ts;tends=NumToStr(tendx);
TkHead= StrCat("Q Listens ",tends);
//********************************

//TextOut(0,LCD_LINE8,"Finished  ");
goto BASIC_Eval;
//TEST SEQUENCE ENDS HERE <<<<<<<<<<<<<<<<<<<<<<<<<<<<<<<<<<
```

```
        }
Reset:
Resettask="Yes";
Wait(2000);
//stop a_BTSignal;

goto Resetmain;
Seq_End:
        }
```

This ends the programming sequences for the Master. Executable motor and action commands are listed and detailed in **Chapter V Interaction between Hardware & Software.** The effort now will be to concentrate on programming for the Slave and the functions available from this device.

PROGRAM SET UP FOR THE SLAVE PROCESSOR
PROGRAM NAME:: U1_SLAVE_00Y1

The elements of the **Slave** coding are detailed in the subsequent headings. They are also listed in the required sequence, similar to that of the **Master,** and are to be assembled and compiled as shown. The text may be copied and pasted directly to the Bricx Command Center working page.

Set up the Bricx Operating System

The Mindstorms NXT OS 3.1 is also used in this Unit1 application. After installation, the default programs should be trimmed away to make space for the **U1_Slave_00Y1**^{TM} version of the Rover software. After trimming the default system programs, the operating queue should look the same as the **Master**:

> ! Click.rso
> ! Startup.rso
> RPGReader.sys
> NVConfig.sys

Set up the Rover Reference Files

After installing the Bricx operating system, reference files which contain matrix Universe states must be written and installed in flash memory. This must take place each time the operating system is updated or replaced. To write the matrix files **K_Mtx.txt** and **MQ_Mtx.txt** the two execution files must be compiled and loaded onto the Bricx. These files are listed above as

> **Basic_Write_KMtx.nxc**
> **Basic_Write_MBMtx.nxc**

When these files are compiled and loaded, execute them on the Bricx. They will create and write the appropriated **.txt** files onto the flash drive of the microprocessor. After the **.txt** files have been written, remove the execution **.nxc** files to make room for the Rover executable files.

Set up the UNIT1 Executable files

The listed files with the block headings **Slave** should now be compiled and loaded onto the microprocessor(s) as executable files. This involves following the directions and procedures outlined in the

Bricx Command Center operations manual that is available for download (**Chapter II, ref: Source Forge Web Site.**)

From the NXT Bricx Command Center NeXT Explorer, the contents of the Bricx flash memory should appear with these contents:

Sound effects

> ! Attention.rso
> ! Click.rso
> ! Startup.rso

System files

> RPGReader.sys
> NVConfig.sys

Text

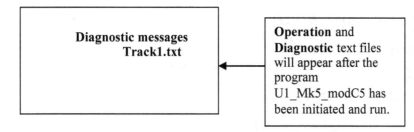

Diagnostic messages
Track1.txt

Operation and **Diagnostic** text files will appear after the program U1_Mk5_modC5 has been initiated and run.

Program

U1_Slave_00Y1.rxe

Declarations
Subroutines (as listed in Chapter V)
task main ( )

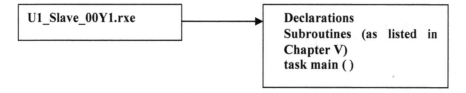

SLAVE:

DECLARATIONS

FUNCTION

Common variable declarations are not necessary when the program consists of the task main ( ) only. Variables are declared as part of the task code.

```
//WrkngSLAVE_00y1
#define BT_Cnx 1
#define INBOX0 3
#define INBOX1 5
#define INBOX2 4
#define OUTBOX 1
#define OUTBOX0 2
#define OUTBOX1 6
```

FUNCTION

The **Slave** runs a single program that acts as a listening post for the slave controlled sensors. Action is taken only upon inquiry from the **Master** microprocessor. The controlled sensors are:

1. Left touch port 4
2. Right touch port 1
3. Magnetic compass port 2
4. Ultra sound looking front port 3

```
task main( )
{
INT MB_MTX[256], MEVENT[19], MQ[27];
INT XCNT,CNT, EVNTIN[19], MTX[361], QOUT[19];
INT TK1_MTX[361];
INT FCE, DEGM0, DEGX,CDEGX, DEGERR0, DEGERR1, DEGZ;
INT DIFF,DIFF1,DIFF2 ;
STRING MAGALGN, MOVE, MAGACTV;
//FLOAT FM;
INT CDIFF, MAGDIFF, TDIFF,XDIFF,YDIFF,TXDIFF;

STRING IN, INQF, OUT, ISTR, TRACKX1, PIN, PINX;
INT I = 0;
INT FSIZE2=30*28*5;
INT QF[10], BYTESWRITTEN;
STRING BUFX, LOCALX, LOCAL0, LOCALX1, TCHX,TCHY;
INT CNTR;
BYTE TRK1;
INT X, DEG0, HDERR;// DEGX;
STRING OKMAG, DEGM, LCLTRUE, LCLRELTV, TCH1, TCH3,TCH4, TCHR_L;
INT MAGREF, DEGTRGT ;
 STRING MAGNOW;
FLOAT FM;
INT X3,XS3;              //THIS IS THE VARIABLE FOR THE USND FWD-CL SENSOR
ARRAYINIT(MQ,0,13);
 MAGREF=0;

TCH4="N";TCH1="N"; TCH3="N";TCHR_L="N";TCHX="N",TCHY="N";
 SETSENSORTOUCH(IN_4);
 SETSENSORLOWSPEED (IN_3);
 SETSENSORTOUCH(IN_1);
IF(CREATEFILE("TRACK1.TXT",FSIZE2,TRK1)==NO_ERR)
{ I=I; CLOSEFILE(TRK1);}
IF (OPENFILEAPPEND("TRACK1.TXT",FSIZE2,TRK1)==NO_ERR)
{
TRACKX1="*****";WRITELNSTRING(TRK1,TRACKX1,BYTESWRITTEN);
}
CLOSEFILE(TRK1);

LISTEN:
//* IF A DIAGNOSTIC TEST IS DESIRED, USE →    GOTO GETMAG;
PIN="";
```

```
CLEARSCREEN();
 TEXTOUT(0,LCD_LINE1,"LISTEN FOR QUEUE") ;
 IF ((SENSOR_4==1)&&(TCHX=="N")) {PLAYTONE(1000,500); TCHX="L";
 MEVENT[3]=1;WAIT(100); }
 IF ((SENSOR_1==1)&&(TCHX=="N")) {PLAYTONE(500,500);TCHX="R";
 MEVENT[2]=1;WAIT(100); }

XS3=250;
REPEAT (10)
{
X3= (SENSORUS(IN_3));          //THESE READINGS ARE ALL IN MM (NOT INCHES)
                               //.3936" PER MM
IF(X3<XS3){XS3=X3;}
}
NUMOUT(0,LCD_LINE3,XS3); WAIT(200);//WAIT(SEC_2);
 IF ((X3<10)&&(TCHY=="N"))
        {
        MEVENT[4]=1;TCHY=STRCAT("F",TCHX);WAIT(100);
        TCHX=TCHY;
        }

TEXTOUT(40,LCD_LINE3,TCHY); WAIT(200);//WAIT(SEC_2);
{
RECEIVEREMOTESTRING(INBOX1, TRUE, PIN);   //INBOX1= 5 RECEIVE MASTER ROUTING
IF (PIN=="") {GOTO LISTEN;}
TEXTOUT(0,LCD_LINE2,PIN); WAIT(200);
IF (PIN=="QF1") {TEXTOUT(0,LCD_LINE3,"FOUND QF1"); WAIT(200);
GOTO QF_FILE;}
IF (PIN=="MQ") {TEXTOUT(0,LCD_LINE3,"FOUND MQ");WAIT(200);
GOTO SND_MQ;}
ELSE IF ((PIN== "MAG")||(PIN=="CALIB"))
        {TEXTOUT(0,LCD_LINE3,"FOUND MAG");WAIT(200);
PINX=PIN;
GOTO GETMAG;}
ELSE IF (PIN=="TCH")  { GOTO TOUCH_R; }
GOTO LISTEN;
}

TOUCH_R:
{
TCHR_L="OK";
//IF ((TCH4=="N")&&(TCH1=="N")) {TCHR_L="N";}
//IF ((TCH3=="N")&&(TCHR_L=="N"))
IF (TCHX=="N")
 { SENDRESPONSESTRING(OUTBOX,"Nx"); WAIT(100);
  GOTO LISTEN;
 }
TEXTOUT(0,LCD_LINE3,"FOUND TOUCH");
TEXTOUT(0,LCD_LINE4,TCHX);
SENDRESPONSESTRING(OUTBOX,TCHX);
TCHX="N";TCHY="N";
WAIT(100);
TEXTOUT(0,LCD_LINE5,"SENT TOUCH"); //WAIT(SEC_2);
}
TOUCHX:
WAIT(2000);     //ADD TIMEOUT TO AVOID DOUBLE ACTION ON TOUCH
GOTO LISTEN;   //SUPPRESS RECEIVE STRING "OKT"
RECEIVEREMOTESTRING(INBOX1, TRUE, BUFX);   //BOX 5 FROM MASTER
```

```
IF (BUFX=="OKT") {TCHx="N";
TEXTOUT(0,LCD_LINE5,"REC'D OKT ");
GOTO LISTEN;}
 ELSE GOTO TOUCHX;


QF_FILE:
CLEARSCREEN();
SENDRESPONSESTRING(OUTBOX,"OKQ");      //OUTBOX = 1 RESPOND TO MASTER
TEXTOUT(0,LCD_LINE2,"QF ARRAY OPEN") ;
WAIT(100);
 CNTR=0;
DO{
RECEIVEREMOTESTRING(INBOX2, TRUE, BUFX);    //INBOX2 = 4 RECEIVE Q[] ARRAY
                         //FROM MASTER
WAIT(100);
IF (BUFX!="")
{ INQF=BUFX;
QF[CNTR]=STRTONUM(INQF);
CNTR=CNTR+1; //INQF="0";
}
}
WHILE (CNTR<6);
MEVENT[1]=QF[0]; //MB STOP_BKUPX
MEVENT[7]=QF[1]; //OBST AHEAD IRED
MEVENT[8]=QF[2]; //ALIGN RIGHT
MEVENT[9]=QF[3]; //ALIGN LEFT
MEVENT[5]=QF[4]; //MOTOR RPMSE3
MEVENT[6]=DEGZ ;  //QF[5]; //DEGZ IS GENERATED IN SLAVE GETMAG>>
IF (QF[4]==1){MEVENT[6]=QF[5];}  //RTAC0 IMPOSES -1 ON DEGZ

MEVENT[0]=1;MEVENT[10]=1;MEVENT[11]=1;MEVENT[12]=1;
TEXTOUT(0,LCD_LINE5,"FINISHED QF");
WAIT(200);
CNTR=0;
                      //CALC THE OBSERVED OUTCOME MQ[]
MATRIX_MATH(13,MEVENT,MB_MTX, MQ);
SENDRESPONSESTRING(OUTBOX,"FMQ");WAIT(100);
ARRAYINIT(MEVENT,0,13);
GOTO LISTEN;

SND_MQ:
CLEARSCREEN();
TEXTOUT(0,LCD_LINE4,"SENDING OKMQ " );
BUFX="OKMQ";
{SENDRESPONSESTRING(OUTBOX,BUFX);
}
CNTR=1;
CNT=13;
WAIT(800);

R_MQ:

MQ_MTX:
{BUFX=NUMTOSTR(MQ[CNTR]);
WAIT(085);
TEXTOUT(0,LCD_LINE5,"           ");
 NUMOUT(0,LCD_LINE5,CNTR);TEXTOUT(30,LCD_LINE5, BUFX);
```

```
{SENDRESPONSESTRING(OUTBOX,BUFX); WAIT(100);}        //THIS SENDS THE MQ VALUE
CNTR=CNTR+1;
IF (CNTR<(CNT+1)) {GOTO R_MQ;}
}
{SENDRESPONSESTRING(OUTBOX,"FMQ"); WAIT(200);}
TEXTOUT(0,LCD_LINE6,"SENT MQ OUTCOMES" );
GOTO LISTEN;


GETMAG:
        //THIS COMMUNICATES WITH MASTER SUBROUTINE POSITION2 ******
{
READ_MAG(DEG0);
NUMOUT(70,LCD_LINE3,DEG0);
WAIT(400);
IF (DEGM0==0) {DEGM0=MAGREF;}

DEGM=NUMTOSTR(DEG0);
SENDRESPONSESTRING(OUTBOX,DEGM);     //SEND MASTER THE CURRENT MAGNOW
WAIT(400);

IF (PINX=="CALIB") {TEXTOUT(0,LCD_LINE3,"CALIBRATION");
IF (MAGREF==0) {MAGREF=DEG0;}
PINX=""; PIN=""; GOTO LISTEN;}

GOTO LISTEN;

  {
                        //THIS DEVELOPS THE ALIGNMENT ERROR/CORRECTION
 MAGX:
RECEIVEREMOTESTRING(INBOX1, TRUE, PIN); //RECEIVE FROM MASTER THE CALC HEADING
                                        //DEGX FROM SUB [POSITION2]
 IF (PIN=="") {GOTO MAGX;}

DEGTRGT=STRTONUM(PIN);        //THIS IS THE CALC MASTER HEADING AFTER THE TURN
GOTO CORRECT;


CORRECT:
DIFF=1;
                //MATCH CALC HEADING DEGX WITH MAGNETIC HEADING DEG0
                //THIS ATTEMPTS TO MOVE THE UNIT AT MAG(0) TOWARDS
                //THE INTENDED CALC(X) HEADING
DIFF=DEGTRGT-DEG0;
IF (DIFF<0) {IF (ABS(DIFF)<181) {MOVE="R";} ELSE {MOVE="L";}}
IF (DIFF>0) {IF (ABS(DIFF)<181) {MOVE="L";} ELSE {MOVE="R";}}
IF (DIFF==0) {DIFF=1; MOVE="0X";}
IF (MOVE=="R") {DIFF=ABS(DIFF)*-1;}
        ELSE {DIFF=ABS(DIFF);}
TEXTOUT(0,LCD_LINE3,"LCL- MAGHD- DIFF");
 NUMOUT(30,LCD_LINE4,DEG0);
 NUMOUT(0,LCD_LINE4,DEGM0);

DEGERR0=(DIFF);

DEGERR0=ABS(DEGERR0) ;        //THIS ALLOWS A +/- 20DEG ERROR
DEGERR1=ABS(DEGM0-DEG0) ;
IF (DEGERR0>20) {DEGZ=1;}        //MAGNETIC DOES NOT AGREE W/ CALC
IF (DEGERR1<21){DEGZ=-1;}        //MAGNETIC HAS NOT CHANGED
```

```
MagAlgn=NumToStr(Diff);
MagActv=NumToStr(DegZ);
DegM0=Deg0;
SendResponseString(OUTBOX,MagAlgn);      //sends to Master at sub position2
TextOut(0,LCD_LINE5,"Algn- Err?- Actv");
Wait(100);
SendResponseString(OUTBOX,MagActv);
NumOut(70,LCD_LINE6,DegZ);
goto LISTEN;
 }}


}
```

V
Programming the Rover
INTEGRATING HARDWARE
and SOFTWARE

BUILDING FUNCTIONAL BEHAVIOUR

We have examined various methods and strategies that give suitable (if not the best) results and responses from the hardware in **Chapter II**. The basis for actions and the interacting programming that supports such actions has been explained and documented in **Chapter IV.** We are now going to assemble software code that allows the hardware to integrate function (i.e. what it does) with the Rover's purpose.

The programming detailed in this chapter focuses on motor and sensor applications, responding to control sequences arising from matrix procedures. These sequences are *called* from the task elements and are formatted as *subroutines.* Each subroutine is presented as a complete entity capable of operating independent of the main program. A testing window is provided in the main task ( ) to call any subroutine and test its function(s).

HARDWARE IS IMPRECISE AND LADEN W/ ERRORS

On some levels, robotic hardware can be very accurate and operate with micrometer like precision. But on most levels, and for many hardware issues on all levels, the accuracy is far from precise and readings can be and are riddled with unwanted interference or "noise." It may also be the case for sensors that have a very limited range, or for those that have a beam spread that picks up all kinds of unwanted reflections. These imperfections and "noise" require some software (programming) tactics to remove the spikes and rumples that develop as output. These are called **smoothing** strategies and include:
- **Dynamic readings**
  - Subroutines
    - Dyno_ShmyL/R
    - Cycle_ChkFwd
    - Power_TurnL/R
    - ScanL_R
- **Controlling the speed of movements**
  - Subroutines
    - StallTurnL_R
    - TShmy_Left/Right
    - Power_TurnL/R
- **Averaging errors**
  - Subroutine
    - Poll_sensors
    - LK_D
- **Rejecting readings**

Motor actions are a special case of hardware imprecision. While the operating code for motor actions may be flawless in its syntax the motor drive mechanism may be so impeded that actual motion is nil. The software must be so integrated with the working of the motor(s) that it is capable of detecting and resolving motoring difficulties. This integration constitutes **motor feed back** and the strategies fall under categories such as:

- **Tires versus tracks**
- **FrontWheelDrive (FWD) or RearWheelDrive (RWD)**
- **Motor drivers and axles**
- **Steering**
- **Turning**
- **Idling with casters**
- **Weight distribution for traction**

MOTOR FEED BACK [MQ]

As the **Unit1** generates specific commands, changes its alignment or initiates motion, motor errors are bound to exist. In some situations, these errors can be kept to a minimum or even rendered negligible if the motion functions are executed in an environment rigidly controlled. However, slight position changes can cause significant errors where the terrain and landscape vary (e.g. the Rover is operating amongst various pieces of furniture and textured floor covering.) All motor errors require programming sensory feedback. Generally these errors fall into categories.

1. Random
2. Frictional slip (the wheels/tracks don't grip well)
3. Change in terrain composition
4. Directional instability (e.g. turns left easier than right.)
5. Perceptional variations due to realignment
6. The Unit is stuck

When the motors are activated, it is intended that movement is initiated and sustained for the duration of the activation. This is not always the case. The processing unit must be alerted to times when the motors are stalled or movement is somehow attenuated. This is accomplished through feed back sensors and position algorithms evaluated in the Motor Matrix **[MQ].**

The execution of a command is expected to change the environment, as registered by sensory polling. Before the Rover can be expected to operate satisfactorily, it must be able to detect whether or not an action has been properly executed. But it is more important that the Rover observes the local conditions regardless of alignment or bearings. This brings up a theoretical approach which proposes that precision of movement and precision of placement are functionally unnecessary, and at best low in priority.

As long as the Unit, functioning as an observer, can locate features of the landscape and conform its movements to the imperative, the introduction of precision would not alter the basic response the Unit, as an Observer, exhibits to the landscape. Where the Rover relies upon some measure of precision is in the *location* and *travel* chores that it performs in association with observations.

MOTOR EVENTS

Motor function events can be represented both as logical states (of the motor) and/or sensory feed back with numerous logical states within a range of (motor sensory) readings. Variations of the motors' states compared to the sensory feed back range provide useful information on the motors' activities. These states would be represented first as hyperset diagrams (**Chapter III, Figs 3-6, 3-7.**) They would be converted to matrix form according to the membership and influence rules. An example of this approach begins by defining the event elements as hyperset drawings, namely the logical sates of the motor itself and the motor as a sensor.

A. Logical States of the Motor: Voltage and Power

Motor commands which call for a specific power input, expressed as a percentage of available power, must be keyed to the power available. If the motor command specifies 100 (or 100% of available power) drops in voltage will cause variations in motor performance. If the command outputs are all calibrated on a power command of 100, the outputs will fail to meet expectations as battery voltage drops. To prevent this, all motor calibrations must be in power demands that are initially below 100. If the Rover is expected to operate within a voltage range of 8.2 to 7.4, a 10% to 15% lower value should be the basis of motor calibration (i.e. power commands of 85 to 90.) This gives the Unit the extra margin to lift the command, up to 100% of available, when voltage drops to 7.4v. (**Chapter IV, Motor Feed Back**)
For example, the motor application for the tractor may be set at 60% of 8.2 volts, or 5.1 volts.
As the battery charge drops, the power must be increased to keep the circuits charged at 5.1v.

xxb = BatteryLevel ()	voltage level
Bratio = 8.2 / xxb	the *boost* required in demand w/ drop in battery
pwr1= 60*Bratio	the revised power percentage of available

As used in any motor command, such as:
OnFwdSync(OUT_BC, pwr1,OUT_REGMODE_SPEED)

In a turn, where motor activity is 2 seconds or less, the tachometer reading is an important indicator of a properly executed turn. This reading must be calibrated by executing various turns while the motor(s) are subjected to stress. Our calibration of **Unit1**[TM] has produced a relationship between the motor power output and the max recorded rpm for the turn.

Rpwr = MotorPower(OUT_C)   power output for the motor C
Rsqpwr=Rpwr/2
Rsqpwr=Sqrt(Rsqpwr)

Experimental readings indicate that when
(Max rpm reading) < (Rsqpwr)
It signals a poor turn execution

The voltage level and power output are both logical states of the functioning motor. When the motor observes itself, the states represent events and are plotted on the event plane of the motor.

Compound Complex

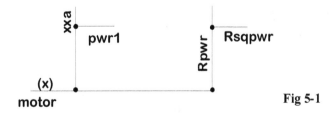

Fig 5-1

B. Logical States of the Motor (sensory) Feed: Revolutions and Tachometer

Basic experiments are performed to calibrate the effective operating range and to resolve the relationship between revs and rpm's,. The experiment consists of recording the maximum rpm for a given period of operation, in association with the total recorded revolutions, while various levels of stress are applied to the motor shaft. Where the range exhibits poor performance, a ratio is established between revs and rpm. Starting with the revolutions, these are clocked for a 2 second period.

Rb = MotorRotationCount(OUT_B)
Rc = MotorRotationCount(OUT_C)

The next states to register are the revolution per minute.

Rtac = MotorTachoCount(OUT_B)

This event state is registered at various levels representing the highest rpm state (Rtacx) and the lowest rpm state (Rtac0.)

If (Rtac<Rtac0) {Rtac0=Rtac;}
If (Rtac>Rtacx) {Rtacx=Rtac;}

A Ratio can be established between
(Total revs) / (max rpm reading)
Ratio = (Rb/Rtacx)

When the *Ratio* falls between (0.4) and (0.66) the revolutions are not consistent with the applied power. While conducting this experiment, it should also be noted that the Rtacx/Rtac0 values compare when the motor is functioning properly and when it is not. These revs become cut off points to signal poor motor function.

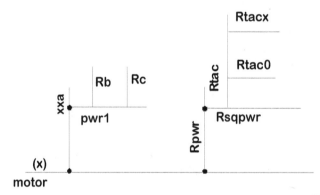

Fig 5-2

Rb < (B mtr total revs @ poor function) = -1
Rc < (C mtr total revs for the lowest allowable function) = -1
Rc > (C mtr total revs for the highest function, not an over-shot turn) = 1

This experiment is also augmented with a reading of the revolutions for a completed stress free turn. When actual revolutions fall below this count, a poorly executed turn is expected. Also to be noted: in a turn, the readings are taken from the servo motor which provides the major turning power. For a right turn, that would be the left motor, forward power, and for a left turn, use the right motor.

129

B. The Command Profile Matrix

A motor action is created when the Observed Outcome matrix **Q[n]** fluoresces at a specific row (**Chapter IV, Example 4-1d**.) There are other inferences when a row fluoresces, such as impending serial events or bringing a heads-up signal to the Rover. The command profile for any outcome can be treated as a bundled event and included in the hyperset as a single event. What this means is that when these alert commands fluoresce, they may be treated as Real events in a sequence that affects motor performance, and included in a hyperset sequence. The **[K]** universe matrix is formed from the hyperset diagram (**Fig 5-2**) and is shown below. This matrix provides snap shot diagnostics for the motor functions. It can be used to initiate motor actions, but here it is presented as **Example 5-1** of a command basis. Included in the example are fictitious event values **[e]** that might be obtained through sampling the motor and its sensory outputs described above.

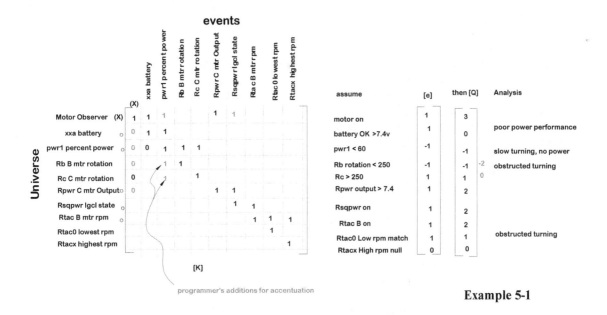

programmer's additions for accentuation

Example 5-1

From this example, it is demonstrated that the **Unit1** Rover makes decisions from consensus. Although the motor action can be isolated to a few parameters the possible errors, external and internal, are best neutralized through consensus.

C. The Command Profile as Specific Instructions

If the command profile is directed from specific commands rather than a consensus approach, the motor events can be expressed as specific outcomes and applied to motor feed back matrix (**Chapter IV, Fig 4-4**) or assigned a direct motor command. The basic coding for sensory readings of tach and revolutions is listed below. This coding can be imbedded in the subroutine Power_TurnL/R.

```
TextOut(0,LCD_LINE1,"Motor Polling");
//motors B and C are tractor drivers
int Rb, Rc, Rtacx, Rtac0;
{ int Rtac;
 Rb=MotorRotationCount(OUT_B);
 Rc= MotorRotationCount(OUT_C);
Rtac=MotorTachoCount(OUT_B);
```

```
if (Rtac<Rtac0) {Rtac0=Rtac;}
if (Rtac>Rtacx) {Rtacx=Rtac;}
}
xxb=BatteryLevel();
Rpwr=MotorPower(OUT_B);
Mevent[11]=0;
if (Rtacx!=0)
{   Rsqpwr=(Rpwr/2); Rsqpwr=Sqrt(Rsqpwr);Ratio=(Rb/Rtacx);
  //if ((Rtacx<Rsqpwr)) {"do what??";}
                              //this relationship doesn't work well
                              //with a straight run. Best with a turn

  if ((Rb<230)||(Rc<230)) { "execute a scan l/r";}
   if ((Ratio>0.4)&&(Ratio<0.66)) {"execute a backup";}
}
```

C. Serial Events

In simple terms, a command profile sponsoring an action is generated when a certain environmental or landscape characteristic is detected. The motor action is intended to change that characteristic so that it is not detected following the action. If a motor action appears to have been executed, perhaps with no negative feed back, and the landscape has not changed, there is reason for the Unit to conclude that the motor action has not been properly executed. This will be reflected in the recurrence of the Command Profile of the outcome matrix **Q[n]**. If, after a motor action, **Q[n]** immediately appears after a new sensory polling, this also may be treated as a Real event that affected motor performance. These are treated as sequences and episodes.

(Ref: Chapter IV, Serial Events Cause Confusion.)

SeqC = the current count of polling episodes
SeqNxx = the current count where row [xx] is activated
Then: if (SeqNxx=0) {SeqNxx=SeqC}
         If ((SeqNxx+Epsxx)==SeqC) {Epsxx=Epsxx+1; }
         Else {Epsxx=0; Seqnxx=0;}

If **Q[xx]** is experiencing serial episodes, back to back, the variable counter (SeqNxx) will continue to build. If it builds beyond a certain number of serial episodes (determined by the programmer) then an action is initiated. (**sub Rep_episode ( )**)

SUBROUTINE SET UP FOR THE MASTER PROCESSOR

Subroutine coding is detailed in the subsequent headings and is listed in the proper sequence. Copy and paste them directly to the Bricx Command Center working page. The sequence should be as follows::

Master Processor::

Write_DegHd(DegRef)
Read_DegHd(DegRef)
StallTurnL_R()

StallTurnL()
StallTurnR()

| Diagnostic text and position markers | → | **Write_Posit0(Posit0)**
Write_Posita(Posita)
Write_Positb(Positb)
Write_Positc(Positc)
Write_Track1(Lk, TkHead, Trackx1, Trackx2, Trackx3, Trackx4) |

Write_FwdAct(hit,pwr)
Read_FwdAct(hit,pwr)
Write_MotrAct(Motr, Lk)
Read_MotrAct(Motr, Lk)
Forward(FCE, Dirx , DegRef, Motr, pwr)
TShmy_Left()
TShmy_Right()
Dyno_ShmyR(Seek)
Dyno_ShmyL(Seek)
Lk_D(Lk, opnxF,opnxD, opnxqD)
Write_FwdTch(hitx)
Read_FwdTch(hitx)
Tch_BT(hitx)
Cycle_ChkFwd(hit, Motr, Lk, GFwd, xyL, xyR)
Matrix_Math(xcnt, EvntIn , Mtx , Qout)
Rep_episode(SeQ, Eps, SeqC)
Back_Up(FCE, Dirx , DegRef)
Power_TurnR(FCE0, FCE, Dirx, Deg0, DegM0, DegZ, M2event,Instr,ShmyA,SMV)
Power_TurnL(FCE0, FCE, Dirx , Deg0, DegM0, DegZ, M2event,Instr,ShmyA, SMV)
About_Face(FCE0, FCE, Dirx, DegRef, Deg0, DegM0, DegZ, Instr, ShmyA)
poll_sensors(event , Mevent , Ratio, Lk, Posit0, Posit1, Motr)
Head_LeftC(opnxL,LEvent,Mevent,Lk,Ratio,Posit0,Posit1)
Head_RightC(opnxR,REvent,Mevent,Lk,Ratio,Posit0,Posit1)
ScanL_R(LEvent,REvent,Mevent,Dirx,DegRef,FCE,Lk,Ratio,Posit0,Posit1)
Eval_GOnoGO(NOgoF, NOgoR, NOgoL, NOgo, LQ , RQ , Q)

The coding details are listed below in the blocked headings.

MASTER Subroutine:
       Write_DegHd

FUNCTION

Compass heading is written to a file for reference. It is not used as a global common variable due to the possibility of unauthorized changes caused by motor errors.

```
sub Write_DegHd(int &DegRef)
{
```

```
byte DegHdT;
int bytesWritten;
int fsize4=100;
bool eof=false;
string DegHd0;
DegHd0=NumToStr(DegRef);
DeleteFile("DegHd.txt");
CreateFile("DegHd.txt",fsize4,DegHdT);
{
WriteLnString(DegHdT,DegHd0,bytesWritten);
}
 CloseFile(DegHdT);
}
```

FUNCTION

Compass heading is read from a file. This keeps heading errors to a minimum.

```
sub Read_DegHd(int &DegRef)
{
byte DegHdT;
int bytesWritten, cnx;
int fsize4=100;
bool eof=false;
string DegHd0, Action0, Hdng0, buf;
hitx=100;
if(OpenFileRead("DegHd.txt", fsize4,DegHdT) == NO_ERR)
    {
Acquire (FileAcc1);
        {
ReadLnString(DegHdT,DegHd0)

DegRef=StrToNum(DegHd0);
        }
    }
Release (FileAcc1);
CloseFile(DegHdT);
}
```

FUNCTION

This is a turning tactic that extracts the Rover from a blocked passage or a dead end. It backs up and turns to the right and left. Other routines will check for clearances.

```
sub StallTurnL_R()
{
int Pwrx=90;
                    // " Stalled L_turn  ";
                    Float(OUT_AB);
                    OnRevReg(OUT_AB,Pwrx,OUT_REGMODE_SYNC);Wait(500);
                    //this goes fwd
                    OnRevSync(OUT_AB,Pwrx,50);Wait(800);
                    //this turns to Right
                    OnFwdReg(OUT_AB,Pwrx,OUT_REGMODE_SYNC); Wait(2600);
                    //this backs up
                    OnRevSync(OUT_AB,Pwrx,-50);
                    //this turns to Left
                    Wait(800);
                    OnFwdReg(OUT_AB,Pwrx,OUT_REGMODE_SYNC); Wait(2600);
                    //this backs up
                    Off(OUT_AB);
}
```

MASTER Subroutine:
StallTurnL

FUNCTION

This is a turning tactic that extracts the Rover from a blocked passage or a dead end. It backs up and turns to the left. Other routines will check for clearances.

```
sub StallTurnL()
{
int Pwrx=90;
                    //Posit1c=" Stalled L_turn  ";
                    Float(OUT_AB);
                    OnRevReg(OUT_AB,Pwrx,OUT_REGMODE_SYNC);Wait(500);
                    //this goes fwd
                    OnRevSync(OUT_AB,Pwrx,70);Wait(1200);
                    //this turns to Right
                    OnFwdReg(OUT_AB,Pwrx,OUT_REGMODE_SYNC); Wait(1600);
                    //this backs up
                    OnRevSync(OUT_AB,Pwrx,-70);
                    //this turns to Left
                    Wait(1700);
                    Off(OUT_AB);
}
```

MASTER Subroutine:
StallTurnR

This is a turning tactic that extracts the Rover from a blocked passage or a dead end. It backs up and turns to the right. Other routines will check for clearances.

```
sub StallTurnR()
{
int Pwrx=90;
        Float(OUT_AB);
        OnRevReg(OUT_AB,Pwrx,OUT_REGMODE_SYNC);Wait(500);
        //this goes fwd
        OnRevSync(OUT_AB,Pwrx,-70);Wait(1200);
        //this turns to the Left
        OnFwdReg(OUT_AB,Pwrx,OUT_REGMODE_SYNC); Wait(1600);
        //this backs up
        OnRevSync(OUT_AB,Pwrx,70);
        //this turns to Right
        Wait(1700);
        Off(OUT_AB);
}
```

MASTER Subroutine:
        Write_Posit0

FUNCTION

The Rover moves through the programming at a pace and direction controlled by various sensory events. Although the discrete task elements are all running at the same time, actions within the tasks are not truly sequential. Task actions are determined by conditions sensed and subroutine calls. In order to provide monitoring of these movements, a set of diagnostic write/read routines create files which track the decisions and actions of the Rover.

This group creates a series of references that allow diagnostic comments and position markers to be imbedded in the progress of the Rover. The string "Posit0" can be any text developed by the programmer to signal and event or location within the program.

```
sub Write_Posit0(string &Posit0)
// Write_Posit0(Posit0);
{
byte Trk1;
int bytesWritten;
if(OpenFileAppend("Track1.txt",fsizex,Trk1)==NO_ERR)
{
WriteLnString(Trk1,Posit0,bytesWritten);
CloseFile(Trk1);
}
Posit0="*W*";
}
```

MASTER Subroutine:
        Write_Posita

FUNCTION

This group creates a series of references that allow diagnostic comments and position markers to be imbedded in the progress of the Rover. The string "Posita" can be any text developed by the programmer to signal and event or location within the program.

```
sub Write_Posita(string &Posita)
{
byte Trk1a;
int bytesWritten;
if(OpenFileAppend("Track1a.txt",fsize2,Trk1a)==NO_ERR)
{
WriteLnString(Trk1a,Posita,bytesWritten);
CloseFile(Trk1a);
}
Posit0="*Wa*";
}
```

MASTER Subroutine:
Write_Positb

FUNCTION

This group creates a series of references that allow diagnostic comments and position markers to be imbedded in the progress of the Rover. The string "Positb" can be any text developed by the programmer to signal and event or location within the program.

```
sub Write_Positb(string &Positb)
{
byte Trk1b;
int bytesWritten;
if(OpenFileAppend("Track1b.txt",fsizex2,Trk1b)==NO_ERR)
{
WriteLnString(Trk1b,Positb,bytesWritten);
CloseFile(Trk1b);
}
Posit0="*Wb*";
}
```

MASTER Subroutine:
Write_Positc

FUNCTION

This group creates a series of references that allow diagnostic comments and position markers to be imbedded in the progress of the Rover. The string "Positc" can be any text developed by the programmer to signal and event or location within the program.

```
sub Write_Positc(string &Positc)
{
byte Trk1c;
int bytesWritten;
if(OpenFileAppend("Track1c.txt",fsizex2,Trk1c)==NO_ERR)
{
WriteLnString(Trk1c,Positc,bytesWritten);
CloseFile(Trk1c);
}
Posit0="*Wc*";
}
```

MASTER Subroutine:
Write_Track1

FUNCTION

This group creates a series of references that allow diagnostic comments and position markers to be imbedded in the progress of the Rover. The string "Track1" can be any text developed by the programmer to signal and event or location within the program. The sub strings, Track1a,1b,1c & 1d are used as markers for the development of a function within the task main( ).

```
sub Write_Track1(string Lk, string TkHead, string &Trackx1,string &Trackx2,string
&Trackx3,string &Trackx4)
{ ClearScreen();
string Track1a, Track1b, Track1c, Track1d;
byte Trk1;
int bytesWritten;
bool eof=false;
Acquire (FileAcc3);
if(OpenFileAppend("Track1.txt",fsizex,Trk1)==NO_ERR)
{

}
Track1a="";Track1b="";Track1c="D"; Track1d="E";

WriteLnString(Trk1,TkHead,bytesWritten);

    if (Trackx1!="xx")
{
```

```
Track1a=StrCat(Lk,Trackx1);
Track1b=StrCat(Lk,Trackx2);

WriteLnString(Trk1,Track1a,bytesWritten);
WriteLnString(Trk1,Track1b,bytesWritten);
}

    if (Trackx3!="xx3")
{
Track1c=StrCat(Lk,Trackx3);
Track1d=StrCat(Lk,Trackx4);

WriteLnString(Trk1,Track1c,bytesWritten);
WriteLnString(Trk1,Track1d,bytesWritten);
}
 CloseFile(Trk1);
 Release (FileAcc3);
 Trackx1="xx";Trackx2="xx2";Trackx3="xx3"; Trackx4="xx4";

}
```

MASTER Subroutine:
                 Write_FwdAct

FUNCTION

Specifics of forward motion are written to a file for reference. It is not used as a global common variable to keep these variables under strict control since they may change locally as the Rover maneuvers or carries out tactical motor actions. The functions are "hit" contact with ultra sound distance limits and power regulation for forward motion.

```
sub Write_FwdAct(int &hit, int &pwr )
// Write_FwdAct(hit,pwr)
{
byte Fwd1;
int bytesWritten;
int fsize4=100;
bool eof=false;
string hit0, sMotr,pwr0;
hit0=NumToStr(hit);
pwr0=NumToStr(pwr);
Acquire (FileAcc1);
DeleteFile("FwdAct.txt");
CreateFile("FwdAct.txt",fsize4,Fwd1);
{
WriteLnString(Fwd1,hit0,bytesWritten);
WriteLnString(Fwd1,pwr0,bytesWritten);

}
 CloseFile(Fwd1);
 Release (FileAcc1);

}
```

The functions are "hit" contact with ultra sound distance limits and power regulation for forward motion.

```
sub Read_FwdAct(int &hit, int &pwr)
//Read_FwdAct( hit,pwr);
{
byte Fwd1;
int bytesWritten, cnx;
int fsize4=100;
bool eof=false;
string hit0, Action0, Hdng0, buf,pwr0;
hit=0;
Acquire (FileAcc1);
if(OpenFileRead("FwdAct.txt", fsize4,Fwd1) == NO_ERR)
  {
  {
  ReadLnString(Fwd1,hit0)
  ReadLnString(Fwd1,pwr0);
  if(StrToNum(hit0)==1){hit=1;}
  hit=StrToNum(hit0);
  pwr=StrToNum(pwr0);
  }
  }
  CloseFile(Fwd1);
  Release (FileAcc1);  //00b3y_1

}
```

MASTER Subroutine:
                    Write_MotrAct

FUNCTION

Specifics of motor condition and direction of travel "Lk" are written to a file for reference. It is not used as a global common variable to keep these variables under strict control since they may change locally as the Rover maneuvers or carries out tactical motor actions. The functions are "Motr" indicating that the motor is under command and "Lk" indicating the direction of travel as in "looking Forward" where Lk="F".

```
sub Write_MotrAct( int &Motr, string Lk )
//  Write_MotrAct( Motr, Lk );
{
```

```
byte Motr1;
int bytesWritten;
int fsize4=100;
bool eof=false;
string  sMotr;

sMotr=NumToStr(Motr);
Acquire (FileAcc2);
DeleteFile("MotrAct.txt");
CreateFile("MotrAct.txt",fsize4,Motr1);
{
WriteLnString(Motr1,sMotr,bytesWritten);
WriteLnString(Motr1,Lk,bytesWritten);
}
 CloseFile(Motr1);
 Release (FileAcc2);
// "MotrAct written"

}
```

FUNCTION

Specifics of motor condition and direction of travel "Lk" are read from a file for reference. The functions are "Motr" indicating that the motor is under command and "Lk" indicating the direction of travel as in "looking Forward" where Lk="F".

```
sub Read_MotrAct( int &Motr, string Lk )
//Read_MotrAct(  Motr, Lk )
{
byte Motr1;
int bytesWritten, cnx;
int fsize4=100;
bool eof=false;
string  Action0, Hdng0, buf;

if(OpenFileRead("MotrAct.txt", fsize4,Motr1) == NO_ERR)
 {
 Acquire (FileAcc2);
// "Reading MotrAct  "
cnx=0;
until (eof == true)
{ // read the text file till the end
if(ReadLnString(Motr1,buf)!= NO_ERR) eof = true;
cnx=cnx+1;
if (cnx==1) {Action0=buf; Motr=StrToNum(Action0);}
if (cnx==2) {Hdng0=buf; Lk=Hdng0;}
```

```
        }
        }
        CloseFile(Motr1);
        Release (FileAcc2);

        }
```

FUNCTION

This is a motor action routine where specifications and direction of travel are set up and recorded for reference within the task elements of execution.

```
        sub Forward(int FCE, int &Dirx[], int DegRef, int &Motr, int &pwr)
        //Forward(FCE, Dirx , DegRef, Motr, pwr) ;
        {
        string Lk;
        int  Rate,Dist, xb,xc,hit,hitx,MQ[];
        float Bratio,xxa, Trvl;
        xxa=BatteryLevel();
        Bratio=xxa/8400 ;
        pwr=88/Bratio;
        if (Motr==1)
        {
        Lk="F";
            Write_MotrAct(Motr,Lk); Wait(500);   //this sets up the motor for Fwd action
            }
            Read_FwdAct( hit,pwr );
                                //this picks up any immediate obstr.
                                //task Chk_FwdUSnd determines the pwr
                                //level
                                //allow time to read file??

            if (hit!=1){
            Acquire (Fwd_Motr);
            OnRevReg(OUT_AB,pwr,OUT_REGMODE_SPEED);
                                //This is a major forward command
            Release (Fwd_Motr);
                    }
        Out_Fwdx:
        }
```

141

A "shimmy" is a slight movement, to the left side, that aligns the Rover with a desired heading. Such a heading may be determined from a dynamic ultra sound scan or magnetic compass readings.

```
sub TShmy_Left()
 {                    //10deg change to Left
 int pwr1,pwr2;
 int Pwrx,pctx;

pctx=90;

Pwrx=pctx*Bxx/100;
//aft (at the drive wheels) looking fwd towards the
//casters, Motor designations are:
//keep motor calls one at a time so power goes to one
     //A is Right Motor
     //B is Left Motor

 repeat(1)
 {
OnRevReg(OUT_B,Pwrx,OUT_REGMODE_IDLE); //Right motor pushes fwd -turn to
left
OnFwdReg(OUT_A,Pwrx,OUT_REGMODE_IDLE); //Left motor pull aft -turn to left
Wait(1200) ;

Off(OUT_AB);
 }
 }
```

MASTER Subroutine:
        TShmy_Right

A "shimmy" is a slight movement, to the right side, that aligns the Rover with a desired heading. Such a heading may be determined from a dynamic ultra sound scan or magnetic compass readings.

```
sub TShmy_Right()       //b2_1
 {                    //10deg change to right
 int pwr1,pwr2;
 int Pwrx,pctx;

     //A is Right Motor
     //B is Left Motor
pctx=90;

Pwrx=pctx*Bxx/100;
 repeat(1)
 {
OnFwdReg(OUT_B,Pwrx,OUT_REGMODE_IDLE); //right motor pulls aft -turn to
right
```

```
OnRevReg(OUT_A,Pwrx,OUT_REGMODE_IDLE); //left motor pushes fwd -turn to
right
Wait(1200) ;

Off(OUT_AB);
}
}
```

MASTER Subroutine:
        Dyno_ShmyR

FUNCTION

A "dynamic shimmy" is a measured movement, to the right side, that aligns the Rover with a clear front
forward looking heading. This heading is determined from continuous ultra sound scanning (dynamic) of
the landscape directly front looking.

```
sub Dyno_ShmyR(string Seek)
{  //no head movement in this turn shimmy
SetSensorLowspeed (IN_2);
int pwr1,pwr2;
 int Pwrx,pctx;
 int xx2,xx2Chk ,sxxL,sxxR,cntr,cntF,Sx2Chk,xChk;
 int zx2,zx3,TimeRd,tsx,zx,tstcnt,timx;
 float zxa,zxb,zxc;
 zxxa=BatteryLevel();
float Bx=(7800/zxxa);
Bxx=Bx*100;
 pctx=80;
 Pwrx=pctx*Bxx/100;  TimeRd=1200;
if (Dx=="Y") {Pwrx=95;TimeRd=500;}   //this forces a turn

goto TURN_ACTIONRd;
//>>>>>>>>>>>>>> START Dyno RIGHT Turn >>>>>>>>>>>>>>>>>>>>>>>>>>>>

TURN_ACTIONRd:              //A is Left Motr, B is Right
{
Float(OUT_AB);
sxxR=0;cntr=0;
repeat(3)              //do a repeat for the USnd
        {          //this takes 644ms to accomplish
xChk= (SensorUS(IN_2))
cntr=cntr+1;
sxxR=sxxR+xChk;
        }
zxa=sxxR/cntr;


        {zx3=zxa+20;}  //for the clearance target, it should
                        //be 20cm greater than the side scan reading
```

```
                        //BUT, if the fwd reading is greater than
                        //LimiT+20, the power turn should be
                        //killed and the Unit should go Forward


ClearScreen();
Acquire (Fwd_Motr);
        Start_TurnRd:        //this starts a steering turn left w/ no stop time
//>>>>>>>>>>>>>>>>>>>>>>>>>>>>>>>>>>>>>>>>>
if(zx3>=225) {TimeRd=1000;}
tsx=CurrentTick();
OnRevSync(OUT_AB,Pwrx,50);
Wait(TimeRd);
 //turn to RIGHT


                poll_TurnRd:
                {
                sxxR=0;cntr=0;
        repeat(3)
        {
xChk= (SensorUS(IN_2))
cntr=cntr+1;
sxxR=sxxR+xChk;     // you can't have two different ranging calcs competing
        }
zx2=sxxR/cntr;
     tstcnt=tstcnt+1;


NumOut(0,LCD_LINE6,zx2);NumOut(20,LCD_LINE6,zx3);NumOut(40,LCD_LINE6,tst
cnt);

        if  ((zx2>=zx3)&&(zx2>=(LimiT+20)))
        {
        Off(OUT_AB);tstcnt=0;goto Turn_OutRd;
        }

timx=CurrentTick()-tsx;
zxb=(0.20)*zxa;   //6Cc4b this represents at least a 12deg change in heading
zxc= (zx2-zxa);   //6Cc4b
if(zx2>=225)  {Off(OUT_AB);tstcnt=0;goto Turn_OutRd;}
if((tstcnt==10)||(tstcnt==20))
  {
        Off(OUT_AB);
        OnFwdReg(OUT_AB,Pwrx,OUT_REGMODE_SPEED);Wait(800);
if(Seek!="N")
   {
        if (abs(zxc)<=zxb)
                {

                StallTurnR();
                //this is a back up and forcing another turn
                //if no significant range change
        goto Start_TurnRd;
                }
                else {
                tstcnt=0;goto Start_TurnRd;
```

```
                    }
        }
        goto Start_TurnRd;
    }
    if(tstcnt==30)
     { tstcnt=20;
      Pwrx=90*Bxx/100;
            Float(OUT_AB);
            OnFwdReg(OUT_AB,Pwrx,OUT_REGMODE_SPEED);
            Wait(1000);
            TimeRd=1500;

                    //this is a back up and forcing another turn
                    //if no significant range change
            goto Start_TurnRd;

     }

    {goto poll_TurnRd;}
    //<<<<<<<<<<<<<<<<<<<<<< END Dyno Turn <<<<<<<<<<<<<<<<<<<<<
    }
    Turn_OutRd:
    Release (Fwd_Motr);
    }}
```

MASTER Subroutine:
        Dyno_ShmyL

FUNCTION

A "dynamic shimmy" is a measured movement, to the left side, that aligns the Rover with a clear front forward looking heading. This heading is determined from continuous ultra sound scanning (dynamic) of the landscape directly front looking.

```
    sub Dyno_ShmyL(string Seek)
    {
    SetSensorLowspeed (IN_2);
    int pwr1,pwr2;
     int Pwrx,pctx;
     int xx2,xx2Chk ,sxxL,sxxR,cntr,cntF,Sx2Chk,xChk;
     int zx2,zx3,TimeLd,tsx,zx,tstcnt,timx;
     float zxa,zxb,zxc;
      zxxa=BatteryLevel();
    float Bx=(7800/zxxa);
    Bxx=Bx*100;
     pctx=80;

     Pwrx=pctx*Bxx/100;  TimeLd=1200;
    if (Dx=="Y") {Pwrx=95;TimeLd=500;}

    goto TURN_ACTIONLd;
    //>>>>>>>>>>>>> START Dyno LEFT Turn >>>>>>>>>>>>>>>>>>>>>>>>>>
```

```
TURN_ACTIONLd:                    //A is Left Motr, B is Right
{
Float(OUT_AB);
sxxL=0;cntr=0;
repeat(3)                //do a repeat for the USnd
        {                //this takes 644ms to accomplish
xChk= (SensorUS(IN_2))
cntr=cntr+1;
sxxL=sxxL+xChk;
        }
zxa=sxxL/cntr;        //3bC

        {zx3=zxa+20;}  //for the clearance target, it should
                        //be 20cm greater than the side scan reading
                        //BUT, if the fwd reading is greater than
                        //LimiT+20, the power turn should be
                        //killed and the Unit should go Forward

ClearScreen();
        Acquire (Fwd_Motr);
Start_TurnLd:      //this starts a steering turn left w/ no stop time
//>>>>>>>>>>>>>>>>>>>>>>>>>>>>>>>>>>>>>
if(zx3>=225) {TimeLd=1000;}
tsx=CurrentTick();
OnRevSync(OUT_AB,Pwrx,-50);
Wait(TimeLd); //turn to LEFT
            poll_TurnLd:
            { zx2=250;
                sxxL=0;cntr=0;
    repeat(3)
      {
xChk= (SensorUS(IN_2))
cntr=cntr+1;
sxxL=sxxL+xChk;    // you can't have two different ranging calcs competing
            //first range and this second range must use the same calc
        }
zx2=sxxL/cntr;
    tstcnt=tstcnt+1;

NumOut(0,LCD_LINE6,zx2);NumOut(30,LCD_LINE6,zx3);NumOut(60,LCD_LINE6,tst
cnt);

    if ((zx2>=zx3)&&(zx2>=(LimiT+20)))
      {
      Off(OUT_AB);tstcnt=0;goto Turn_OutLd;
      }

timx=CurrentTick()-tsx;
zxb=(0.20)*zxa;  // this represents at least a 12deg change in heading
zxc=(zx2-zxa);   // this is the delta distance from the turn
NumOut(0,LCD_LINE6,zxa);NumOut(30,LCD_LINE6,zx2);
NumOut(55,LCD_LINE6,zxc);NumOut(75,LCD_LINE6,zxb);
if(zx2>=225) {Off(OUT_AB);tstcnt=0;goto Turn_OutLd;} //6Cc4b1
if((tstcnt==10)||(tstcnt==20))
 {
        Off(OUT_AB);
```

```
                    OnFwdReg(OUT_AB,Pwrx,OUT_REGMODE_SPEED);Wait(800);
        if(Seek!="N")
          {
              if (abs(zxc)<=zxb)
                      {

                      StallTurnL();
                      //this is a back up and forcing another turn
                      //if no significant range change
                 goto Start_TurnLd;
                           }
                       else {
                       goto Start_TurnLd;
                           }
          }
        goto Start_TurnLd;
      }

    if(tstcnt==30)
     { tstcnt=20;
     Pwrx=90*Bxx/100;
          Off(OUT_AB);
          OnFwdReg(OUT_AB,Pwrx,OUT_REGMODE_SPEED);
    //do not use "_SYNC"
                                      //on the motor command
                                      //If one wheel is stuck
                                      //the other won't turn

          Wait(500);
          TimeLd=1500;
              //this is a back up and forcing another turn
              //if no significant range change
              ClearScreen();
          goto Start_TurnLd;

     }
    {goto poll_TurnLd;}
    //<<<<<<<<<<<<<<<<<<<<< END Dyno Turn <<<<<<<<<<<<<<<<<<<<<
    }
    Turn_OutLd:
    Release (Fwd_Motr);

    }}
```

MASTER Subroutine:
                Lk_D

FUNCTION

The Rover scans the landscape with a head movement in front, to the right or left. Quarter points are also registered at 45 degrees to the front. It ends with a clear front forward looking reading with the head centered. The ultra sound scanning of the landscape takes place as the head is turning, hence "dynamic."

```
sub Lk_D(string Lk, int &opnxF,int &opnxD, int &opnxqD)      //2;
// insert Standard power functions
//Lk_D( Lk, opnxF,opnxD, opnxqD)
//this is a "Directional" looking routine
//It is automatically self centering with physical stops on the Head
   //In the calling sub, if (Ratio==0.5) then opnxF=-1;
   //As a "-1", a flag is sent to bypass an USnd reading and position the head
   //to the side
   //This is used when the head turn is for side polling
   //Turn to the side and stay there.Do not take readings
{ int xxy,xxz,xx,xx2,xxq,cnt,Lkr;
  int pctj,Pwrj;
cnt=0;
               //this is the UltraS routine
//It is possible to scan while the head is turning. Use a "while" condition
//in a time mode ""while (time<800)"" for the do loop. Within the loop, nest a
//USnd reading looking for the highest value. At the end of the time, when the head
//is at a quarter turn, evaluate the reading
pctj=80;
Pwrj=pctj*Bxx/100;

 xsampleUSx:
{
xxy=250;
xx2=250;
xxq=250;
xx=0;
cnt=cnt+1;

if ((Lk=="RR") || (Lk=="LR")) {goto ReturnXx;}  //"RR" or "LR" is a self-centering
                                                //return from a polling turn
if (cnt==1) {goto xQsamplex;}
if (Lk=="L") {
{OnFwdReg(OUT_C,Pwrj,OUT_REGMODE_IDLE);Wait(500); }
                              //This overshoots the stops
                              //at 50pwr and allows extra
                              //torque in the neck shaft
                              //to be released in counter
                              //rotation
         } //Look to the left
if (Lk=="R") {
{OnRevReg(OUT_C,Pwrj,OUT_REGMODE_IDLE);Wait(500); }
//800 is a quarter point rotation
} //Look to the right

     Off(OUT_C); if (cnt==3) {Wait(1500);}
                                 //in an overshoot: give the shaft
                                 //time to release the torque
   if ((cnt==3)&&(opnxF==-1)) {goto xOut_US;}
                    //as a "-1", a flag is sent to bypass an USnd reading
                    //This is used when the head turn is for side polling
                    //Turn to the side and stay there.Do not take readings

     xQsamplex:
     if (opnxF==-1) {goto xsampleUSx;}
```

```
                    repeat(10)
                    {

                    xx=SensorUS(IN_2);
                    if(xx<xx2){xx2=xx;}
                    }
                    x=x2;
                    if (xx<xxy) {if (xx!=0) {xxy=xx;}}
                    if (cnt==1) {opnxF=xxy;goto xsampleUSx;}
                    if (cnt==2) {opnxqD=xxy;goto xsampleUSx;}   //this examines quarter point
                    if (cnt==3) {opnxD=xxy;}
                    }
ReturnXx:
 if ((Lk=="R")||(Lk=="RR")) {
OnFwdReg(OUT_C,Pwrj,OUT_REGMODE_IDLE);Wait(920);
} //1400: full rotation to the left timed from the stops, allowing centering
 if ((Lk=="L")||(Lk=="LR")) {
 OnRevReg(OUT_C,Pwrj,OUT_REGMODE_IDLE);Wait(850);
}
Off(OUT_C);
xOut_US:
}
```

MASTER Subroutine:
Write_FwdTch

FUNCTION

This functions keeps track of physical touch episodes (hitx) as opposed to ultra sound distance events. The variable "hitx" is True when the SLAVE signals that a touch sensors has been contacted. This event is written to the file FwdTch.txt.

```
            sub Write_FwdTch(int &hitx)
            {
            byte FwdT;
            int bytesWritten;
            int fsize4=100;
            bool eof=false;
            string hitx0;
            hitx0=NumToStr(hitx);
            DeleteFile("FwdTch.txt");
            CreateFile("FwdTch.txt",fsize4,FwdT);
            {
            WriteLnString(FwdT,hitx0,bytesWritten);
            }
             CloseFile(FwdT);
            }
```

MASTER Subroutine:
Read_FwdTch

The variable "hitx" is written to the file FwdTch.txt. At various times, the Rover checks the file for information on obstructions directly ahead that are out of ultra sound peripheral range.

```
sub Read_FwdTch(int &hitx)
{
byte FwdT;
int bytesWritten, cnx;
int fsize4=100;
bool eof=false;
string hitx0, Action0, Hdng0, buf;
hitx=100;
if(OpenFileRead("FwdTch.txt", fsize4,FwdT) == NO_ERR)
    {
Acquire (FileAcc1);
        {
ReadLnString(FwdT,hitx0)

hitx=StrToNum(hitx0);
        }
    }
Release (FileAcc1);
CloseFile(FwdT);
}
```

MASTER Subroutine:
Tch_BT

FUNCTION

The variable "hitx" is created when the MASTER interrogates the SLAVE for peripheral events. This includes touches to the set of sensors on the front bumper of the Rover.

```
sub Tch_BT(int &hitx)
{
int pcnt;
string Pin, pinx;
Pin="";pcnt=0;
 hitx=100;
SendRemoteString(BT_Cnx,OUTBOX1,"Tch"); Wait(800);   //box 5 to Slave
Chk_PinTch3:
{ReceiveRemoteString(BT_Cnx,INBOX,Pin);Wait(300);}     //box 1 from Slave
if (Pin=="") {pcnt=pcnt+1;
        if (pcnt<5) {goto Chk_PinTch3;}
        else goto Tch_Out3;
```

```
                }
    if(Pin!="Nx") { Off(OUT_AB);
                if (Pin=="L") {hitx=1;}
                if (Pin=="R") {hitx=-1;}
                if (Pin=="F") {hitx=-10;}
                }
    Tch_Out3:
    Write_FwdTch(hitx);
       goto SkipCalib;
            SendRemoteString(BT_Cnx,OUTBOX1,"Calib");
            Check_Pin0x:
            ReceiveRemoteString(BT_Cnx,INBOX,Pin);
            DegRefs=Pin;
            DegRef=StrToNum(Pin);
            if(DegRef==0) {goto Check_Pin0x;}
        SkipCalib:
    }
```

FUNCTION

As the Rover maneuvers about the landscape, motor events and sensory perceptions lack precision. The consequence is an action command that is executed but does not achieve the desired result. After specific action commands, the Rover is directed to check its position with reference to obstructions and/or peripheral clearances. The cycle concept of the subroutine is the side to side quarter turn of the head as it scans the vicinity for clearances.

```
sub Cycle_ChkFwd(int &hit, int Motr, string Lk, int &GFwd,int &xyL,int &xyR)   //2;
{

//It is possible to scan while the head is turning. Use a "while" condition
//in a time mode ""while (time<800)"" for the do loop. Within the loop, nest a
//USnd reading looking for the highest value. At the end of the time, when the head
//is at a quarter turn, evaluate the reading

//This also initiates side shifts based upon USnd readings

int xx,hitx,MQ[16];
int xx2,xx2Chk ,sxxL,sxxR,cntr,cntF,Sx2Chk,xChk;
int  diffhi ;
int cnt, hiL, hiR, lwR, lwL,bku,trn;
long tmr,tmcnt;
string Posit0;
byte Trk1;
int fsize2=30*28*10;
int bytesWritten;
int pctk,Pwrk;
```

151

```
SetSensorLowspeed(IN_2);
cnt=0;

pctk=60;
Pwrk=pctk*Bxx/100;    //6Cc4b1x
Cycle:

GFwd=0,bku=0;
xx2=250;
hiL=0;hiR=0;lwR=250;lwL=250;sxxL=0;sxxR=0;
 //use this routine to locate Chk_Fwd points

// "  Cycle scan         "

cntF=0;Sx2Chk=0;

repeat(10)
 {
xChk= (SensorUS(IN_2))
cntF=cntF+1;
     xChk=SensorUS(IN_2);
     Sx2Chk=Sx2Chk+xChk;
        }
xx2Chk=Sx2Chk/cntF;
NumOut(3,LCD_LINE1,xx2Chk);

             if(((xx2Chk-10)>=LimiT)||(Lk=="N"))
             {trn=1;goto Lkng_Fwd;}
{
tmcnt=CurrentTick();
cntr=0;
do {
tmr=CurrentTick()-tmcnt;
             if (tmr<325)
             {OnFwdReg(OUT_C,Pwrk,OUT_REGMODE_IDLE);
             } //left swing
      //the time
      //of the swing
      //must be beyond
      //the side lobe
      //effect > 800sec
cntr=0;sxxL=0;
repeat(3)              //do a repeat for the USnd
        {              //this takes 644ms to accomplish
xChk= (SensorUS(IN_2))
cntr=cntr+1;
sxxL=sxxL+xChk;
      }
}
while (tmr<725);       //this keeps the head lkng left for 200ms
sxxL=sxxL/cntr;
NumOut(20,LCD_LINE1,sxxL);
Off(OUT_C);

//"Inside Cycle 1";
```

```
tmcnt=CurrentTick();
cntr=0;
do {
tmr=CurrentTick()-tmcnt;
if (tmr<1050) {OnRevReg(OUT_C,Pwrk,OUT_REGMODE_IDLE);}
                                              //from left
cntr=0;sxxR=0;                                //to right swing
repeat(3)
        {                         //1100+800=1900
xChk= (SensorUS(IN_2))
cntr=cntr+1;
sxxR=sxxR+xChk;
        }
}
while (tmr<1375);
sxxR=sxxR/cntr;
NumOut(60,LCD_LINE1,sxxR);
Off(OUT_C);
                                //center head
OnFwdReg(OUT_C,Pwrk,OUT_REGMODE_IDLE);Wait(800);
                                //from right back to center
                                //very sensitive to turn back time
Off(OUT_C);
}

//"Inside Cycle 2"

if  ((xx2Chk-10)<LimiT)     //current position is too close
{                    //Less than LimiT
 {xyL=sxxL; xyR=sxxR;}
//Left and Right options
Posit0=StrCat(QGOcnts," sub:Cycle Options ",NumToStr(xyL),"/",NumToStr(xyR));
Write_Posit0(Posit0);
goto Cycle_Out;
}


  //forward
 if (((xx2Chk-10)>=LimiT)&&(abs(trn)>=1))      //use a counter [bku] to avoid
{GFwd=1;hit=0;
goto Cycle_Out; //3zZ
}                         //selecting a cleance merely because
                          //the Unit has backed away from the
                          //obstr


 xx2=250;Sx2Chk=0;cntF=0;
repeat(10)
 {
xChk= (SensorUS(IN_2))
cntF=cntF+1;
     xChk=SensorUS(IN_2);
     Sx2Chk=Sx2Chk+xChk;
        }
xx2Chk=Sx2Chk/cntF;
NumOut(3,LCD_LINE5,xx2Chk);
```

```
Lkng_Fwd:
if (((xx2Chk-10)>=LimiT)&&(abs(trn)>=1))        //this will only give a clear flag
                               //after a turn, when bku is set to 0,
                               //Or at the start of a cycle w/o a
                               //back up
{ GFwd=1;hit=0; }
if (Lk=="N") {
        Posit0=StrCat(QGOcnts," sub:Cycle Fwd Snap-Shot
GFwd=",NumToStr(GFwd));
          Write_Posit0(Posit0);
          goto Cycle_Out;
        }

Cycle_Out:
}
```

<table>
<tr><td>MASTER Subroutine:
                Matrix_Math</td></tr>
</table>

FUNCTION

This procedure multiplies the universe matrix **[K]** by the event column matrix **[e]** to obtain the observed outcome matrix **[Q].** The outcome matrix is the basis for evaluation and action and is characterized as the variable **Qout** from the subroutine.

```
sub Matrix_Math(int xcnt, int EvntIn[], int Mtx[], int &Qout[] )
 {
 int zcnt=xcnt+1;
 ArrayInit(Qout,0,zcnt);

 int cnt, cntr, xdx,Q1, xd,Q2;
 cnt=0;  //6Ce_b1_x
 do
  {cnt=cnt+1 ;
cntr=0;
 xdx=((cnt-1)*xcnt);

 do
 { xd=xdx+cntr;
//event[n] always starts from EvntIn[0]

 Q1= Mtx[(xdx+cntr)]*EvntIn[cntr] + Q1;  //this calculates each row value
 cntr=cntr+1  ;

 }
 while (cntr<(xcnt+0));
                     //Qout[] is arranged starting from [1], not [0]
                     //Not (cnt-1). (cnt) is the real Q array #
                     //displayed as a column, not row
                     //remember- the first element in a
```

```
                    //row is "0"
    Qout[(cnt)]=Q1;

     Q1=0  ;cntr=0;

     }
     while(cnt<(xcnt+0))
     cnt=0 ;
       //"End of Math"
     }
```

FUNCTION

This develops a method of counting the recurrence of any specific task or variable element.

```
    sub Rep_episode(int &SeQ, int &Eps,int SeqC)
    {
    //it is important to decide where the Global event counter is incremented
    //Normally this would be at the start of each poll cycle

    //SeQ;   //this is the event of interest that was last counted: SeQ
    //SeqC;  //this is the sequence currently in the ongoing count qeue: SeqC
        //In a sequential test, if the current event and last event
        //counted do not match the ongoing count plus the episode marker
        //counted from the last event,
        //then intervening events have taken place, breaking the sequence.
    //Eps;   //the numbers of events in an unbroken sequence of similar events

     if (SeQ==0) {SeQ=SeqC;Eps=1;goto SeqOut; }
                    //if the event last counted SeQ is 0,or not counted
                    //then set it (=) to the Global sequence SeqC
     if ((SeQ+Eps)==SeqC) {Eps=Eps+1;}
                    //if the event counter SeQ plus the episode is the
                    //same as the global sequence SeqC, then this is
                    //an event within the stream of current episodes.
                    //So the episode counter increments by +1
     else { Eps=0;SeQ=0;}
     SeqOut:
     }
```

FUNCTION

This is a straight back up command with a front clearance large enough for a full turn with the front bumper clearing an obstruction ahead.

```
sub Back_Up(int FCE, int &Dirx[], int DegRef)
//this is a pure "back up" command
{
string Lk="F";
int hit, Motr,pwr;
Read_FwdAct( hit,pwr );
NumOut(70,LCD_LINE6,hit);
if(hit==1)
{ Motr=-1; Write_MotrAct( Motr, Lk );      //where a Read_FwdAct shows hit==1
                                           //then Motr is set to -1 with a write

}
int Trvl;
float Bratio,xxa;
OnFwdReg(OUT_AB,85,OUT_REGMODE_SYNC);
Wait(1200);                                //chassis requires 13" back up
Float(OUT_AB);
}
```

MASTER Subroutine:
            Power_TurnR

FUNCTION

Execute a dynamic turn to the left. Dynamic turning is not a motor action that is constant in its power demands. Unless the Rover is operating on a smooth unimpeded surface, turns are subject to variations in surface, traction, obstructions and internal power drains. To assist the Rover in handling these problems and execute a relatively reliable turn, a system of sensor events are for power monitoring and ultra sound range gauging.

```
sub Power_TurnR(int &FCE0, int &FCE,int &Dirx[], int &Deg0, int &DegM0, int
&DegZ, int &M2event[],string &Instr, int &ShmyA, string SMV)
//Power_TurnR( FCE0, FCE, Dirx, Deg0, DegM0, DegZ, M2event,Instr,ShmyA,SMV)
{    int FCEx;
 //this is a Dynamically steered turn Right w/ USnd ranging through turn
 float Md,Mp,Mi,Rc,Rpwr, Rtac;
 float Rtac0,Rtacx,Rsqpwr;
int tsx,timx, Trvl,zx,zx2,zx3,Limtx,tstcnt;
int pwr1,pwr2;
int CDegx,TimeR;
string ActionR="Steering R @ USnd= ";
int Pwrx,pctx;
zx2=250;
tstcnt=0;
SetSensorLowspeed(IN_2);
zxxa=BatteryLevel();
                //Bratio=4680/zxxa  ;
                //ratio of optimum output to scaled pwr demand
```

156

```
                    //Scaled pwr demand == .60 of 7800 ==4680
                    //pwr1 == 4680
float Bx=(7800/zxxa);
Bxx=Bx*100;
Pwr1= 70*Bxx/100;              //power output equivalent to 4680 mv (4.68v)

Limtx=1500;
if(SMV=="AF") {Limtx=6000;} //in About_Face [AF] allow a complete turn around
TURN_ACTIONR:                 //A is Left Motr, B is Right
{
repeat(3)                     //this sets the min target USnd reading
     {
     zx= (SensorUS(IN_2));
     if(zx<zx2){zx2=zx;}
     }
      if (zx2<220) {zx3=zx2+20;}  //for the clearance target, it should
                         //be 20cm greater than the side scan reading
                         //BUT, if the fwd reading is greater than
                         //LimiT+20, the power turn should be
                         //killed and the Unit should go Forward

         else {zx3=zx2;}
             zx2=250;
ClearScreen();
TimeR=1000;
Read_DegHd(DegRef);
         DegM0=DegRef;
         Start_TurnR:
//>>>>>>>>>>>>>>>>>>>>> this starts a steering turn left w/ no stop time
tsx=CurrentTick();
if (tstcnt<=20) {OnRevSync(OUT_AB,Pwr1,50);}
Wait(TimeR); //turn to RIGHT
             poll_TurnR:
if(zx3>=(LimiT+20)) { //ActionR=" go Forward ";
                                  }
             { zx2=250;
    repeat(3)
    {
    zx= (SensorUS(IN_2));
    if(zx<zx2){zx2=zx;}
    }
    tstcnt=tstcnt+1;
    Read_DegHd(DegRef);       //00b
    DeltaDeg=abs(DegM0-DegRef);
    TextOut(0,LCD_LINE7,"                ");

NumOut(0,LCD_LINE7,zx2);NumOut(30,LCD_LINE7,zx3);NumOut(65,LCD_LINE7,tst
cnt);
    NumOut(80,LCD_LINE7,DeltaDeg);

timx=CurrentTick()-tsx;

if((zx2>=zx3)&&((zx2-20)>=LimiT))
     {
     if ((Instr=="L")&&(DeltaDeg<8)) {goto ForcedR;}
                                     //This forces a turn away from "L"
                                     //if Unit doesn't move then go
```

```
                                        //into the Stall_Turn sequences
        Wait(500);Off(OUT_AB);
        TextOut(0,LCD_LINE8,"Test Exit ");
        if(tstcnt>1) {goto Turn_OutR;}
        } //this stops the turn after 1500ms

    ForcedR:
    if((tstcnt==10)||(tstcnt==20))
        {if(DeltaDeg>7) {Instr="Null";}
        Float(OUT_AB);//TimeR=1200;    //3v2a
        if(DeltaDeg<8) {goto Stall_TurnR;} //00b
        pctx=90;
        Pwrx=pctx*Bxx/100;
        Read_DegHd(DegRef);
        DegM0=DegRef;
        NumOut(0,LCD_LINE4,DegRef);
        OnFwdReg(OUT_AB,Pwrx,OUT_REGMODE_SPEED); Wait(700);
        Float(OUT_AB);
        goto Start_TurnR;
        }
          if (tstcnt==30)
          {tstcnt=20;
          pctx=90;
          Pwrx=pctx*Bxx/100;
          Stall_TurnR:
            if (DeltaDeg<8)
                  {
                  StallTurnR();
                  }
                                        // chassis requires 13" back up
          else
                  {OnFwdReg(OUT_AB,Pwrx,50);
                  Wait(1200);
                  }
          Float(OUT_AB);
          TimeR=200;
          goto Start_TurnR;
          }
    {goto poll_TurnR;}

              }
            //while (x2<=60)   //keep turning as long as USnd reading
                    //is 20cm less than the target x3

    Turn_OutR:
    Float(OUT_AB);
    }

    Instr=StrCat(ActionR,NumToStr(zx2)," ",NumToStr(zx3));
        //END OF TURN_ACTION
    }
```

MASTER Subroutine:
        Power_TurnL

FUNCTION

Execute a dynamic turn to the left.

```
sub Power_TurnL(int &FCE0, int &FCE,int &Dirx[], int &Deg0, int &DegM0, int
&DegZ, int &M2event[],string &Instr, int &ShmyA, string SMV)
{
int DegRef,
 int FCEx;
 //this is a Dynamically steered turn Left w/ USnd ranging through turn
 float Md,Mp,Mi,Rc,Rpwr, Rtac;
 float Rtac0,Rtacx,Rsqpwr;
int tsx,timx, Trvl,yx,yx2,yx3,Limtx,tstcnt;
int pwr1,pwr2;
int CDegx,TimeL;
string ActionL="Steering L @ USnd= ";
int Pwrx,pctx,DegRef;
yx2=250;
tstcnt=0;
SetSensorLowspeed(IN_2);
zxxa=BatteryLevel();
                //Bratio=4680/zxxa  ;
                //ratio of optimum output to scaled pwr demand
            //Scaled pwr demand == .60 of 7800 ==4680
            //pwr1 == 4680
float Bx=(7800/zxxa);
Bxx=Bx*100;
Pwr1= 70*Bxx;          //power output equivalent to 4680 mv (4.68v)
Limtx=1500;
if(SMV=="AF") {Limtx=6000;} //in About_Face [AF] allow a complete turn around
TURN_ACTIONL:              //A is Left Motr, B is Right
{


repeat(3)
    {
    yx= (SensorUS(IN_2));
    if(yx<yx2){yx2=yx;}
    }
    if (yx2<220) {yx3=yx2+20;}    //yx3 is the snap shot of fwd clearance
     else {yx3=yx2;}
          yx2=250;
TimeL=1000;
NumOut(30,LCD_LINE7,yx3);
Read_DegHd(DegRef);
     DegM0=DegRef;
     Start_TurnL:
//>>>>>>>>>>>>>>>>>>>>> this starts a steering turn left w/ no stop time
tsx=CurrentTick();
OnRevSync(OUT_AB,Pwr1,-50);
Wait(TimeL); //turn to LEFT
             poll_TurnL:
if(yx3>=(LimiT+20)) {
                           }
{ yx2=250;
    repeat(3)
      {
```

```
        yx= (SensorUS(IN_2));
        if(yx<yx2){yx2=yx;}
        }
        tstcnt=tstcnt+1;
        Read_DegHd(DegRef);
        DeltaDeg=abs(DegM0-DegRef);
        NumOut(0,LCD_LINE7,yx2);//NumOut(30,LCD_LINE7,yx3);
        NumOut(65,LCD_LINE7,tstcnt);
        NumOut(80,LCD_LINE7,DeltaDeg);
timx=CurrentTick()-tsx;


if((yx2>=yx3)&&((yx2-20)>=LimiT))
        {
        if ((Instr=="R")&&(DeltaDeg<8)) {goto ForcedL;}
                                        //This forces a turn away from "L"
        Wait(500);Off(OUT_AB);
        TextOut(0,LCD_LINE8,"Test Exit ");
        if(tstcnt>1) {goto Turn_OutL;}
        }                               //this stops the turn after 1500ms

ForcedL:
if((tstcnt==10)||(tstcnt==20))
        {if(DeltaDeg>7) {Instr="Null";}
        Float(OUT_AB);//TimeL=1200;    //3v2a
        if(DeltaDeg<8) {goto Stall_TurnL;}
        pctx=90;
        Pwrx=pctx*Bxx/100;
        Read_DegHd(DegRef);   //00b
        DegM0=DegRef;
        NumOut(0,LCD_LINE4,DegRef);
        OnFwdReg(OUT_AB,Pwrx,OUT_REGMODE_SYNC); Wait(700);
        Float(OUT_AB);
        goto Start_TurnL;
        }
          if (tstcnt==30)
          {tstcnt=20;
          pctx=90;
          Pwrx=pctx*Bxx/100;
          Stall_TurnL:
            if (DeltaDeg<8)
                    {
                    TextOut(0,LCD_LINE8,"Call StallTurnL ");
                    StallTurnL();

                    }
        // chassis requires 13" back up
          else
                    {OnFwdReg(OUT_AB,Pwrx,-50);
                    Wait(1200);
                    }
        Float(OUT_AB);
        TimeL=200;
        goto Start_TurnL;
        }
{goto poll_TurnL;}
```

```
                        }
                //while (x2<=60)  //keep turning as long as USnd reading
                        //is 20cm less than the target x3
Turn_OutL:
Float(OUT_AB);
}

Instr=StrCat(ActionL,NumToStr(yx2)," ",NumToStr(yx3));
        //END OF TURN_ACTION

}
```

MASTER Subroutine:
        About_Face

FUNCTION

Execute a complete 180 degree turn to reverse the Rover's front facing direction. Check for clearances and power needs. Use a series of dynamically controlled power turns.

```
sub About_Face(int &FCE0, int &FCE,int &Dirx[], int DegRef, int &Deg0, int
&DegM0, int &DegZ,string &Instr, int &ShmyA)
// About_Face(FCE0, FCE, Dirx, DegRef, Deg0, DegM0, DegZ, Instr, ShmyA)
{ string SMV;
  int FCEx, cnt, tEXs,tEXf,xaa,x2aa,nx, Bkcnt;
   int pwr1,pwr2,Trvl;
   int opnxF,opnxqR,opnxqL,opnxR,opnxL,Sopnx;
   int M2event[0];
    string Lk,Positxa,Posit1xa;
float Bratio,xxa;

SetSensorLowspeed(IN_2);
ClearScreen();

 Bkcnt=0;
 nx=1;
 if (Instr=="BkO") {nx=3;}
 goto Clear_Ahead;   //BackOut;

 ScanLR:   //Scan L/R for clearances
 Positxa="About_Face > scan ";
 Write_Posit0(Positxa);
 Lk="L";
 Lk_D( Lk, opnxF,opnxL, opnxqL);
 NumOut(5,LCD_LINE3,opnxL);
 Lk="R";
 Lk_D( Lk, opnxF,opnxR, opnxqR);
 NumOut(40,LCD_LINE3,opnxR);
 Lk="F";
```

```
Sopnx= (opnxR+opnxL);          //This is the Sum of R/L readings
                               //if the sum is less than 94cm 37in then back up
                               //for 32cm chassis width.
                               //For fat tire 38cm chassis width use 112
if(Sopnx>=112) {goto Turn_Exe;}
goto BackOut;                  //don't repeat this backup


if (Sopnx<112){nx=2;}
if (Instr=="BkO") {nx=3;}      //first BackOut command BkO uses 3 reps

BackOut:
{
{Bkcnt=Bkcnt+1;
        repeat(nx){Back_Up( FCE, Dirx,  DegRef);}
        nx=1;
        if (Bkcnt==1) {Positxa="Back_up @ ta ";Write_Posit0(Positxa);
        goto ScanLR;}
}
        //after 3 backups, set nx ==1 & scan L/R,
        //test for clearances. if Sopnx is still <94cm, back up again
            //Bkcnt>2 is exit count and/or a major extraction effort
            //change the backout sequence to 1

Turn_Exe:
   //repeat(2)     //this double repeat in power turn executes a 180
   { Posit1xa=StrCat(NumToStr(opnxR),"/",NumToStr(opnxL));
    SMV="AF";
// do a USnd dynamic turn where x3 will be based upon the reading from
 //the blind turn, not the backup distance
if (opnxR>opnxL)
{repeat(1) {
Power_TurnR(FCE0, FCE,Dirx,  Deg0, DegM0, DegZ, M2event,Instr, opnxR, SMV);}
Posit1xa=Instr;}
else if (opnxL>opnxR)
{repeat(1){
Power_TurnL(FCE0, FCE,Dirx,  Deg0, DegM0, DegZ, M2event, Instr, opnxL, SMV);}
Posit1xa=Instr;}

  Positxa=StrCat("A_F Power Turn ",Instr); //," ",Posit1xa);
  Write_Posit0(Positxa);

  //check for clearance ahead. If clear, abort movement, goto Out_ta
  Clear_Ahead:
   int Sx2aa,cntx;
     x2aa=250;
     cntx=0;Sx2aa=0;
      repeat(3)
      {
      cntx=cntx+1;
      xaa=SensorUS(IN_2);
      Sx2aa=Sx2aa+xaa;
            }
      x2aa=Sx2aa/cntx;

      if (x2aa>60)
```

162

```
        {
      goto Out_ta;
      }
     else goto BackOut;
   }


}

Out_ta:
 ShmyA=x2aa;
 Posit1xa=StrCat("Exit_ta ",NumToStr(x2aa));
      Write_Posit0(Posit1xa);
 int CDegx;

SMV="ta";

 FCE=FCEx;
 Trvl=0;


}
```

FUNCTION

Gather sensory input from the main battery of the oculus (observation platform.) This includes motor action for the head and may include reduction in forward movement to allow time for the sensor polling. Output is in the form of event **[e]** logical states (+1, -1, 0, & null.)

```
sub poll_sensors(int &event[], int &Mevent[], float &Ratio, string &Lk, string Posit0,
string Posit1, int &Motr)
//Posit0 & Posit1 are merely carry thru variables when this sub is used in other
subs
//also event[ ] can be used to carry info into this sub for use in an ACTion.
//for example event[16-18] carries info about IR ahead when looking to the side
    {
//int event[25]  ;
int s1,s2,s3,s4;
  int s3A1_13  ;
  int s1A1_30   ;
  int s1A1_50    ;
  int s1A1_80    ;
  int s2A1_30, s2A1_50, s2A1_80 ;


  int s4A1_L, s4A11_L, s4A1_F, s4A11_F, s4A1_R, s4A11_R ;
int xs, xq, x2;
float x, xx;
int cntr;
int hitxPS,opnxF;
float y,xxx,Rsqpwr,xxb;
```

163

```
string buf,SMV,Lkk;

int xy; int xxy;
int pwr;

cntr=0; hit=0;

byte Trk1;
int bytesWritten;
Lkk=Lk;
hitxPS=110;


Trackx1="xx";Trackx2="xx2";Trackx3="xx3"; Trackx4="xx4";
Track1a="";Track1b="";Track1c=""; Track1d="";

event[0]=1;
event[9]=0;event[10]=0; event[26]=1;
event[21]=1;event[22]=1;event[23]=1;event[24]=1;event[25]=1;   //Initilize all motor
                                                //actions
// "USnd      "

s3=1  ;  event[9]=s3;




//,"Sound buds");
//calibrate ears. They do not register
//the same db accurately
//for this set up

SetSensorSound(IN_4); //left ear
SetSensorSound(IN_1); //right ear
event[1]=0;event[2]=0;event[3]=0;event[4]=0;
event[5]=0;event[6]=0;event[7]=0;event[8]=0;
s1=1;
s2=1;
xy=0;
xxy=0 ;
              //,"Listen do loop");


do{
  {
  //send a sonic ping
  //PlayTone(800,500);
  //Wait(200);
  }
x=SND1+x;                              //receive the ping
xx=((SND2)*1.1)+xx;                    //right ear must be notched UP
cntr=cntr+1;

}
              //end of Listen do loop
while(cntr<3) ;
```

```
if (x>xx)
{
  if (x<2) {s1A1_30=1;
          }
  else if (x>2) {s1A1_50=1; s1A1_30=0;
              }

  if (x>5) {s1A1_80=1; s1A1_50=0;
          }
  event[0]=1;event[1]=s1;event[2]=s1A1_30;
  event[3]=s1A1_50;event[4]=s1A1_80;event[23]=1;
  if (Lk=="L") {event[1]=-1;event[4]=-1;}
}

if (xx>x)
{
  if (xx<2) {s2A1_30=1 ;
          }
  else if (xx>2) {s2A1_50=1; s2A1_30=0;
               }
  if (xx>5) {s2A1_80=1; s2A1_50=0;
          }
   event[0]=1;event[5]=s2;event[6]=s2A1_30;
   event[7]=s2A1_50;event[8]=s2A1_80;event[22]=1;
if (Lk=="R") {event[5]=-1;event[8]=-1;}
 }


int Tcntr=0;
{
}

SetSensorLowspeed (IN_2);

Acquire (USndAcc);
//This segment registers distance based upon a fixed looking position
//It is not a side scanning sequence. The head is either Front or SideL/R
//If Lk=="R/L", the head has already been turned in the calling routine. There
//is no quarter point reading, only a side L/R reading

  //this finds the smallest value (closest mark)

if (Lk!="F") {Lk="FF";}          //Lk is already defined
                                 //When Lk="R"/"L" it must be replaced with "FF"
                                 //Lk must be suppressed to prevent head turn
xs=250;
repeat (10)
{
x= (SensorUS(IN_2));             //these readings are all in cm (not inches)
                                 //.3937" per cm
if(x<xs){xs=x;}
}
          //Use Posit0 as a string to carry QAction for use as a trigger
if (Posit0=="Qhitx")
```

```
{
if ((Lkk=="R")&&(xs<30)) {TShmy_Left();Trackx3="Left";}
                              //align away from side walls/obstr
if ((Lkk=="L")&&(xs<30)) {TShmy_Right();Trackx3="Right";}
                                  //when an IR signal shows obstr
}                                 //ahead


//These readings are prioritized by clearance and local looking "Lk"

if ((xs>120)&&(Lk!="F")) {event[9]=-1;Trackx1="S3-1";Trackx2="null";}
  //this is a portal
  //It is restricted to side scan where ((xs>120)&&(Lk!="F"))
if (Lk=="F"){
if ((xq<120)&&(xq>59)) {event[13]=-1;event[9]=-1;
     //this is a clearance that is slightly off heading. It requires a slight alignmnt
   //It is preferred to a full turn
   goto Out_USnd;}
   }
 if ( (xs>100)) {event[12]=1;
            }
 if ((xs<100)&&(xs>44)) {event[11]=1;
                }
 if (xs<45) {event[10]=1;
        }

Out_USnd:
Lk=Lkk;                     //Lk is reestablished for use in Lk_D
Release (USndAcc);
{
}

float se5, se6, se7, se8, se9;
float dir, se1, se2, se3, se4 ;
float se1x ,se2x ,se3x ,se4x ,se5x,sxx,Sx,Sxx,Scnt,dirSxx ;
int str;
int active ;
cntr=0;
float dirx,Sdirx;
event[14]=0;
event[15]=0;event[16]=0;
event[17]=0;event[18]=0;
event[19]=0;event[20]=0;

SetSensorLowspeed(SNX4);
{
 float dir, se1, se2, se3, se4, se5, result, cnt,IRcntr;
IRcntr=0;
 SetSensorLowspeed(IRSEEKER);
Sdirx=0;Sxx=0;Scnt=0;sxx=0;
 IRrpt:
 se1=0;se2=0;se3=0;se4=0;se5=0;
 Sx=0;
  do
 {
   ReadSensorHTIRSeeker2AC(IRSEEKER, dir, se1x, se2x, se3x, se4x, se5x);
  if (se1x>se1 ) {se1 =se1x*10;}    //this chooses the Highest value
```

```
      if (se2x>se2 ) {se2 =se2x*10;}
      if (se3x>se3 ) {se3 =se3x*10;}
      if (se4x>se4 ) {se4 =se4x*10;}
      if (se5x>se5 ) {se5 =se5x*10;}
     cntr=cntr+1;
   }
  while (cntr<5);
                   if (se1==sxx) {Sx=Sx+1;Scnt=Scnt+1;}
         if (se1>sxx) {sxx=se1; Sxx=0;Sx=1;Scnt=1;}
                   if (se2==sxx) {Sx=Sx+2;Scnt=Scnt+1;}
         if (se2>sxx) {sxx=se2;Sxx=0; Sx=2;Scnt=1;}
                   if (se3==sxx) {Sx=Sx+3;Scnt=Scnt+1;}
         if (se3>sxx) {sxx=se3;Sxx=0; Sx=3;Scnt=1;}
                   if (se4==sxx) {Sx=Sx+4;Scnt=Scnt+1;}
         if (se4>sxx) {sxx=se4;Sxx=0; Sx=4;Scnt=1;}
                   if (se5==sxx) {Sx=Sx+5;Scnt=Scnt+1;}
         if (se5>sxx) {sxx=se5;Sxx=0; Sx=5;Scnt=1;}

  IRcntr=IRcntr+1;
  Sxx=Sxx+Sx;
  int xse=0;

  if (IRcntr<5) {goto IRrpt; }

  dirSxx=Sxx/Scnt;
  //dirSxx is the pricipal direction of the heat source
  //sxx is the maximum recorded strength
  }

    s4=1  ;

  active=0;
  {
   {
      if ((dirSxx >=4)||(dirx>3))
      {
      s4A1_R=1;
      str=sxx;
      event[14]=s4;event[15]=s4A1_R;event[16]=1;event[22]=1;event[24]=1;
           if (Lk=="R") {event[15]=-1;event[16]=-1;}
         if (sxx>30) {event[26]=1;} //this is the backup command for IRseeker
         active =1 ;
         goto Out_IR;
       }

   }
                 {
                    if (dirSxx>=2)
                    {
                    s4A1_F=1 ;
                    event[14]=s4;event[17]=s4A1_F;event[18]=1;
                    if (Lk!="F") {event[17]=-1;event[18]=-1;}
                    str=sxx;
                    if (str>30) {event[26]=1 ;}
                    active =1 ;
                    goto Out_IR;
```

```
                        }
                }


                {
                        if ((dirSxx >= 1)||(dirSxx==2))
                        {
                        s4A1_L=1 ;
                        event[14]=s4;event[19]=s4A1_L;event[20]=1; event[23]=1;
                        event[25]=1;

                        str=sxx;
                        if (Lk=="L") {event[19]=-1; event[20]=-1;}

                        if (str>30) {event[26]=1; }
                                        }
                }

}
Out_IR:
active =0 ;
int Q[29] ;
int Q1;
cntr=0;
Mevent[0]=1;
}
```

MASTER Subroutine:
HEAD_LEFTC

FUNCTION

This is a motor action initiated by sensors (Infra red or motor stall) to move the head to the left (left looking) to check for near obstacles and move away from them

```
sub Head_LeftC(int &opnxL, int &LEvent[], int &Mevent[], string Lk, float &Ratio,
string Posit0, string Posit1)
{
int x,x2,y,opnxR,opnxF,opnxqL,opnxqR,opnxqF;
int xy=250, Trvl=1;
int FCEa, Dix, Fa;
 int pwr1,pwr2, Motr;
float Bratio,xxa;
xxa=BatteryLevel();
Bratio=xxa/8400 ;
pwr1= 26/Bratio;pwr2=88/Bratio;
Lk="L"; opnxF=0;

SetSensorLowspeed (IN_2);
if (Ratio==0.5) { opnxF=-1;}
                        //as a "-1", a flag is sent to bypass an USnd reading
                        //This is used when the head turn is for side polling
                        //Turn Left and stay there.Do not take readings
```

```
Lk="L";Lk_D( Lk,opnxF, opnxL, opnxqL);
if (Ratio==0.5) {   //Ratio = 0.5 for polling sacnning only
poll_sensors(LEvent, Mevent, Ratio, Lk, Posit0, Posit1, Motr);
goto Out_2b;
}
                        //The Dyno_ShmyR() aims the front towards the Right
                        //and in so doing swings the back in an arc to the left.
                        //For FrntWhlDrv the close obstr <35 on the left
                        //will block the rear casters from a complete
                        //swing. The first move must be a 1.) TShmy_Left
                        //2.) Backup and the 3.) Dyno_ShmyR(). This will
                        //provide clearance for the rear to swing in a clear arc.
if (opnxL<41)
{
TShmy_Left();
OnFwdReg(OUT_AB,85,OUT_REGMODE_SYNC);
Wait(1200);        //new chassis requires 13" back up
Float(OUT_AB);

Seek="N";
Dyno_ShmyR(Seek);
//this is a simple pivot to the right
opnxL=0;}

else if (Ratio!=-1)
{
OnRevReg(OUT_AB,85,OUT_REGMODE_SYNC);Wait(800);       //G5_FWD_02
Float(OUT_AB);                             //go straight to Dyno_Shmy

TextOut(0,LCD_LINE1," Left Pivot ");
Dyno_ShmyL(Seek);
//this is a simple pivot into a clear field on the left

}
Out_2b:
if (opnxF==-1) {Lk="LR";Lk_D( Lk,opnxF, opnxF, opnxqF);}
                        //Where opnxF==-1, this brings the head
                        //turn back to center without a reading
}
```

MASTER Subroutine:
        Head_RightC

FUNCTION

This is a motor action initiated by sensors (Infra red or motor stall) to move the head to the left (left looking) to check for near obstacles and move away from them

```
sub Head_RightC(int &opnxR, int &REvent[], int &Mevent[], string Lk, float &Ratio,
string Posit0, string Posit1)
//Head_RightC(opnxR,REvent,Mevent,Lk,Ratio,Posit0,Posit1)
{
```

```
int x,x2,y,opnxL,opnxF,opnxqR,opnxqL,opnxqF ;
int xy=250;
 int pwr1,pwr2, Motr;
float Bratio,xxa;
xxa=BatteryLevel();
Bratio=xxa/8400 ;
pwr1= 26/Bratio;pwr2=88/Bratio;
Lk="R";
opnxF=0;

SetSensorLowspeed (IN_2);

if (Ratio==0.5) {opnxF=-1;}                    //this is a turn to the right w/o a return
Lk="R";Lk_D( Lk,opnxF, opnxR, opnxqR);         //Turns head to look Right

if (Ratio==0.5) {
//Ratio=0.5 allow polling scanning only. No head scanning
poll_sensors(REvent, Mevent, Ratio, Lk, Posit0, Posit1, Motr);
goto Out_2a;
}

if (opnxR<41)    //For fat tire 38cm width chassis use 41
{
TShmy_Right();
OnFwdReg(OUT_AB,85,OUT_REGMODE_SYNC);
Wait(1200);      //new chassis requires 13" back up
Float(OUT_AB);

//This is the complex motr
//1.) TShmy_Right
//2.) Backup and then
//3.) Dyno_ShmyL(). This will
//provide clearance for the rear to swing in a clear arc.

Dyno_ShmyL(Seek);
//this is a simple pivot to the left
opnxR=0;}
                              //Ratio==1 allows side shimmy
                              //Ratio==0.5 is for scanning only
                              //Ratio==-1 allows side shimmy for
                              //obstructed side only

else if (Ratio!=-1)    //6Cc4b1
{
OnRevReg(OUT_AB,85,OUT_REGMODE_SYNC);Wait(800);
Float(OUT_AB);
Dyno_ShmyR(Seek);
//this is a simple pivot into a clear field on the right
}
Out_2a:
if (opnxF==-1) {Lk="RR";Lk_D( Lk,opnxF, opnxF, opnxqF); }
}
```

FUNCTION

This is a motor action initiated by sensors to move the head to the left and right in one cycle to check for near obstacles and move away from them

```
sub ScanL_R(int &LEvent[], int &REvent[], int &Mevent[],int &Dirx[], int DegRef, int
FCE, string Lk, float &Ratio, string Posit0, string Posit1)
//ScanL_R(LEvent,REvent,Mevent,Dirx,DegRef,FCE,Lk,Ratio,Posit0,Posit1)
{
int x,x2 ;                    //this polls sensors with left-right head swings
int y ;
int opnxL;
int opnxR;
int Rnd;
int xy=250;
long active;
string buf;
SetSensorLowspeed (IN_2);
if (Ratio==1) {Back_Up(FCE,Dirx,DegRef);}  //if no side adjustments, then
                            //no back up
                            //Ratio==1 allows side shimmy
                            //Ratio==0.5 is for scanning only
                            //Ratio==-1 allows side shimmy for
                            //obstructed side only
Head_LeftC(opnxL, LEvent, Mevent, Lk, Ratio, Posit0, Posit1);
Head_RightC(opnxR, REvent, Mevent, Lk, Ratio, Posit0, Posit1);
}
```

FUNCTION

This routine evaluates **[Q]** and **[MQ]** outcomes as they create consensus patterns of recognition for peripheral and forward looking obstructions. Motor stalls and left/right looking **[LQ/RQ]** consensus patterns are also evaluated. The decisions are either "open," closed "L, R, & F," or "boxed." The subroutine returns these instructions to the main task. The decision to proceed is registered in GOgate (true==1 false ==0) (**Chapter IV Programming,** sect COORDINATING CODEPENDENT THREADED TASKS) and GOcnt for the sequence that prevents over writing motor events that are in progress.

```
sub Eval_GOnoGO(string &NOgoF, string &NOgoR, string &NOgoL, string &NOgo,
int LQ[], int RQ[], int Q[])
//Eval_GOnoGO( NOgoF, NOgoR, NOgoL, NOgo, LQ , RQ , Q )
{
int x1,x2,GOcnt, Qbox;
NOgo="clear";
 NOgoR="clear-R";NOgoL="clear-L";
```

```
//,"Slv Scan Matrix"


  //NOgoF has been removed and placed alone as a "Fwd_Eval"


//x1 Left ear
//x2 Right ear
//Looking left: Left ear checks behind; Right ear checks ahead
//If left ear is dominant (x1>x2) LQ[5] (x1) ; then obst is behind "ta"
//Right ear dominant (x2>x1) LQ[9] (x2) ; then obst is ahead "F"
//Looking right: rules are opposite of left

x1=LQ[5];x2=LQ[9];
GOcnt=x1-x2;          //left views to the left: clustered behind
{
if ((GOcnt>0)||(LQ[26]==3)) {NOgo="ta";}
else if ((x2>x1)&&(x2>3)) {NOgo="F"; } //obstruction ahead - clustering
if (LQ[2]==4) {NOgoL="L";}
if ((LQ[26]>1)||(LQ[10]<0)) {NOgoL="L";}   //obstruction to the left
if ((LQ[26]>1)&&(LQ[27]>1)) {NOgoL="L";}
if ((LQ[10]==1)&&(LQ[11]!=2)) {NOgoL="Opn";}
}
//NumOut(10,LCD_LINE2,LQ[10]);

x1=RQ[5]+1;x2=RQ[9]+1;
//,"Test R_Q"
GOcnt=x2-x1;          //right views to the right: clustered behind
{
if ((GOcnt>0)||(RQ[25]==3)) {NOgo="ta";}
else if ((x1>x2)&&(x1>3)) {NOgo="F"; } //obstruction ahead - clustering
if (RQ[6]==4) {NOgoR="R";}
if ((RQ[25]>1)||(RQ[10]<0)) {NOgoR="R";}   //obstruction to the right
if ((RQ[25]>1)&&(RQ[27]>1)) {NOgoR="R";}
if ((RQ[10]==1)&&(RQ[11]!=2)) {NOgoR="Opn";}
}

if ((RQ[25]>1) && (LQ[26]>1)){ NOgo="ta";}
Qbox=Q[11]+LQ[11]+RQ[11];
if (Qbox>=4) {NOgo="Bxd";}
}
```

SUBROUTINE SET UP FOR THE SLAVE PROCESSOR

Slave subroutine coding is listed in the proper sequence. Copy and paste them directly to the Bricx Command Center working page. The sequence should be as follows::

Slave Processor::

SUB READ_MAG(INT &DEG0)

SLAVE Subroutine:
Read_Mag

FUNCTION

The magnetic compass heading is registered in the sensor reading. It is corrected for deviation, which is the compass error caused by local magnetic disturbances. Variation is the error caused by Earth's magnetic field as it varies from true geographic North and it is not corrected.

```
SUB READ_MAG(INT &DEG0)
{
INT X, DEGMAG, DEGMX;
FLOAT FM;
DEGMAG=0;
REPEAT (10){
CLEARSCREEN();
SETSENSORLOWSPEED(IN_2);
X=SENSORUS(IN_2);
DEGMAG=DEGMAG+(2*X);
}
DEGMAG=(DEGMAG/10) ;
CLEARSCREEN();
TEXTOUT(0,LCD_LINE1,"READ");
TEXTOUT(0,LCD_LINE2,"MAG HEADING");NUMOUT(70,LCD_LINE2,DEGMAG);
//WAIT(SEC_10);
//CORRECT MAGNETIC HEADING
DEGMX=0 ;
//THIS CALIBRATION IS FOR SPECIFIC POSITIONS OF THE UNITS AND WIRING
{
IF ((DEGMAG<361)&&(DEGMAG>300)) {DEGMX=(DEGMAG-300)*0.45;}
IF ((DEGMAG<151)&&(DEGMAG>0)) {DEGMX= (DEGMAG)*0.45;}
IF ((DEGMAG<201)&&(DEGMAG>150)) {DEGMX= (DEGMAG)*0.75;}
IF ((DEGMAG<250)&&(DEGMAG>200)) { DEGMX=DEGMAG;}
IF ((DEGMAG<300)&&(DEGMAG>250)) { DEGMX=DEGMAG*1.14;}
//IF ((DEGMAG<300)&&(DEGMAG>200)) {DEGMX=(210)*0.45+(DEGMAG-
200)*1.2+(50*1.5);}
```

```
//IF ((DEGMAG<200)&&(DEGMAG>149)) {DEGMX=(210)*0.45+(100)*1.3+((DEGMAG-
150)*1.65);}
 }
DEG0=DEGMX ; IF (DEG0==0){DEG0=1;}
IF (DEG0>360) {DEG0=DEG0-360;}
 }
```

VI
TECHINCAL APPROACH

MAKING SENSE OUT OF NONSENSE

A method is presented dealing with Event streams having No Rhyme or Reason to a creature observing the events. In the case of an automaton (robotic computer,) this involves a series of computational steps which enable the machine to choose to initiate actions after sorting a stream of sensory signals.

UNIVERSES OF POSSIBILITIES

This method of programming constructs a row and column array based upon the results of a disconnected, random input of sensory signals. These signals are sorted in such a way that the final array contains information leading to actions and movement. This is accomplished by:

> 1. A reasoned set of arguments describing the association of events and how they may be symbolically depicted.
> 2. A programmed model of the hypothesis that an **observer** is associated with the events by shared vectors linking qualities of membership and influence.

In 1985 I was inspired to develop a mathematical model of a method that arranged random experiences in such a way that *meaning* could be inferred from the total experience.

This method led to certain theoretical universe models. In a sense, the universes referred to here are logical states. Rather than one universe, where a concept either belongs (1) or doesn't (0), my universes are many. A TRUE concept can be Converse and belong to a currently examined universe (+1) or Adverse and not belong to the current logical universe (-1). The concept may close the logical stream as FALSE (0) or allow a pass through the logical gate as not evaluated (null).

The concepts referred to involve events. An event can be any state of any item or particle that can be detected by any other item or particle. It can also be any concept in a abstract state as long as it can be detected. The detected state of any event is considered the *logical state.* The model postulates that:

> **1) All possible events exist in multiple parallel universes;**
> **2) All universes are in a steady state;**
> **3) Experiences consist of observing existing events in a series and**
> **4) Time as we know it is a delusion.**

I developed the symbolic logic of this postulate and tested it using a computer to sort, in an extremely disconnected frame of reference, all the events submitted to it, random or otherwise.

At the time, I was running my professional work on a Cray at Control Data in Minneapolis. But I didn't need that power for this, so in 1985, I bought a Radio Shack TRS-80 desk top computer running at 4.2 MHz. The process to solve *equations of state* was initially coded in Fortran for the Cray, later in Basic for the TRS-80, QuickBasic, and C. This began as an elementary maze-like problem of random experiences. In no time it became much more complex.

The model currently in use involved some fundamental definitions and concepts on how an event is observed and how the observation affects the event. For a detailed explanation and examples of this model, refer to the publication **Hyperbolic Event Structures for Artificial Intelligence, Book I**

But for the moment the following explanations are offered. To begin, there is the stipulation that events exist as elementary units of any phenomenon. An "event" is fundamental and has no intrinsic meaning outside of itself. An event also must be observable and detectable. This stipulates that all events to be true require an observer. And lastly, the event is not altered by variations in observation, or the absence of observation.

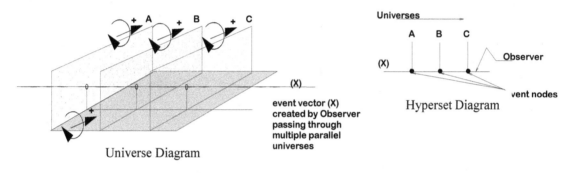

event vector (X) created by Observer passing through multiple parallel universes

Universe Diagram

Hyperset Diagram

Fig 6-1

ALL POSSIBLE EVENTS EXIST IN MULTIPLE PARALLEL UNIVERSES;

Parallel universes do not interact or exert influence between universes. Universe events may be detected by an Observer (x) only through an intersecting (hyperbolic) plane of the Observer (X).

Events are linked by the observational plane that passes through parallel universes. The link is not causal. It is simply a series of registered logical states. Since there is no indication of cause or inherent influence between the events, they can be observed in any sequence. *Influence* is assumed to exist only between event observations and their sequence with the observer. In a parallel universe, where there is no physical contact between universes, influence cannot extend beyond any single universe.

ALL UNIVERSES ARE IN A STEADY STATE

An **equation of state** can be used to express the relationship between an event and an influence which becomes apparent as a result of an observation. The event is observed through the characteristics of its "logical state." An example of a logical state would be a "snap-shot" reading from a sensor that is continuously receiving signals.

$$q_n = a_n(e_n)$$
where

- **(q)** is the logical state of the observation or the description of the observed state (such as a sensor output or signal activated switch.)

- **(e)** is any observed event (such as a signal.)
- **[a, b …..]** are relationships that influence the shared events **(e)** to the alternative observers/observation (such as periodic reading, directional control, etc.)

Compatibility of the observed system is achieved by the observer's relationship to the logical state as simply an experience of any event.

EXPERIENCES CONSIST OF OBSERVING EXISTING EVENTS IN A SERIES

INFLUENCE
Any event, with any observed state, may be observed by any number of observers. Because of the discrete nature of an event, it does not require any protocol in order for its observation. This means that two observers may be aware of the same event, but in completely different states. Also, an event (or node) may be shared by any number of alternative observers in any number of different states.

$$a_1e_1 = q_1$$
$$a_2e_1 = q_2$$

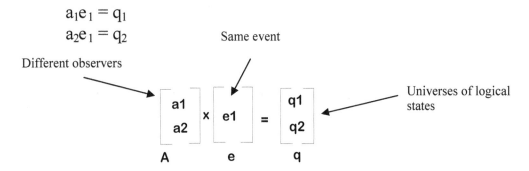

In the example above, the matrix **[A]** will be referred to as the *Influence* matrix. The array **[q]** will be designated as competing *universes*.

In terms of *Influence,* if the outcome result is a series of observations, a matrix **[A]** can be identified as a link connecting the various events.

Then   **[q] = [A] e**

MEMBERSHIP

Consider now that an *Experience* can be defined as a plurality of observations. As an observation progresses through a series of events a body of assembled logical states, or "what is observed," accrues. The body which constitutes an *experience* exhibits a quality of realities which is comprised of logical states **[q]**. There is a distinction within this membership. Realities, although shared, may not be compatible events. Consequently realities must be identified in terms of their compatible qualities. For example, observations of the *same events* may not belong to the same sequence and may be described by different states.

The problem now is to bring this equation of state into a representative field where an experience can be evaluated as a logical element. This can be done by introducing compatibility through **membership.**

Incompatibility of observed states does not alter the fact of the event nor the observation, meaning that the event remains true. But the notation of that event, within either event state, is altered. Compatible event states can be considered converse (+). Incompatible event states are considered adverse (-), yet both are considered True. This raises the question how are events related? In the initial proposal defining equations of state, the events lie on a vector created by an observer plane passing through universes. Consequently an event is a **member** of an observation. This introduces the concept of *Membership.*

A membership can be shared qualities of any collection being "observed," say by a micro-processor reading sensors at periodic intervals. An *Observed Outcome* (Q), expressed as a product of the events' membership in universes [k] and the logical state (q) of the events due to the observation, assembles the inherently meaningless event points into an experiential grid.

$$Q_n = k_n q_n$$

An observed outcome (Q) is a result of the logical state (q) of the competing universes and the event membership (k) of the relative universe states, and comprises what you end up "seeing."

Compatibility in this case is determined by the outcome of the observation(s) (Q). The **observed outcome** (Q) is altered by variations in the arrangement of converse and adverse events according to the **membership [k]** of events within the context of the observation. If you are observing only green balls (+1) and a red one shows up, that red ball is adverse (-1) to the membership of the observation, although it is still true |1|.

If an experience is a plurality of events, all of which manifest an *influence,* and belong to a specific membership of observers, the product of this combination of influence and membership would produce a specific **outcome** based upon the experiences. So even though the observed events have no inherent meaning by themselves, the event series exhibits meaning based upon membership with the plane of observation.

These are the components of an observational vector:
1. When a logical state (q) (a sensing apparatus,)
2. composed of influenced events [A] (e) (a directional signal,)
3. can be expressed in a membership [k] (a common processor,)
4. a random series of observed events can be expressed as an outcome (Q.)

So that   Q = k [A] e

This expression involves two column matrices, [e] and [Q] It expresses conditions within **universes,** due to influences upon the logical states. The matrix [k] is a *Membership* matrix and [A] is the *Influence.*

In any given **universe** of observations an **Observed outcome [Q]** exists which is a product of membership [k] and influence [A] within that **universe.** The variable e is a discrete event of the universe

Also since

$$q_n = a_n (e_n)$$

It follows that

$$Q_n = k_n a_n (e_n)$$

Where: (k) is the quality of the assembled events, or *membership*
             (a) is the relationship between shared events, or *influence*
             (e) is a discrete signal, impulse, point, etc. or *event*

The **observed outcome** model builds all the elements of an observation that belong to a specific series of events into a **structure**. This leads to the formation of the *Experience* matrix **[K]**, as the product of *membership* and *influence*.

$$A_n^T \, k_n \; = \; K$$

TIME AS WE KNOW IT IS A DELUSION

The experience of observation is now assembled into a matrix set that can be manipulated and "solved." The discovery of "meaning" rests in the series itself. The important element of this model is there is no cause and effect. Since all possible events already exist, and need only be observed, the sequence is irrelevant to the **truth** of the event. The *fact* of observation as a sequence is important.

$$Q_n = K \, (e_n)$$

$$\text{when} \;\; |\,K\,| <> 0$$

If the determinant of **[K]** is not singular (equal to zero) then:

$$(e_n) = K^{-1} Q_n$$

This proposes that the *experience matrix* **[K]** can be inverted, and more specifically a past event may be deduced (i.e. solved) from a current observation outcome **[Q]**. In fact the lines between past, present and future become blurred when it is seen that **[K]** can be inverted and reverted. An observed outcome **[Q]** may be the inverted solution of a "future" event. The notion that the automaton is unaware of time as a quality would beg the argument that there is no awareness of whether or not the discovered "meaning" has anything to do with any logical state other than what is currently "now." To the automaton, the possibilities of state all exist simultaneously and can be sorted as a factual collection of series. Without a psychology there is no extended time frame.

CATAGORIZING EVENTS AND RECORDING THEIR STATES

The elements of **[K]**, notably the assembly of logical states, can be represented by any *quality* which is inherent in the observation. In the examples used here,

[K] represents:
- a) sensors,
- b) the respective sensor readings,
- c) motor responses,
- d) head rotation, right or left
- e) motor actions.

Quite simply, this format arranges the sensory devices in an array where they can be triggered by readings. Rather than one sensor reading triggering a motor reaction, multiple sensor readings can be assessed simultaneously, triggering a more comprehensive motor reaction(s).

For example if the experience/membership matrix (or bundle of events) **[K]** is known, it can be inverted. Underlying events **(e)** which produced a known outcome can be discovered. This causes specific issues to arise from this model **in terms of the robot's reality.**

- Inversion of the experience matrix **[K]** reveals past and future observation sets.

179

- Causality is an aberration, not a quality of the observation.
- Time is an experience of serial space.

This calls into play the expression:

$$(e_n) = K^{-1} Q_n$$

If the robot is searching for the proper motor response, this expression would be used to identify which sensors should be polled

LEARNING

This model restricts the learning of the automaton to what it has experienced. When it functions as an observer only, the learning process is limited to sequences (or sequence segments) which reflect converse (+1) events or logical states. In a fixed system of sensors, the experience matrix **[K]** can be "hard wired" to the program. These matrices take the form of structures, and can be manipulated, inverted and "solved" for any variation of experience(s) constituting a learned reality.

FORMAL BASIS FOR BUILDING EXPERIENCE

The model under consideration does not attach meaning to the event/experience itself but has imbued the experience sequence with the significance of embodying a "solution." Meaning is only implied from the observation itself as it relates to past and future manipulations of the founding experience.

Event Structures

As a practical aspect, the automaton looks to its experience matrix **[K]** to evaluate its past and future. There is no meaning beyond this application and no insight available other than this basis (i.e. its own experience.)

The advantage of the matrix format is the ability to take the results of a current observation and determine the events that produced it. This in itself is a learning experience for the observing unit.

The matrix comprises a structure where the observing unit is provided a formal standard which can be accessed in developing solutions and alternative actions.

MANIPULATING AND "SOLVING" EVENT STRUCTURES

The matrix formats that have been proposed are
- Event   **[e]**
- Experience   **[K]**   or $[A^T k]$
- Observed Outcome   **[Q]**

Each has its own characteristic, leading to a decision by the observing Unit. The event column matrix **[e]** can only be sensed. The experience matrix **[K]** can be altered and inverted. The Observed Outcome **[Q]** can be manipulated through variations in the sensory environment. The one concept overshadowing the others is that the greater the density of the sensate event column, the greater the awareness of the automaton Unit.

In line with this concept, the greater the sophistication of the experiential links to the events, the greater the powers of observation in the Unit.

There are two basic types of structural formats which can be manipulated in a manor that produce information and actionable stimuli.

REAL AND TRANSLATIONAL FORMATS (OBSERVER & NAVIGATOR)

1. A **Real** experience links a series of events with an observed outcome. An **Observer** develops awareness solely on the basis of sequence. When the **Observing Unit's (Unit1)** memory of the task (matrix) is established, it is indexed in a way that allows a specific recovery. The task itself (which may simply be a position in space or a sensor reading) is identified in each event structure (matrix.). In all cases the event experience, and becoming aware of a series of events, is formatted to frame the series so the sequence can unfold in a way that can be replicated by the **Unit1.** Examples of a productive exercise in a real set of observed outcomes are:
   a. Reacting to a series of sensor impulses,
   b. searching for predefined outcome thresholds in **[Q]**.

The results of a **Real** experience consisting of a multiple parallel universes are referred to as a **Grid** matrix (**Chapter IV, Programming, art: Linking Multiple Sensors.**)

2. A **Translational** experience manipulates a series of events for the purpose of reaching an outcome and is the foundation of abstraction, especially if the examined outcome was originally not associated with any current event series. A **Navigator** develops decisions through a programming core called a **logical element (LE).** It performs the interpretive functions of the experience matrix **[K].** Examples of a productive exercise in a hyperbolic set of event structures are:
   a. Repetitive reviewing of event series,
   b. searching for a different outcome than the primary experience.

The results of a **Translational** experience, where events (and multiple universes) intersect forming a logic vector and causation, are referred to as a **Velox (vectored logic)** matrix.

Once the experience matrix **[K]** of either format is created, it may be polled using specific event truth (e = 1) for any single event (n). This polling will cause associated events to light up or "**fluoresce**" as observed outcomes **[Q.]**

REASONING

A set of logical (*if / then*) gates, in the model presented (**Chapter IV, Programming,**) deal with event structures and matrices of experienced episodes that generally relate to initiating an action. Each identifiable action can be maintained in memory as a matrix structure or as a repeated response. (ref: <u>Auto-Robot Programming</u>)

Once the memory of the task (matrix) is established, it can be indexed in a way that allows a specific recovery. In all cases the event experience, and becoming aware of a series of events, is formatted to frame the series so the sequence can unfold in a past-present relationship.

a. In a **Grid**, *if* the observed outcome **[Qn]** in a specific event series (n) reaches a certain threshold, *then* the **Observing Unit (Unit1)** performs an **action** (e.g. look to the left.)

b. In a **Velox**, *if* the observed outcome **[Qn]** can be identified with any other outcome, *then* the Unit follows a pattern of actions called a **task**. This interpretive function is handled by the vectored logic of the **Logical Element (LE).**

Primitive insights about the event or task pathways are achieved in both Grid and Velox systems when specific events **(e)** are set equal to 1 (*illuminated*) causing certain observed outcomes **[Q]** to return a (scalar) value equal to or greater than 1 (*fluoresce.*) This means that if event **(e)** at position (n) is set to (1) or True, then following a matrix multiplication of

$$[K] \, [e_n] = [Q_n]$$

for the **n**th row, will cause **Q** of that row **(n)** to return a value equal to or greater than 1.

$$\begin{pmatrix} K_{11} & K_{12} \\ K_{21} & K_{22} \end{pmatrix} \times \begin{pmatrix} e_1 \\ e_2 \end{pmatrix} = \begin{pmatrix} K_{11} \, e_1 + K_{12} \, e_2 \\ K_{21} \, e_1 + K_{22} \, e_2 \end{pmatrix} = \begin{pmatrix} Q_1 \\ Q_2 \end{pmatrix}$$

For example, given the matrix operation shown in   Fig. 6-x1,

Fig 6-2a

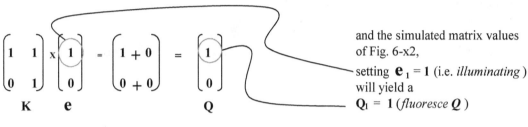

and the simulated matrix values of Fig. 6-x2,

setting $e_1 = 1$ (i.e. *illuminating*) will yield a

$Q_1 = 1$ (*fluoresce Q*)

Fig 6-2b

 Executing an **action** based upon a consensus of events (in a Grid) is specifically related to the observed outcome **[Q]**. **Task** performance (in a Velox) is a global series of events that can be deconstructed and/or inverted to determine isolated events. The matrix indexed and related to the Task is the Experience (symbolized by **[K]**). Isolated events within either **[Q]** or **[K]** matrix can be "illuminated" or separated from the series. When they are reintroduced to the experience matrix, specific observed outcomes **[Qn]** are caused to exhibit True observed states, or "fluoresce."

Note: Keep in mind that all this is going on as a result of programming. The robot or automaton is fundamentally ignorant of the process. The matrix math result of illumination verses fluorescence may seem obvious to you, but the machine knows nothing of this outside of the process just described.

The two types of formats yield different *observational outcome* matrices. Grid systems only fluoresce the system being illuminated. Velox systems exhibit a higher density *experience* **[K]** matrix, where one illuminated event causes nearby or related events to fluoresce. Although Grid and Velox systems are shown to differ in the depth of abstract association, each has definite uses in forming event paths.

CAUSALITY AND LOGICAL TIME

In the parallel grid type of multiple universe system, a universe plane can have compound event nodes that form an *Experience*. The system can be complex as well, where an event range (i.e. more than two) [e] combine from one universe plane to form an *Experience*. This type of event structure takes on the appearance of causality, since following the sequence of events will always lead to a specific **Observed outcome.** In a TRUE *Experience,* where the matrix of |**K**| <>0, the inversion of the *Experience* leads to the same sequence of events and vice-versa. A recreation of those events continues to lead to the **Observed**

outcome. This gives rise to the notion that the sequence of events involves an inherent causality. But the notion is false, since the events exist as discrete elements. It is only the path (basically the *Experience*) followed that leads to an outcome that is predictable in terms of a TRUE observation.
It is much like an understanding that in following a road, road side monuments, although comprising specific outcomes, have not caused each other to exist.

Causality appears to be a synthesis of the *Experience* and is a false impression, not a characteristic of the event elements.

The synthesis of a **logical Causation** takes the form of a **velox** universe system, where an intersection is created at a common event node.

Corollary of CAUSALITY

Causality appears to be a synthesis of the *Experience* and is a false impression, not a characteristic of the event elements. The falsehood lies in the model which assumes the events are specifically related and converging, rather than parallel with no commonality.

The synthesis of a **logical Causation** takes the form of a **vectored-logic** or *velox* universe system, where an intersection is created at a common event node.

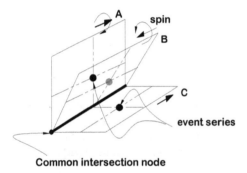

Fig 6-3

COROLLARY OF TIME in a Causal Universe

In this model system, **time passes in only one direction: from present to past**. Inverted matrices of present events can represent events of the past, but they cannot in turn be reverted. Each inversion in turn produces a matrix unassociated with any root experience. Consequently there is no interchangeability between *Experience* matrices, where inversion and reversion correctly reflect reciprocals. Consequently current [K] matrices cannot be considered an inverted event array of the future.

VECTORED Logic Systems

CONVERGENT universes intersect at a common point and create rotational (vectored) patterns.

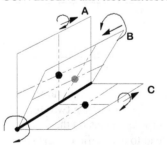

Fig 6-4

Rotationally Vectored pattern

In a vectored-logic (to be referred to as velox) system of intersections, the Observational vector can be rotating across the intersecting planes. If the Observer lies normal to the plane of rotation then the vector is linear (similar to a parallel system.) If the Observer lies in the plane of rotation then the vector is rotational.

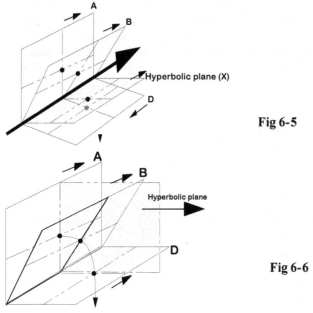

Fig 6-5

Fig 6-6

In either type of universe system, grid or velox (vectored-logic,) the system is TRUE only if the series of shared events is continuous. An event encounter is Adverse (-) if the vector of the *Observer* crosses a plane where no event is shared, or if an event changes state, and the progression of the Observation stops.

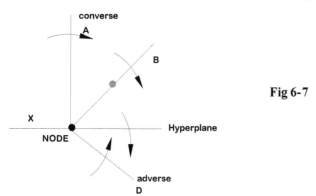

Fig 6-7

The difference between the two types of intersections is that the parallel grid has universes that share an event but do not interact directly. The velox universe system shares events and interact directly at a common intersection.

TIME AS A FUNCTION OF THE PRESENT

The *Experience* of "reality" is in terms of the present. Even if the observer were to become an observer of a so called past phenomenon, the conditional of the *Experience* would be in present terms (its happening *NOW.*)

On the other hand, past events can be viewed as in a frame, but not observed as an event in terms other than the present.

184

The matrix operation that describes logical observed outcomes can be inverted to describe origins as well as outcomes. This suggests that observed events comprise both past, present (event moment) and future (observed outcome.) This may be called the **PPF** phenomenon. The characteristics of *Duration* and *Time* may be the echoing or reverberation of past-present-future observations. There may also be a threshold for actually observing an event. The instant moment that an event takes place may be undetectable to instruments, including organic systems. The **density** of a PPF sequence as a multiple and exact outcome may enable an otherwise unobservable moment to be *Experienced*. The fact that it is *Experienced* in some density allows the sensory mechanism (brain for instance) to store the PPF as an imprint. This creates *Duration*.

This notion forces the idea of *time travel* as a reality. However the underlying concept is that the event phenomenon is basically timeless. In addition, the event is layered with all possible states. This prevents paradox in the experience of the past-future interfering with the present by allowing any and all possible states to overlap, canceling conflicting observations.
An example of the time travel paradox is: Returning to a time past before the observer was born and killing the great grandfather. This would be prevented in a world of infinite possible states, since the entity killed would be merely one of many possible causes for the observer's presence. In addition, since the observer can Experience events only in the present sense, the present would not be altered. The only logical result would be that the entity killed could not be the great grandfather.

Event outcomes which are not **observed** are not significant ($|K| = 0$)
Logical TIME which is not observed is not significant.

A series of events, existing on a plane of possibilities, is brought into the realm of the Observer's experience when the plane the Observer occupies, a hyperbolic plane, intersects the event plane. The Observer Plane possess all the characteristics of the event plane and interacts with it through sharing of events. The intersection of the event plane and the hyperbolic Observer Plane creates a *vectored* sequence of shared events in a three dimensional state. This state establishes a *structure* to the *experience* of events, and can be expressed in a matrix product of universe membership and influence.

Due to the three dimensional characteristic of the vector, it can be considered to occupy *space*. Also because of its vector it can be considered to have *duration,* a characteristic of *Time*. The vector structure of events leads to the concept that Time is a characteristic of space, not coexisting as a separate but linked element, and that Time is a construct of the Observer's event sequence. Basically then, Time is a method the sensing device (or any observer) synthesizes in order to sort the Observed Outcomes of the experienced events.

In developing the structure of the experienced events (membership and influence) a matrix **[K]** of possibilities is created that must be real or TRUE where the determinant $|K| <> 0$. This leads to a second observation that if **[K]** can be inverted, then the perception of space as a vector (Time) can be reversed, traveling both forward and back, along the vectored space.

However since all real experience is in the present (now), the progression of the observation vector cannot be discerned as passing into the past or future. All that can be detected is that the **vector moves away from the *moment of Now*. Past and future are interchangeable.**

Time can be modeled as an Observer's synthesis of vectored space, not as a property of that space. This forces a revision of time as a concept belonging to **Logical Time.**

Details and programming of a **Unit1 Observer** are covered in the preceding Chapters. Complete information regarding event links, Velox matrices, **[K]** matrix inversion and **Navigator** programming can be found in **Hyperbolic Event Structures for Artificial Intelligence, Book I**

MOZILLA PUBLIC LICENSE
Version 1.0

----

1. Definitions.

  1.1. ``Contributor'' means each entity that creates or contributes to the creation of Modifications.

  1.2. ``Contributor Version'' means the combination of the Original Code, prior Modifications used by a Contributor, and the Modifications made by that particular Contributor.

  1.3. ``Covered Code'' means the Original Code or Modifications or the combination of the Original Code and Modifications, in each case including portions thereof.

  1.4. ``Electronic Distribution Mechanism'' means a mechanism generally accepted in the software development community for the electronic transfer of data.

  1.5. ``Executable'' means Covered Code in any form other than Source Code.

  1.6. ``Initial Developer'' means the individual or entity identified as the Initial Developer in the Source Code notice required by Exhibit A.

  1.7. ``Larger Work'' means a work which combines Covered Code or portions thereof with code not governed by the terms of this License.

  1.8. ``License'' means this document.

  1.9. ``Modifications'' means any addition to or deletion from the substance or structure of either the Original Code or any previous Modifications. When Covered Code is released as a series of files, a Modification is:

      A. Any addition to or deletion from the contents of a file containing Original Code or previous Modifications.

      B. Any new file that contains any part of the Original Code or previous Modifications.

  1.10. ``Original Code'' means Source Code of computer software code which is described in the Source Code notice required by Exhibit A as Original Code, and which, at the time of its release under this License is not already Covered Code governed by this License.

  1.11. ``Source Code'' means the preferred form of the Covered Code for making modifications to it, including all modules it contains, plus any associated interface definition files, scripts used to control compilation and installation of an Executable, or a list of source code differential comparisons against either the Original Code or another well known, available Covered Code of the Contributor's choice. The Source Code can be in a compressed or archival form, provided the appropriate decompression or de-archiving software is widely available for no charge.

  1.12. ``You'' means an individual or a legal entity exercising rights under, and complying with all of the terms of, this License or a future version of this License issued under Section 6.1. For legal entities, ``You'' includes any entity which controls, is controlled by, or is under common control with You. For purposes of this definition, ``control'' means (a) the power, direct or indirect, to cause the direction or management of such entity, whether by contract or otherwise, or (b) ownership of fifty percent (50%) or more of the outstanding shares or beneficial ownership of such entity.

2. Source Code License.

2.1. The Initial Developer Grant.
The Initial Developer hereby grants You a world-wide, royalty-free, non-exclusive license, subject to third party intellectual property claims:

(a) to use, reproduce, modify, display, perform, sublicense and distribute the Original Code (or portions thereof) with or without Modifications, or as part of a Larger Work; and

(b) under patents now or hereafter owned or controlled by Initial Developer, to make, have made, use and sell (``Utilize'') the Original Code (or portions thereof), but solely to the extent that any such patent is reasonably necessary to enable You to Utilize the Original Code (or portions thereof) and not to any greater extent that may be necessary to Utilize further Modifications or combinations.

2.2. Contributor Grant.
Each Contributor hereby grants You a world-wide, royalty-free, non-exclusive license, subject to third party intellectual property claims:

(a) to use, reproduce, modify, display, perform, sublicense and distribute the Modifications created by such Contributor (or portions thereof) either on an unmodified basis, with other Modifications, as Covered Code or as part of a Larger Work; and

(b) under patents now or hereafter owned or controlled by Contributor, to Utilize the Contributor Version (or portions thereof), but solely to the extent that any such patent is reasonably necessary to enable You to Utilize the Contributor Version (or portions thereof), and not to any greater extent that may be necessary to Utilize further Modifications or combinations.

3. Distribution Obligations.

3.1. Application of License.
The Modifications which You create or to which You contribute are governed by the terms of this License, including without limitation Section 2.2. The Source Code version of Covered Code may be distributed only under the terms of this License or a future version of this License released under Section 6.1, and You must include a copy of this License with every copy of the Source Code You distribute. You may not offer or impose any terms on any Source Code version that alters or restricts the applicable version of this License or the recipients' rights hereunder. However, You may include an additional document offering the additional rights described in Section 3.5.

3.2. Availability of Source Code.
Any Modification which You create or to which You contribute must be made available in Source Code form under the terms of this License either on the same media as an Executable version or via an accepted Electronic Distribution Mechanism to anyone to whom you made an Executable version available; and if made available via Electronic Distribution Mechanism, must remain available for at least twelve (12) months after the date it initially became available, or at least six (6) months after a subsequent version of that particular Modification has been made available to such recipients. You are responsible for ensuring that the Source Code version remains available even if the Electronic Distribution Mechanism is maintained by a third party.

3.3. Description of Modifications.
You must cause all Covered Code to which you contribute to contain a file documenting the changes You made to create that Covered Code and

the date of any change. You must include a prominent statement that the Modification is derived, directly or indirectly, from Original Code provided by the Initial Developer and including the name of the Initial Developer in (a) the Source Code, and (b) in any notice in an Executable version or related documentation in which You describe the origin or ownership of the Covered Code.

3.4. Intellectual Property Matters

(a) Third Party Claims.
If You have knowledge that a party claims an intellectual property right in particular functionality or code (or its utilization under this License), you must include a text file with the source code distribution titled ``LEGAL'' which describes the claim and the party making the claim in sufficient detail that a recipient will know whom to contact. If you obtain such knowledge after You make Your Modification available as described in Section 3.2, You shall promptly modify the LEGAL file in all copies You make available thereafter and shall take other steps (such as notifying appropriate mailing lists or newsgroups) reasonably calculated to inform those who received the Covered Code that new knowledge has been obtained.

(b) Contributor APIs.
If Your Modification is an application programming interface and You own or control patents which are reasonably necessary to implement that API, you must also include this information in the LEGAL file.

3.5. Required Notices.

You must duplicate the notice in Exhibit A in each file of the Source Code, and this License in any documentation for the Source Code, where You describe recipients' rights relating to Covered Code. If You created one or more Modification(s), You may add your name as a Contributor to the notice described in Exhibit A. If it is not possible to put such notice in a particular Source Code file due to its structure, then you must include such notice in a location (such as a relevant directory file) where a user would be likely to look for such a notice. You may choose to offer, and to charge a fee for, warranty, support, indemnity or liability obligations to one or more recipients of Covered Code. However, You may do so only on Your own behalf, and not on behalf of the Initial Developer or any Contributor. You must make it absolutely clear than any such warranty, support, indemnity or liability obligation is offered by You alone, and You hereby agree to indemnify the Initial Developer and every Contributor for any liability incurred by the Initial Developer or such Contributor as a result of warranty, support, indemnity or liability terms You offer.

3.6. Distribution of Executable Versions.

You may distribute Covered Code in Executable form only if the requirements of Section 3.1-3.5 have been met for that Covered Code, and if You include a notice stating that the Source Code version of the Covered Code is available under the terms of this License, including a description of how and where You have fulfilled the obligations of Section 3.2. The notice must be conspicuously included in any notice in an Executable version, related documentation or collateral in which You describe recipients' rights relating to the Covered Code. You may distribute the Executable version of Covered Code under a license of Your choice, which may contain terms different from this License, provided that You are in compliance with the terms of this License and that the license for the Executable version does not attempt to limit or alter the recipient's rights in the Source Code version from the rights set forth in this License. If You distribute the Executable version under a different license You must make it absolutely clear that any terms which differ from this License are offered by You alone, not by the Initial Developer or any Contributor. You hereby agree to indemnify the Initial Developer and every Contributor for any liability incurred by the Initial Developer or such Contributor as a result of any such terms You offer.

3.7. Larger Works.
You may create a Larger Work by combining Covered Code with other code not governed by the terms of this License and distribute the Larger Work as a single product. In such a case, You must make sure the requirements of this License are fulfilled for the Covered Code.

4. Inability to Comply Due to Statute or Regulation.

If it is impossible for You to comply with any of the terms of this License with respect to some or all of the Covered Code due to statute or regulation then You must: (a) comply with the terms of this License to the maximum extent possible; and (b) describe the limitations and the code they affect. Such description must be included in the LEGAL file described in Section 3.4 and must be included with all distributions of the Source Code. Except to the extent prohibited by statute or regulation, such description must be sufficiently detailed for a recipient of ordinary skill to be able to understand it.

5. Application of this License.

This License applies to code to which the Initial Developer has attached the notice in Exhibit A, and to related Covered Code.

6. Versions of the License.

6.1. New Versions.
Netscape Communications Corporation (``Netscape'') may publish revised and/or new versions of the License from time to time. Each version will be given a distinguishing version number.

6.2. Effect of New Versions.
Once Covered Code has been published under a particular version of the License, You may always continue to use it under the terms of that version. You may also choose to use such Covered Code under the terms of any subsequent version of the License published by Netscape. No one other than Netscape has the right to modify the terms applicable to Covered Code created under this License.

6.3. Derivative Works.
If you create or use a modified version of this License (which you may only do in order to apply it to code which is not already Covered Code governed by this License), you must (a) rename Your license so that the phrases ``Mozilla'', ``MOZILLAPL'', ``MOZPL'', ``Netscape'', ``NPL'' or any confusingly similar phrase do not appear anywhere in your license and (b) otherwise make it clear that your version of the license contains terms which differ from the Mozilla Public License and Netscape Public License. (Filling in the name of the Initial Developer, Original Code or Contributor in the notice described in Exhibit A shall not of themselves be deemed to be modifications of this License.)

7. DISCLAIMER OF WARRANTY.

COVERED CODE IS PROVIDED UNDER THIS LICENSE ON AN ``AS IS'' BASIS, WITHOUT WARRANTY OF ANY KIND, EITHER EXPRESSED OR IMPLIED, INCLUDING, WITHOUT LIMITATION, WARRANTIES THAT THE COVERED CODE IS FREE OF DEFECTS, MERCHANTABLE, FIT FOR A PARTICULAR PURPOSE OR NON-INFRINGING. THE ENTIRE RISK AS TO THE QUALITY AND PERFORMANCE OF THE COVERED CODE IS WITH YOU. SHOULD ANY COVERED CODE PROVE DEFECTIVE IN ANY RESPECT, YOU (NOT THE INITIAL DEVELOPER OR ANY OTHER CONTRIBUTOR) ASSUME THE COST OF ANY NECESSARY SERVICING, REPAIR OR CORRECTION. THIS DISCLAIMER OF WARRANTY CONSTITUTES AN ESSENTIAL PART OF THIS LICENSE. NO USE OF ANY COVERED CODE IS AUTHORIZED HEREUNDER EXCEPT UNDER THIS DISCLAIMER.

8. TERMINATION.

This License and the rights granted hereunder will terminate automatically if You fail to comply with terms herein and fail to cure such breach within 30 days of becoming aware of the breach. All sublicenses to the Covered Code which are properly granted shall survive any termination of this License. Provisions which, by their nature, must remain in effect beyond the termination of this License shall survive.

9. LIMITATION OF LIABILITY.

UNDER NO CIRCUMSTANCES AND UNDER NO LEGAL THEORY, WHETHER TORT (INCLUDING NEGLIGENCE), CONTRACT, OR OTHERWISE, SHALL THE INITIAL DEVELOPER, ANY OTHER CONTRIBUTOR, OR ANY DISTRIBUTOR OF COVERED CODE, OR ANY SUPPLIER OF ANY OF SUCH PARTIES, BE LIABLE TO YOU OR ANY OTHER PERSON FOR ANY INDIRECT, SPECIAL, INCIDENTAL, OR CONSEQUENTIAL DAMAGES OF ANY CHARACTER INCLUDING, WITHOUT LIMITATION, DAMAGES FOR LOSS OF GOODWILL, WORK STOPPAGE, COMPUTER FAILURE OR MALFUNCTION, OR ANY AND ALL OTHER COMMERCIAL DAMAGES OR LOSSES, EVEN IF SUCH PARTY SHALL HAVE BEEN INFORMED OF THE POSSIBILITY OF SUCH DAMAGES. THIS LIMITATION OF LIABILITY SHALL NOT APPLY TO LIABILITY FOR DEATH OR PERSONAL INJURY RESULTING FROM SUCH PARTY'S NEGLIGENCE TO THE EXTENT APPLICABLE LAW PROHIBITS SUCH LIMITATION. SOME JURISDICTIONS DO NOT ALLOW THE EXCLUSION OR LIMITATION OF INCIDENTAL OR CONSEQUENTIAL DAMAGES, SO THAT EXCLUSION AND LIMITATION MAY NOT APPLY TO YOU.

10. U.S. GOVERNMENT END USERS.

The Covered Code is a ``commercial item,'' as that term is defined in 48 C.F.R. 2.101 (Oct. 1995), consisting of ``commercial computer software'' and ``commercial computer software documentation,'' as such terms are used in 48 C.F.R. 12.212 (Sept. 1995). Consistent with 48 C.F.R. 12.212 and 48 C.F.R. 227.7202-1 through 227.7202-4 (June 1995), all U.S. Government End Users acquire Covered Code with only those rights set forth herein.

11. MISCELLANEOUS.

This License represents the complete agreement concerning subject matter hereof. If any provision of this License is held to be unenforceable, such provision shall be reformed only to the extent necessary to make it enforceable. This License shall be governed by California law provisions (except to the extent applicable law, if any, provides otherwise), excluding its conflict-of-law provisions. With respect to disputes in which at least one party is a citizen of, or an entity chartered or registered to do business in, the United States of America: (a) unless otherwise agreed in writing, all disputes relating to this License (excepting any dispute relating to intellectual property rights) shall be subject to final and binding arbitration, with the losing party paying all costs of arbitration; (b) any arbitration relating to this Agreement shall be held in Santa Clara County, California, under the auspices of JAMS/EndDispute; and (c) any litigation relating to this Agreement shall be subject to the jurisdiction of the Federal Courts of the Northern District of California, with venue lying in Santa Clara County, California, with the losing party responsible for costs, including without limitation, court costs and reasonable attorneys fees and expenses. The application of the United Nations Convention on Contracts for the International Sale of Goods is expressly excluded. Any law or regulation which provides that the language of a contract shall be construed against the drafter shall not apply to this License.

12. RESPONSIBILITY FOR CLAIMS.

Except in cases where another Contributor has failed to comply with Section 3.4, You are responsible for damages arising, directly or indirectly, out of Your utilization of rights under this License, based on the number of copies of Covered Code you made available, the revenues you received from utilizing such rights, and other relevant factors. You agree to work with affected parties to distribute responsibility on an equitable basis.

EXHIBIT A.

`` The contents of this file are subject to the Mozilla Public License Version 1.0 (the "License"); you may not use this file except in compliance with the License. You may obtain a copy of the License at http://www.mozilla.org/MPL/

Software distributed under the License is distributed on an "AS IS" basis, WITHOUT WARRANTY OF ANY KIND, either express or implied. See the License for the specific language governing rights and limitations under the License.

The Original Code is _____.

The Initial Developer of the Original Code is _____.
Portions created by _____ are Copyright (C) _____
_____. All Rights Reserved.

Contributor(s): _____.''